# CHILDREN IN SLAVERY THROUGH THE AGES

# CHILDREN IN SLAVERY THROUGH THE AGES

Edited by

*Gwyn Campbell*

*Suzanne Miers*

*Joseph C. Miller*

OHIO UNIVERSITY PRESS

ATHENS

Ohio University Press, Athens, Ohio 45701
www.ohioswallow.com
© 2009 by Ohio University Press
All rights reserved

To obtain permission to quote, reprint, or otherwise reproduce or distribute material from
Ohio University Press publications, please contact our rights and permissions department
at (740) 593-1154 or (740) 593-4536 (fax).

Printed in the United States of America
Ohio University Press books are printed on acid-free paper ⊛ ™

16 15 14 13 12 11 10 09   5 4 3 2 1

Library of Congress Cataloging-in-Publication Data
Children in slavery through the ages / edited by Gwyn Campbell, Suzanne Miers, Joseph
C. Miller.
    p. cm.
Includes bibliographical references and index.
ISBN 978-0-8214-1876-5 (hbk. : alk. paper) — ISBN 978-0-8214-1877-2 (pbk. : alk.
paper)
    1. Child slaves—History. 2. Slavery—History. I. Campbell, Gwyn, 1952- II. Miers, Suzanne.
III. Miller, Joseph Calder.
HT861.C45 2009
306.3'6208309—dc22

2009023495

# CONTENTS

# EDITORS' INTRODUCTION

This is the first of two volumes on children in slavery—a subject that has only recently become the focus of academic research. Scholarly attention has up to now centered primarily on adult male slaves, first in the Americas and the Caribbean, then in Africa, and more recently on women in slavery.[1] Throughout the known history of slavery, children were in a minority. However, as the chapters in these volumes show, at least for the transatlantic, Indian Ocean, and internal U.S. trades, they were increasing in numbers and importance from the late eighteenth century as slavery in its classic form came increasingly under attack. Moreover, it is possible that children currently constitute a large proportion of the victims of the various forms of "modern" slavery. Our aim here is to provide comparative examples of child slavery, from the eighth to the twentieth centuries. Child slavery is surely the most pitiful form of slavery, since children are the most malleable of slaves and have the least powers of resistance. Most slave children, however, have a high degree of adaptability, which, as will be seen, was and is central to survival in a world in which they were, and still are, valued and thought of as trade goods, possessions, and generators of wealth, rather than as human beings with needs of their own.

We have space in these two volumes for only a few examples of the role and fate of child slaves. Whole regions, and whole sections of the economy in which children were, and still are, enslaved, remain to be explored. This is a pioneer work and we hope that other scholars will follow us in the search for information on this little-known subject.

OUR SOURCES

Apart from the uses to which children were put, how they were affected by their slave experiences has been little researched, and our sources are often sketchy. Children did not keep diaries or other records of their lives and treatment while in bondage. Adult slaves, particularly freed slaves, recorded facts about their childhood, but their reminiscences, albeit highly valuable, are filtered through later experiences. However, there is some firsthand information on those children who were freed from captured slave ships or slave caravans and handed over by the British to missionaries in Sierra Leone, East Africa, and India after the trade became illegal, during the nineteenth century. There are also the accounts of those who, at the same time, sought refuge with the European colonial authorities, particularly if, as in Mauritius, a protector of slaves had been appointed. More recently, there are the stories of children who fled to British consulates in Arabia, or to British officials in the Persian Gulf states, where slavery was legal until the 1960s. The last country to outlaw slavery was Oman, in 1970. Unfortunately, the full accounts of these children's experiences in Arabia were either unrecorded or not sent back to the Foreign Office by British officials. However, future research on the ground will surely yield much valuable information.

Slavery took many forms, some crueler than others. On the one hand, unknown numbers of children in many lands have, over the centuries, been torn from, or even sold by, their natal families, taken far from home, often resold—sometimes many times—and raised among strangers. They were often overworked, poorly fed and housed, and exposed to sexual abuse, cruelty, disease, and other dangers. Their welfare has always been subordinated to the interests—economic, political, or social—of their owners. Child slaves were, and sadly still are, the defenseless victims of poverty, wars, raids, and trickery, as well as greed and a thirst for power. However, as the following chapters show, this picture of brutality and suffering must be modified by the fact that for some children life in slavery was preferable to a life of poverty at home. Moreover, some boy slaves were trained to wield power and some girl slaves ended up leading lives of luxury. Sadly, they represented a small minority of the children in bondage.

## DEFINITION OF SLAVERY

A number of the contributions to this volume underscore one of the major problems in comparative slavery studies: the definition of *slavery*. In the conventional historiography that has focused on European forms of bondage, a reasonably clear consensus has arisen as to the meaning of the term. This consensus is assisted by the common linguistic origin of the term *slave* in most European languages. A slave is generally taken to constitute a chattel, deprived of civic rights, and whose status is inherited by his or her children. Further definitions have concentrated on the social death and the ubiquity of violence in the slave experience. However, it is becoming increasingly evident that there existed, notably in the non-Atlantic world, many different forms of bondage, which changed according to time and place and which often overlapped with one another. These systems, some of which are examined in this volume, at times approximated to the Atlantic concept of slavery but often differed significantly from it. Slaves were not always chattels or deprived of basic civic rights; they did not always pass their slave status on to their children; and some could rise to positions of considerable wealth and influence. Such systems thus challenge researchers to reexamine the meaning of slavery through the adoption of more holistic and comparative analytical paradigms.[2]

## THE DEFINITION OF A CHILD

Our first task here is to define what we mean by a child. Today, the United Nations and many Western countries define a child as anyone under the age of eighteen. However, this is not a universal yardstick. For instance, the age of consent to marriage for girls in some countries is as low as twelve. The legal age at which children of either sex enter the work force, are conscripted for military service, are allowed to marry, vote, or drive varies from country to country. The legal school leaving age could be an indicator of legal adulthood, but in many countries education is not compulsory, and in some countries few if any girls attend school. Many children do not have birth certificates and their age is not officially known.

The difficulty of defining childhood is even greater when discussing the past. In part this stems from the paucity of records. However, it also derives from concepts of childhood often radically different from modern Western concepts. Even in Enlightenment Europe, which stressed the capacity to reason as the test of the civilized human being, children, alongside females and nonwhite males, were considered irrational and "animal-like" and thus debarred from civic rights and responsibilities. Children required "domestication," and slavery, it was often argued, was the protected status best suited to that end for nonwhite children. The definition of a slave child was frequently determined by widely varying criteria, including "appearance" and height. A vivid example of how difficult it can be to judge a child's age by his or her appearance is provided by George Michael La Rue's chapter in this volume.[3] He describes a slave boy who arrived in the northern Sudan without parents or relations and was believed to be anywhere from three to six years old—a surprisingly large age range. In the Atlantic slave trade, foremost among the determinants of a child's age was the individual's height. In the Indian Ocean traffic it was height and apparent maturity.[4] However, in Enlightenment thinking the nonwhite remained uncivilized, even after attaining physical maturity. Indeed, physical maturity accentuated the "animallike" characteristics of the barbarian. Thus, the adult slave continued to be viewed as mentally and spiritually undeveloped and infantile; often a more dangerous and volatile version of the child slave.[5]

## THE ORGANIZATION OF THIS VOLUME

There is no chronological sequence to slavery. It has taken many forms and has often overlapped with other types of servitude, some of which are still widespread. We start this first volume with a description of children in different slave trades, beginning with António de Almeida Mendes' pioneer study of children in the early Portuguese slave trade between North and West Africa, the Iberian Peninsula, and America in the fifteenth and sixteenth centuries. This is followed by Richard B. Allen's study of the European traffic across the vast Indian Ocean, which brought victims all the way from China and the East Indies to India, the Mascarenes, and the African coasts. Next we have chapters on two different African trades in the nineteenth century: Fred Morton analyzes the East African traffic supplying markets on the Swahili coast, the offshore islands of the Indian Ocean, Arabia, and India;[6] La Rue studies the Egyptian traffic supplying slaves from the southern Sudan to markets in the northern Sudan, Egypt, and the Middle East;[7] and the first section of this volume ends with Susan Eva O'Donovan's description of children in the U.S. slave traffic between 1820 and 1860.[8]

The second section provides examples of the very varied uses and treatment of slaves in different parts of the world over time. The first two chapters discuss forms of elite slavery in the medieval Middle East. Thus Kristina Richardson deals with a form of female servitude in the 'Abbasid Empire (AD 750-1258),[9] while Gulay Yilmaz describes the recruitment and use of certain highly privileged male slaves in the Ottoman Empire between the early fifteenth and the late sixteenth centuries.[10] Kim Bok-Rae discusses the use and powers of eunuchs in the Chinese Empire as late as the early twentieth century.[11] In her turn, Pauline Pui-ting Poon describes the fate of unwanted girls in poor Chinese families who were often adopted by richer families to serve as ill-used domestic servants in a system known as *mui tsai*.[12]

The last section opens with a discussion by Pierre H. Boulle of the various uses of child slaves in late-eighteenth-century France, from playthings of the court and aristocracy to servants of a variety of owners.[13] Kenneth Morgan's chapter explains the reasons for the high infant mortality in the British Caribbean colonies in the eighteenth and nineteenth centuries, which fueled the demand for imported slaves.[14] Calvin Schermerhorn, writing on America's Southern states in the last decades of plantation slavery, paints a horrifying picture of the impact on child slaves of the selling away of their parents and natural guardians.[15]

### CHILDREN IN THE SLAVE TRADES

We begin our discussion of the place of children in the slave trade with Mendes' pioneer study of children in the Portuguese slave trade in the fifteenth and sixteenth centuries. Originally a trade in slaves, many of them Muslim, captured in Mediterranean wars, this developed into a large-scale traffic involving slaves from both interior and coastal Africa. It linked North and West Africa and even central Africa with the Iberian Peninsula and the Americas, resulting in a "cultural and economic bridge" between the three continents. This created what Mendes sees as a "single, integrated Atlantic civilization." Since black slaves became the principal source of labor, he sees them as "the main agents of social change" in all three regions. He begins by tracing the changing sources and role of slaves in the Iberian Peninsula, from Saracens—often Muslims, captured in Mediterranean conflicts, who usually served the elite—to Africans, many of them captured or kidnapped in the far interior and brought to the coast by African traders. The captured Africans were considered to be savages. They eventually permeated all levels of society and changed European attitudes toward slaves and their uses. Iberian societies absorbed large numbers of slaves and shipped hundreds of thousands to the New World. Only a small minority were children, though they were the easiest to capture and the first to adapt to their new roles. As adults, most remembered their African childhood but also saw their own future and that of their descendants as rooted in Europe or the Americas rather than in a return to their homeland, even when that became possible with the abolition of slavery in the nineteenth century. Much research remains to be done on the actual experiences of children in this early European trade in Africans, in which children were a small minority of the captives. Mendes' chapter, however, provides the setting for further research.

In our second chapter, Allen analyzes the role of children in the Indian Ocean slave trade during the eighteenth and early nineteenth centuries. Sources are scarce, as Allen makes clear, so that, although this traffic predated the transatlantic slave trade by centuries, much less is known about it. Its victims were both drawn from and sold in regions as far apart as China, India, the Mascarenes, and eastern and southern Africa. The traders comprised people from all over the Indian Ocean world, including Arabs, Indians, and Africans, as well as Europeans. The children were enslaved in various ways. Many were sold by their own, often impoverished, relations. Some, sold in times of famine to ensure their survival, cost less than cats or dogs.

The slave populations of the importing areas were not self-sustaining, and children were overall only a minority of those imported. However, their proportion varied considerably according to time and place. Thus there was a higher percentage of children in cargoes from Africa than in those from India and Malaysia and, significantly, as in the case of the Atlantic trade, the proportion of children in slave cargoes increased as the trade came under attack. Numbers were also imported illegally after the traffic was outlawed. Nevertheless, unlike the victims of the transatlantic trade, most slave children traded across the Indian Ocean were wanted as servants rather than field hands and the girls were valued for their sexual and reproductive potential. Like adults, many child slaves died on the way to their destinations. This traffic has resulted in populations of very mixed descent in former European colonies in, and bordering, the Indian Ocean. The two chapters that follow, on the slave trade in eastern Africa, illustrate the degree to which the experiences of children in these traffics could vary.

Morton describes a relatively humane part of the usually cruel trade from east-central Africa to markets either on the east African coast or, via the Indian Ocean, to Arabia, the Persian Gulf, and India. The march from the interior to the coast was arduous, with the adults shackled and the children struggling to keep up with them; they were sometimes killed if they failed to do so. This chapter demonstrates that children in the nineteenth-century East African slave trade functioned not simply as servants or laborers but also as small capital, used by traders to settle debts, establish credit, and as bargaining chips in other transactions. The value of these slave children appreciated the longer they remained in the interior, for they grew bigger and more useful. Typically separated from their parents, they subsequently identified with their masters. They might change hands several times and take months or even years to reach the coast, where they were primarily bought for domestic service. Some remained in eastern Africa but others were sold to slavers and taken on to Middle Eastern and other Indian Ocean world markets.

By contrast, La Rue, writing on the period between 1820 and 1835, discusses the terrible experiences of children bought or captured in the southern Sudan and bound for markets in the northern Sudan, Egypt, and the Ottoman Empire. Those who survived the grueling journey to the markets in the north were used to pay off soldiers, kept as slaves in the northern Sudan, or sent for sale to Egypt and the Middle East, where they usually ended up as domestic servants. Many were orphaned en route, as their enslaved mothers or other relatives died from disease, starvation, ill treatment, or simply the rigors of the journey. As in the Atlantic trade, children who arrived at their destination showing pockmarks were more valuable than those who had not previously contracted smallpox, as the latter would prove more vulnerable should an outbreak of the disease occur.

La Rue concentrates on the story of a little orphan called 'Ali, an extraordinary figure who, although he had survived the long and difficult journey, and like his companions was filthy and covered with vermin, managed to retain an aristocratic air, a happy countenance, and impeccable manners. Hence he was thought to be the child of a ruling family—although nohing is known of his background. As noted above, his age was variously estimated as three or six. He was, apparently, unusually resilient. It was believed that the trader who owned him was anxious to sell him because he was clearly Muslim and, under Islamic law, should not have been enslaved. He charmed William Holt Yates, a member of the British Royal College of Physicians and an abolitionist, who bought him for research on phrenology. At a time when science was often invoked to justify racial inequalities, this chapter shows how science (including the pseudoscience of phrenology) could be invoked to disprove the charge that Africans were innately inferior to Europeans. 'Ali was sent to school in England, where he appears to have been much liked, and became a leader among his peers. Sadly, he died of whooping cough at the age, estimated by his British acquaintances, of six—which if correct would have made him three to four years old when purchased. His is surely a unique story in the history of the particularly inhumane trans-Saharan slave trade.

The children in all these trades were acquired in a number of similar ways. Many were captured in wars and raids—alone, with their parents, or with siblings and friends. Some were captured in the far interior, others near the coast. Poverty-stricken parents and relatives also sold their children to better their fate or, in times of famine, to save their lives or feed the rest of the family. Others were sold by debtors to their creditors if they failed to repay their debts. Some were kidnapped and sold by unscrupulous relatives. Others were exacted as tribute by chiefs, who sold them to dealers. Some were acquired in the far interior and forced to make a long and arduous trek to the coast. Others were captured by coastal people in local raids.[16]

We have no chapter on the transatlantic slave trade after the sixteenth century, but that topic is amply covered in other, more conventional accounts of the history of the slave trade. Suffice it to note that research on this traffic is plentiful and that the databases are constantly providing new material. They clearly show that children were only a fraction of the slaves transported. They were not the slaves of choice, because buyers had to wait, often many years, before they were old enough to become fully fledged field hands—the job for which most of these slaves were wanted. Only in the nineteenth century, in the cocoa plantations of Latin America, were they especially valued because their small fingers were more nimble at picking beans from the pods than those of their elders. However, from the late eighteenth century the New World demand for children grew, and they became an increasingly important part of slavers' cargoes. Several reasons are suggested for this. One is that, although the number of children born in the New World was an important factor in the proliferation of slaves, as Morgan's chapter makes clear, the infant survival rate among slaves was very low in the Caribbean.[17]

O'Donovan, writing on the internal market in the United States, underlines the rise in demand for native-born children in the last decades of slavery—between 1820 and 1860. This gave rise to a trade in children that formed part of the Second Middle Passage—the movement of a million slaves from the Atlantic coast and upper South, some short distances, some into the Old Southwest. This process preyed particularly hard on children who were frequently separated from their families.[18] When combined with slave hiring, the number of separations grew even greater. Children, O'Donovan shows, were viewed as especially desirable for "manning" plantations because they were less likely to run away. They did not have the experience of adults and were more easily exploited. Indeed, in the last years of slavery children became the slaves of choice precisely because of their vulnerability, since they had not acquired the "run away & fortune-making natures of men."[19]

## EXAMPLES OF THE USES AND TREATMENT OF SLAVE CHILDREN THROUGH THE AGES

The second section of this volume gives examples of the very different uses of child slaves through the ages. They illustrate the wide variety of roles performed by slave children of both sexes, besides their ubiquitous use as unskilled labor and as domestic servants.

Richardson's contribution is the first of two exclusively discussing girls. She describes a very particular type of female slavery—the recruitment, by force, of young girls as entertainers for Middle Eastern rulers and other wealthy patrons during the 'Abbasid era (ca. AD 750-1258). These girls, whose ages when recruited are not known, were chosen because they were both young, hence trainable, and "entrancingly beautiful," with sex appeal. Since Muslims could not legally be enslaved, many of these girl slaves originated outside the Islamic heartland, from areas such as India and Ethiopia, although some were recruited from the local slave population. Such girls fetched high prices, and their value increased as they were given an expensive education, being trained in poetry, music, and Arabic to perform for elite males. They thus occupied an intermediate position between the secluded sphere of women and the visible sphere of male belletrists. The essay provides significant evidence that these young women, who were hired out as performers, as well as prostitutes, "exploited their sexuality and their proximity to the politically powerful" to their personal and material advantage.

The road to success for these girls was to become the concubines of their owners, who sometimes freed them. The most successful were those who bore their master a child. By Muslim law, they could not then be sold, and the child usually acquired free status.[20] However, most singing girls remained slaves, many despised as prostitutes.

Yilmaz discusses the *devşirme*–a particular group of male slaves conscripted from the early fifteenth century from among Christian Serbs, Greeks, and Albanians living in the Ottoman Empire, to serve as administrators and soldiers. Every three to four years, peasant boys from within the Ottoman domain were forcibly recruited to become "servants of the sultan." They had to be between ten and eighteen years old, able-bodied, handsome, clever, unmarried, uncircumcised, well brought up, and of "good birth." To ensure that the land would still be cultivated, only one boy could be taken from each family and, in any given year, only one from every forty families. Some parents tried to prevent their sons from being conscripted, although others asked that they be chosen.

This fascinating essay explains why the Ottomans adopted this system and challenges many misconceptions about the devşirme. The boys were taken to the capital, given Muslim names, circumcised, and converted to Islam. Those considered the most talented were trained as palace servants while the rest became janissaries. Yilmaz describes the careful training given to both groups. The most successful were eventually promoted to the higher grades of the army and administration; the rest were drafted into the sultan's army. Devşirme might fill all posts from grand vizier to laborer. Those who rose to positions of influence were thus vitally involved in what Yilmaz calls the "power dynamics" of the Ottoman Empire. Eventually, population increase, sharp inflation due to the influx of American silver, and military developments in Europe (including the use of firearms) caused the empire to change the system by "opening the doors" to Muslim commoners. Yilmaz attributes this to the sultan's desire to change the power relations within the ruling elite.

The chapters by Richardson and Yilmaz clearly deal with children destined to become privileged slaves with opportunities for advancement denied to most persons in servitude. Nevertheless, they were slaves, with no control over their futures, and were trained to fill particular niches—social in the case of the singing girls; political and military in the case of the devşirme. Slavery in the Muslim world was governed by Islamic law, which forbade the enslavement of fellow Muslims and urged owners to treat their slaves well and even to free them. Actual treatment, however, depended on the use to which the slaves were put. While slave servants were on the whole treated better than those in plantation colonies, there were many exceptions. Conspicuous among them were the small boys used for pearl diving in the Red Sea far into the twentieth century. They were not only exposed to constant danger but were often harshly treated.[21]

In the next chapter Kim focuses on those eunuchs who served the emperor of China as slaves until the overthrow of the empire in 1911. Other eunuchs made up the retinues of nobles and princes in both China and Korea. Although little is known about their early years, we include them in this volume because they were prepared for a life of servitude as children. Most were boys whose parents had them castrated in order to promote their chances, as slave eunuchs, of rising to positions of power and influence at the imperial court. Castration was usually done in infancy or early childhood, as survival rates were higher than for boys castrated later in life—although there were boys who had themselves castrated in adolescence. It would seem that child eunuchs must have had an education that prepared them for high office, but sadly little is as yet known about this. The most successful eunuchs rose to positions of considerable power: a few ruled through pliant emperors. And some attempted to regain at least some normalcy by adopting children to create families of their own. However, they were always at the mercy of the emperor and court politics. They could at any time fall from favor and, as Kim shows, could lose their lives. In sum, Kim's chapter offers an important insight into the "adoptive system" for recruiting eunuchs and will hopefully pave the way for more research into the experiences of child victims central to the "making" of eunuchs.

Pauline Pui-ting Poon, writing about Hong Kong in the early twentieth century, looks at the "mui tsai" system. This was a type of bondage closer to modern slavery.[22] The chapter is included here as it was a form of slavery designed for, and in theory limited to, children. It was originally developed to save the lives of unwanted girls. The survival of Chinese families depended on sons, who looked after aged parents and performed rituals to the deities. Girls were often considered an unnecessary burden since they had to be kept until they could be married—when they joined their husbands' families. To save the lives of those female infants, whose parents either could not or would not support them, a custom developed whereby they were transferred for a small fee from their natal family into a richer one. Originally, when the two families remained in the same village, the treatment of the children could be monitored, but as people moved, many of these girls were ill treated by their adoptive parents and the most unfortunate were traded—some more than once.[23] To all intents and purposes such girls were slaves. In the worst cases they were worked at all hours, given jobs beyond their strength, isolated in the household, and often almost starved. Their servitude, theoretically at least, ended when they grew up and their adoptive family was supposed to arrange a suitable marriage for them. One advantage these girls derived from the system was that their feet were not usually bound—so that, unlike their mistresses, they were not crippled. However, this meant they were often bought as hardworking wives by poor men. The stigma of having been a mui tsai was so great that even in the late twentieth century many former mui tsai tried to hide the fact from their children.[24]

Poon discusses the attempts made by the British colonial government in Hong Kong early in the twentieth century to regulate the system. The government's efforts were always limited by its desire not to alienate the Chinese elite, on whose goodwill and support the colonial rulers depended. On the other hand, welfare organizations were constantly exhorting the colonial government to greater efforts. Poon also discusses the efforts by the Hong Kong Chinese, who were anxious to reform the system. In particular, she considers its uses and abuses and the impact of a Chinese organization—Po Leung Kuk—organized to fight for the girls' rights. The British eventually demanded that the girls be registered and visited by welfare workers. In China this form of child slavery ended only after the communist government was established.

Boulle, writing about slaves in late-eighteenth-century France, deals with child slaves in a very different setting. He begins with a description of slave children who were treated as playthings of the royal court and aristocracy, supplanting monkeys and toys. This opens a discussion of the fate of nonwhite children in France. There were twice as many male as female "colored" children, the largest group being between the ages of eight and twelve. Most nonwhite children were not playthings but were destined to be domestic servants or trained for a particular job, such as wig making, and dressmaking for girls, and cooking and grooming of men's hair or wigs, for boys. Surprisingly, such apprenticeships normally excluded carpentry or other occupations essential to colonial economies, possibly indicating a more intimate slave-master relationship. Most children of African descent were registered as slaves, as were the darker children of East Indian descent. Some were born in France of mixed parentage; others were children of planters, often by mulatto mothers, who were sent to France for their education by their white fathers—who sometimes accompanied them.

Legally, only plantation owners could bring slaves to France, and these slaves had to be returned within three years. However, the laws were brazenly flouted, especially by the elite. Many child slaves were imported by officials, naval officers, and particularly slave traders, to become servants, interpreters, and cabin boys. As they grew up, some successfully appealed to courts for manumission. Some were freed by their owners and left to fend for themselves in France. Others simply absconded. Boulle suggests that male owners who freed their slaves did so because they feared they might develop relationships with their wives, who had petted them in childhood. Parallel fears on the part of French women may also account for the greater number of girls sent back to the colonies once they reached maturity.

Morgan's contribution to this volume addresses a very different and much better known theme: the very high mortality rate of slave infants in the British Caribbean—which in turn necessitated a continuous supply of imported slaves. He offers an extremely compelling explanation for high slave mortality. In 1790 nearly half the slave children born in the West Indies died before the age of two. Morgan compares these appalling statistics with the much lower death rate of infants in Britain at the same period. He dismisses the theory that the deaths were due to mothers willfully neglecting their children because they were unwilling to condemn them to a life of slavery, or to bear the extra burden of looking after them, or because they were more interested in "amorous adventures." Rather, he attributes the high death rate chiefly to unhygienic conditions in the slave quarters, to insufficient diet for slave mothers and children, and to medical ignorance. He suggests, for example, that African practices that mandated that a baby's clothes remain unchanged for three days after birth, and that the child not be nurtured until it was nine days old, contributed to the high mortality rate. However, he emphasizes that slave mothers normally looked after their children as best they could in the appalling circumstances in which they lived.

Schermerhorn's chapter, with its very apt title "Left Behind but Getting Ahead," complements that of O'Donovan on the antebellum South in the years leading up to the Civil War and the legal end of slavery. Where she is concerned with the trade in infant and child slaves, he discusses the impact on native-born slave children of the separation, through sale, from their parents and other relatives or guardians. He focuses on the Chesapeake, where the children were separated from their parents, who, as young adults, had been traded west and south. These parentless children became an increasingly large proportion of the remaining population. Left to fend for themselves, they formed successive bonds with networks of caregivers. First they turned to grandparents and extended family members or even bonded with the children of their owners. Subsequently, they learned to form networks of ever-changing "informal kin" in place of families. Churches sometimes functioned as such networks, even though slave pastors were also liable to be sold away.

As each generation reached its "prime," it was sold or hired out to work far from home. Thus in their turn orphans became parents and were separated from their own children in the same fashion. Tragically these children and subsequently their offspring came to think of themselves as property with a cash value rather than as human beings. The tragedy of their lives is alleviated only by the picture Schermerhorn paints of their strength, strategic know-how, and resilience in the face of one inevitable parting after another. His account turns a history of endless sorrow into an inspirational tale of the strength of the human spirit and the ability to overcome tragedy. With its stress on agency, as well as victimization, this chapter effectively rebuts the argument that slavery had devastating effects on children, inflicting what the historian Nell Painter has called "soul murder."[25]

This volume, with its studies of childhood slavery, invites further research into a fascinating, if harrowing subject. Our opening section on the slave trade is a tale of horror, deprivation, and sadness. Even the relatively good treatment of children on the transatlantic voyage compared to the suffering of their parents,[26] and of those attached to traders in East Africa, described here by Morton, does not mitigate this picture. It merely shows that persons involved in all branches of this cruelest of trades could be humane if it suited their purposes.

The next section comprises examples of different forms of slavery. Our samples have been chosen, first to show the reasons why children were bought, even when their labor might not cover the purchase price for many years; and second to illustrate the wide variety of children's experiences of bondage. Some forms of slavery, such as that practiced in the Southern United States, were based simply on the owners' need to make a profit—no consideration being shown for the child victims of the system. There doubtless were considerate owners but the system did not encourage or reward such sentiments. By contrast, in the trade in Chinese child slaves, the treatment of the mui tsai varied according to their owners. Other forms of slavery, as shown in the contributions in this volume on the devşirme in the Ottoman Empire and the eunuchs in imperial China, could open the way to high political office and influence. By contrast, the singing girls of the 'Abbasid Empire were apparently a solely cultural phenomenon, with no political or monetary significance, except that the girls could be hired out as prostitutes. In all three of these cases the children were relatively well treated.

It appears clear throughout that the numbers of child slaves traded increased from the late eighteenth century, as the abolitionist movement expanded, presaging the development of modern forms of slavery in which child victims have been central. This theme will be explored more fully in the companion volume, *Children in Modern Servitude*, in which we consider examples of child servitude in the nineteenth and twentieth centuries. The second volume investigates in particular the transition from slavery to freedom—a transition that today is still not complete because, although the institution is illegal everywhere, children are currently being born into slavery in parts of Africa. Owners can no longer exert all their former powers, but they can, and do, treat the descendants of slaves as inferiors and in some countries still control their lives. We include some case studies of modern slavery that clearly demonstrate that the outlawing and virtual disappearance of classic slavery has not ended child servitude. These and other forms of modern bondage are being attacked by international organizations, governments, and other concerned bodies, including NGOs. Current forms of servitude involve many more children than did traditional forms of bondage, largely as the result of conventional preoccupations with adults as victims of slavery and changed circumstances—notably population growth, growing disparity between rich and poor areas of the world, and the development of modern systems of communication. As interest in child slavery continues to grow, and as research, particularly doctoral research, proceeds, more sources will surely be found and more studies will undoubtedly appear to cast more light on this vitally important subject.

## NOTES

1. See Gwyn Campbell, Suzanne Miers, Joseph C. Miller, eds., *Women and Slavery*, vol. 1, *Africa, the Indian Ocean World, and the Medieval North Atlantic* (Athens: Ohio University Press, 2007); vol. 2, *The Modern Atlantic* (Athens: Ohio University Press, 2008).

2. For a start in this direction, see Gwyn Campbell, ed., *The Structure of Slavery in Indian Ocean Africa and Asia* (London: Frank Cass, 2004); Campbell, ed., *Abolition and Its Aftermath in Indian Ocean Africa and Asia* (London: Routledge, 2005).

3. George Michael La Rue, "The Brief Life of 'Ali, the Orphan of Kordofan: The Egyptian Slave Trade in the Sudan, 1820–35," chapter 4 below.

4. Richard B. Allen, "Children and European Slave Trading in the Indian Ocean during the Eighteenth and Early Nineteenth Centuries," chapter 2 below.

5. Gwyn Campbell, "Children and Slavery in the New World: A Review," *Slavery and Abolition* 27, no. 2 (2006): 261–62.

6. Fred Morton, "Small Change: Children in the Nineteenth-Century East African Slave Trade," chapter 3 below.

7. La Rue, "Brief Life of 'Ali."

8. Susan Eva O'Donovan, "Traded Babies: Enslaved Children in America's Domestic Migration, 1820–60," chapter 5 below.

9. Kristina Richardson, "Singing Slave Girls (*Qiyan*) of the 'Abbasid Court in the Ninth and Tenth Centuries," chapter 6 below.

10. Gulay Yilmaz, "Becoming a *Devşirme*: The Training of Conscripted Children in the Ottoman Empire," chapter 7 below.

11. Bok-Rae Kim, "The Third Gender: Palace Eunuchs," chapter 8 below.

12. Pauline Pui-ting Poon, "The Well-Being of Purchased Female Domestic Servants (*Mui Tsai*) in Hong Kong in the Early Twentieth Century," chapter 9 below.

13. Pierre H. Boulle, "Slave and Other Nonwhite Children in Late-Eighteenth-Century France," chapter 10 below.

14. Kenneth Morgan, "The Struggle for Survival: Slave Infant Mortality in the British Caribbean in the Late Eighteenth and Nineteenth Centuries," chapter 11 below.

15. Calvin Schermerhorn, "Left Behind but Getting Ahead: Antebellum Slavery's Orphans in the Chesapeake, 1820-60," chapter 12 below.

16. For an example see A. Diptee, "African Children in the British Slave Trade during the Late Eighteenth Century," *Slavery and Abolition* 27, no. 2 (2006): 183-96.

17. Morgan, "Struggle for Survival."

18. O'Donovan, "Traded Babies."

19. Ibid.

20. This was not the case in all branches of Islam.

21. See A. B. Wylde, '83 to '87 in the Sudan, 2 vols. (London: Remington, 1888).

22. For further discussion of modern slavery, see *Children and Slavery*, vol. 2.

23. For a firsthand account by a former mui tsai, see Janet Lim, *Sold for Silver: An Autobiography* (Singapore: Oxford University Press, 1985).

24. Janet Lim to Suzanne Miers, pers. comm.

25. Nell Irvin Painter, *Soul Murder and Slavery* (Waco, TX: Baylor University Press, 1998).

26. Paul Lovejoy, "The Children of Slavery—The Transatlantic Phase," in *Slavery and Abolition* 27, no. 2 (2006): 197-217.

# THE TRADES IN
# SLAVE CHILDREN

# 1

# CHILD SLAVES IN THE EARLY NORTH ATLANTIC TRADE IN THE FIFTEENTH AND SIXTEENTH CENTURIES

ANTÓNIO DE ALMEIDA MENDES

Traditional historiography presents us with a stereotyped picture of Atlantic slavery, in which black slaves generally appear as a category of dominated people who neither speak nor think for themselves, but rather are spoken and thought about. In the fifteenth century shipping routes in the North Atlantic created a cultural and economic bridge of humanity between the Iberian Peninsula, West Africa, and the Americas, which resulted in the emergence of a single, integrated Atlantic civilization. Movements of slaves, indentured servants, and voluntary migrants between the three continents, whether forced or not, profoundly changed the people and economies of the three continents. Black slaves became the principal source of labor and so became the main agents of social change in the Americas, southern Europe, and North and West Africa.

In Portugal the presence of slaves is attested from the earliest years of the kingdom in the twelfth century. Bequests made by members of the upper nobility in the thirteenth century contain many references to Saracen (Muslim) slaves. To take two examples, in 1273 Martim Gil de Coreixas bequeathed a Saracen slave called Maphomede to the monastery of Saint Peter of Cete (north of Oporto); while in the same year Teresa Rodrigues of Urrô[1] bequeathed a Saracen slave called Aly to a religious institution at Barcelos.[2] These Moorish slaves had been captured and enslaved either by corsairs in the Mediterranean or in the wars of reconquest conducted by Christians in the Iberian Peninsula and its North African presidios.[3] Did these instances of slavery in the Mediterranean world have much connection with slavery later in the Atlantic?[4] Certainly, there was no question as yet of an organized trading system with regular ports of call and trading agents, even though Pedro de Meneses, the governor and captain of Ceuta, on the North African side of the Straits of Gibraltar, shipped more than two thousand Moorish captives to Portugal between 1415 and 1437. The Muslims among them were intended for the ransoming of Christian captives, but some were reexported to Valencia and Barcelona, where Meneses had agents, notably a certain João de Lamego.[5]

The first trade in black people, linking the Mediterranean with Guinea via the Sahara, took place at the end of the thirteenth century. It was controlled in the Sudan by Arabs and in Sicily by Catalans and Genoese. But it was certainly the maritime expansion of the Portuguese in the fifteenth century that established an enduring line of communication between the West African coast and Iberian Europe. At the root of this modern trade link were five centuries of the transatlantic trade. Between the middle of the fifteenth century and the end of the sixteenth, Portuguese ships brought between 300,000 and 350,000 African men, women, and children to the Iberian Peninsula, compared with 400,000 to the New World.[6] But whereas medieval Moorish slavery was limited to serving a social elite and confined to domestic work in the palaces of the very rich—as one later found black slaves in the New World among every sector of society—in the sixteenth century slave labor fundamentally changed the social and economic structures of the Iberian world and became one of the main economic strategies in the metropolis. In Lisbon, Africans joined numerous other dependents, captives, serfs, and day laborers of every origin and color in urban centers and noble households[7] and eventually came to monopolize certain jobs. Black women and children found themselves confined to menial domestic tasks of the most unpleasant and degrading kind—they worked as minor domestics, hawkers (regateiras), washerwomen, porters, street vendors, figures encountered everywhere in the city of Lisbon.[8] This pervasive presence led to a lasting semantic shift from male slave to negro and criado as well as from child slave (escravito) to cria.[9]

This vocabulary reveals the servile condition of blacks and the opinion of the time about non-Europeans living in the metropoles and the American colonies. Moorish slaves had been converted to Christianity only when opportunities presented themselves and remained assimilated only superficially; they were a shifting population, still liable to be used for the ransoming of Christians held captive in North Africa. In contrast, Africans from south of the Sahara who reached Europe were regarded as boçais, raw savages—uncivilized, having had no contact with Islam, who had to be led through a long process of latinization (*ladinisação*), catechization, and literacy and socialization before they could become full subjects of the realm. Baptism and the taking of a Portuguese first name gave the slave a Christian identity. The choice of the Christian name was left neither to chance nor to the discretion of the master but was controlled by the church, to ensure that the first name was neither profane nor ridiculing but rather that of a Christian saint, either male or female depending on the slave's sex, so that the recipient could enjoy divine protection. But even when integrated into Christian society, the African slave was not integrated into the nation. The adjective *negro* remained not only as a physical description but was also used as a surname referring to his or her racial and geographic origins.

To understand the fates of a few of the hundreds of thousands of Africans who reached European shores it is important for us to know who they were and from whence they came, and thus to recover some knowledge of the past lives of these men and women. In 1650 Sebastian Bran, a black man, then some fifty years old, was interrogated by the Inquisition at Cartagena, in modern Colombia. He declared that he had been born in Guinea and around the age of thirteen had been captured by African merchants, who sold him to Portuguese traders. Having been taken to the Portuguese island of Santiago, Cape Verde, he had been baptized and then bought by a white master, who gave him a new name and shipped him across the Atlantic.[10] Sebastian, like many Africans, had not forgotten the land of his ancestors and, after forty years away from Africa, he still remembered his early life, his village, and his family. How can one thus explain why after the nineteenth-century abolition of slavery in Spain and Portugal, freed slaves did not return to Africa, even though racial prejudice, stereotyping, and social inequality had been constant features of their lives in Europe? We do not know Sebastian's precise origins in Africa, but he had forgotten nothing of his African past, of his journey by sea, or of his forced departure from Africa. Displaced thousands of miles from the land of his birth by other black people, treated as a stranger by the Africans who had sold him, and perceived by white men as a man of the "black race," yet Sebastian regarded himself as a composite, torn between two cultures and three continents, who knew that his own future and that of his descendants lay in the Hispanic world rather than in any return to Africa.

African merchants and their prisoners could be of the same color and the same ethnic origin, but if they were from different areas or of different social standings they could still be foreign to one another. In 1541, Leonor Rodrigues, a black woman, appeared before the Inquisition of Lisbon. She

denounced her mistress, Maria Rodrigues, a recently converted New Christian (one at least nóminally converted from Judaism), who had sworn an
oath against Manuel, the king, who had forcibly converted both of them.
To the stupefaction of her slave, Maria Rodrigues ironically asked her if
she would like to become white, to which she replied yes,[11] thus expressing
the blatant wish for cultural whitening of those of the black population
who lived with Portuguese names, practiced Christianity, or mastered the
Portuguese language in hopes of being freed and integrated. Cultural assimilation, as well as biological mixing, allowed some "latinized" slaves to
profit from the existing means of social advance and as individuals to nurse
the hope of economic and social mobility. Assimilation into the family and
household of the master, learning to read and write, and acceptance into
religious confraternities (brotherhoods) inscribed the slave and the freed-
man, whether black or half-caste, into the metropolitan social hierarchy. Some
slaves achieved fabled positions as soldiers, sailors, scholars, and ecclesias-
tics. Thus the African Juan Latino (1518-94), who arrived in Spain at the
age of twelve as the son of a slave mother, became a brilliant humanist.

The demography and the patterns of this first Atlantic trade yield important evidence about the dynamism of slavery in European and African
societies. First, the almost complete figures we possess for slaves arriving
in Portugal between 1499 and 1522 (table 1.1 and fig. 1.1) show a regular
and massive trade. Children and women constituted more than 70 percent
of those imported,[12] whereas in the later transatlantic trade there were on
average two men for every woman, although that ratio changed according
to time and place.[13] The contact between Europeans and Africans in the fifteenth century did not reduce the trade in women and children but rather
strengthened it. In southern Europe and North Africa, the exploitation

TABLE 1.1
## Slaves embarked at Arguin to Portugal (1499–1520)

| Dates | Numbers |
| --- | --- |
| May 1499–December 1501 | 668 |
| March 1505–November 1508 | 526 |
| December 1508–June 1511 | 1,540[a] |
| July 1511–August 1514 | 1,002[a] |
| November 1514–September 1517 | 2,336 |
| September 1517–October 1520 | 3,792 |

Sources: Arquivo Nacional/Torre do Tombo; Corpo cronológico.
[a]Includes all slaves leaving Arguin.

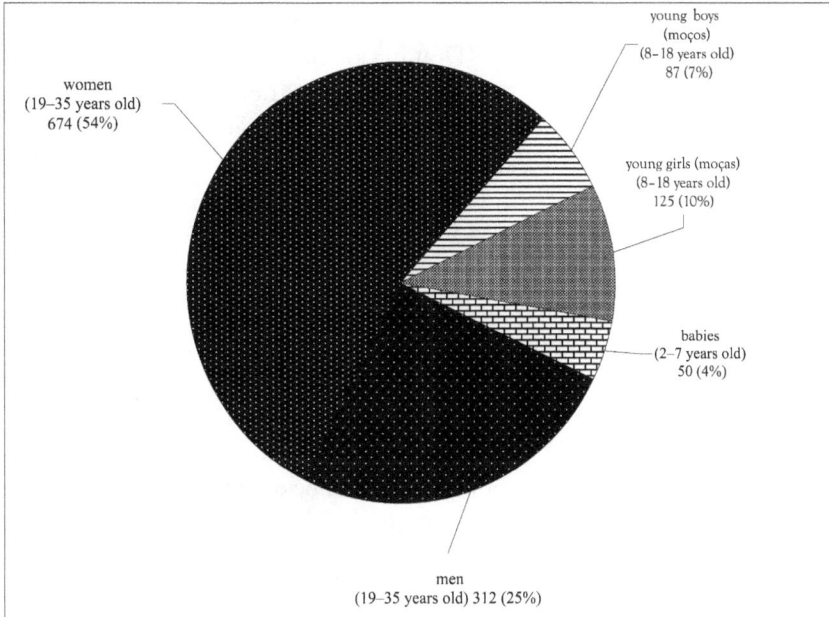

FIG. 1.1. Gender and age of 1,248 slaves, Arguin to Lisbon, 1511–22

of women and children, whether black or white, for domestic work or for sexual purposes, was a long-standing and common feature, fed by piracy in the Mediterranean and onshore raiding. From then until 1575 nearly 70 percent of all slaves who crossed the Atlantic to destinations in Europe or the Americas were shipped from the trading ports of Senegambia or else from the Portuguese entrepôt of Santiago in Cape Verde.[14] These slaves, introduced into Portugal, were designated as *Jolofos*. Whether used by Portuguese or Africans, the term *Jolofo* signified a geographical area—the great Jolof Empire, which comprised the Wolof, Sereer, and Malinke homelands in and south of the Senegal River basin, rather than only the Wolof ethnic group near the coast.

This forced transfer between the Iberian Peninsula and Senegambia was the result of economic, social, and political differences on the two sides of the Atlantic. In Portugal the victory over the Muslims in the twelfth century had left a consciousness among the military and civilians of a unified political, economic, and cultural sphere centered on themselves as Christians. In the fifteenth and sixteenth centuries the West was Christendom. Iberian Christian society was a hierarchical one of orders and distinctions of rank, founded on the inequality of birth, but in practice there was an integration that included all Christians irrespective of color. Didier Lahon emphasizes that African slaves could achieve social integration through embracing the

cult of the Virgin Mary. The black Confraternity of the Rosary, Nossa Sen-
hora do Rosário, based on the Dominican convent of Lisbon, asked no
more of those who wished to join it than that they profess Catholicism,
without distinctions of sex or origin.[15] In Senegambia invasions and other
military conflicts, the circulation of women, and itinerant merchants and
the trans-Saharan trade disrupted the stability of frontiers. These military
and religious conflicts redefined the dominance of the various ethnic
communities, inflamed social tensions, and turned entire groups of members within the communities into "foreigners." The Wolof political identity
included ethnically and linguistically distinct Berbers, Sereer, Fulbe, Mandingo, and Lebu. The spread of Muslim law and faith along the commercial
routes established a principle of inequality based on stratification between
Muslims and non-Muslims and between slave and free. Slavery, as Roger
Botte has pointed out, "was not one labor regime among others but became
the very basis of the social order as a result of the demographic bulk of the
[large] servile population."[16] Portuguese traders, on their arrival on the West
African coast in the fifteenth century, thus entered a system of trading networks, whether commercial or not, that animated the scene in West Africa.
Coastal states developed an economic system based entirely on internal
slavery and the slave trade overseas. So it was with the kingdoms of Gaabu
and Fuuta Jaloo at the end of the eighteenth century,[17] and doubtless also
those of Siin, Saalum, and Kajoor from the fifteenth century onward.

Thus, many Africans had their first experience of slavery in Africa and
not in Europe. Before their embarkation in Portuguese ships, most had
traveled long distances from the places where they had been captured to
the ports whence they departed. For many African captives their arrival
in Portugal must have presented the possibility of a way out of slavery,
which in Africa was a condition inherited through the generations. In fact
the men concerned no longer thought of themselves as Africans or Europeans, as blacks or whites, but as individuals integrated into the ties of
dependence and location according to the laws and norms of behavior of
their new societies. Our unequal knowledge of the societies of Europe and
Africa does not permit us to retrace the complete circuit from the interior
of Africa to Portugal. Nevertheless, various kinds of sources bear witness to
the slaves' experiences. These include certificates of marriage, baptism, and
manumission, civil and criminal law suits, and nearly complete listings of
slaves imported from Senegambia during two decades (1499 to 1520).

The sources explored for this study point to the need for further research showing slavery not as confined to black people but as including the
whole range of men, women, and children who arrived in Portugal. There

is also the need to work out the internal itineraries of the traffic in slaves, as well as their genders, classes, ages, and social and ethnic origins. These are fundamental evidence for the formation of the complex identities that developed in the Mediterranean region.

## THE NORTH ATLANTIC TRADE BETWEEN PORTUGAL AND AFRICA

In the thirteenth century an early trade in black people connected the two shores of the Mediterranean, between the Maghreb and southern Europe, through the islands of Majorca and Sicily. The African trade routes across the Sahara are relatively well known. They joined the heart of the African continent all the way from Senegambia to the great bend of the Niger River and as far east as Darfur to the ports of the North African coast. Most of the captives who crossed the Sahara by these routes were destined to be sold into the Muslim communities of North Africa, but blacks from the Barca Mountains[18] were seen in Barcelona and Sicily. We know, for example, that at Palermo in Sicily, between 1440 and 1460, Henry Bresc noted the sale of eighty-four black men and thirty-seven black women from Barca.[19] And in 1441 two Portuguese mariners, Antão Gonçalves and Nuno Tristão, sailed their caravel down the coast of the western Sahara beyond the River of Gold, where they captured eleven black Moors and one black female, whom they carried north to Lagos in southern Portugal. And on Friday, 8 August 1444, the first slave cargo, consisting of 235 Africans, arrived in Lisbon. The North Atlantic trade thus became the vital link in a chain connecting the medieval Mediterranean trade in slaves, the trade across the Sahara, and the transatlantic trade of modern times. The southward advance of the Iberian caravels through the North Atlantic began with the brutal Spanish conquest of the Canary Islands in 1402.[20] Portuguese and Spanish incursions multiplied from 1420 onward and by the end of the fifteenth century led to the virtual extermination of eighty thousand native Guanches. The male Guanches were killed in battle, and their wives and children were carried off to the ports of the Iberian Peninsula. Of a sample of 515 Guanche slaves who reached Valencia between 1489 and 1497, 47 percent were women from seventeen to thirty years old, 32 percent were young boys and girls between six and sixteen, 11 percent were boys between two and sixteen, while only 10 percent were men between seventeen and thirty.[21]

This first organized deportation from the Canary Islands to the Iberian Peninsula led to a much larger traffic along the coasts of Mauritania and Guinea. A thorough search of thousands of notices in the *Corpo cronológico*, preserved in the Portuguese National Archives, enabled a detailed reconstruction, slave by slave, of the trade that linked the port of Lisbon with the Saharan entrepôt of Arguin and the internal slave trade within Africa between the beginning and the middle of the sixteenth century. Developed from 1440 onward on a small rocky island off the coast of modern Mauritania, the entrepôt became a very active market for slaves, gold, and fish. Here the Portuguese made contact with Berber merchants who had organized themselves around a long-distance trade in slaves, gold, salt, and cola nuts as well as for predation.[22]

Between 1444 and 1456 fewer than a thousand black slaves had left the shores of Mauritania and Upper Guinea. Around 1456, Alvise de Cadamosto estimated the annual arrival of slaves in Portugal at 700 to 800. Between 1486 and 1493 arrivals numbered 3,539. Thus the yearly average arrivals were 440.[23] These slaves, called in the texts Wolof and Mandingo,[24] formed the largest number of those found in Lisbon, Seville, and Valencia, more than other slaves called Benin, Mina, or Congo shipped from the Gulf of Guinea or from Kongo. For more than half a century (1470-1540) the entrepôt of Arguin was the principal port of departure for African slaves destined for Portugal. Table 1.1 summarizes the arrivals of these slaves in Lisbon, and shows that within the space of twenty years (1499-1520) at least ten thousand individuals, known as peças (equivalent to "pieces" of the textiles used to purchase them) arrived at the entrepôt and that in a half-century perhaps twenty to twenty-five thousand slaves were exported to Portugal from Arguin. The supplies of human merchandise reaching Arguin, and also of gold, varied from year to year, depending on what was happening hundreds of miles away, south of the Sahara in the African hinterland. The trade from Arguin, and thus also that reaching Portugal, depended on regional political and economic conditions in Africa and on the deliveries of the Berber intermediaries, whom the Portuguese called al-formas,[25] the Muslim caïds,[26] and the Jewish intermediaries who controlled the supply of textiles (haïks, hambels) produced in Morocco.[27]

The Portuguese traded slaves for merchandise in four centers: the bay of Saint-Jean (in the village of Awguej), Tofia, Cabo da Area, and Anterote (near Nouakchott), situated respectively at 17, 24, 39, and 51 leagues from Arguin. Commercial transactions were made piece by piece and slave by slave in lengthy bargaining processes. Once agreement had been reached, the Muslim vendor made his choice from the articles displayed in the fort within a schedule of equivalences between given articles and gold. Written in both Arabic and Portuguese, this schedule was displayed in the trading chamber in full view of all, effectively providing the legal framework for transactions. Each article had a single "use value," which corresponded to a monetary standard expressed in gold (table 1.2). A young, clean, healthy male

TABLE 1.2
## Slave Merchandise Equivalents

TEXTILES AND GARMENTS

| Merchandise | Value (gold doubloons) |
| --- | :---: |
| Alentejo carpets (3 sizes) | 5 |
| | 2.5 |
| | 2 |
| Hambel (rug) | 5 |
| Burnoose | 3 |
| Haik | 1.25 |
| Djellaba (robe) | 5 |
| Woolen hat | 0.25 |
| Toque | 1 |
| Gallabiya | 1.25 |
| Bordat (cotton fabric, cubits) | 0.6 |

TACK AND METALWARE

| Merchandise | Value (gold doubloons) |
| --- | :---: |
| Stirrup | 5 |
| Saddle | 8 |
| Bridle | 2 |
| Spur | 1.25 |
| Chamber pot | 0.5 |
| Shaving basin | 1.25 |
| Fabric | 5 |
| Moroccan Safi cotton | 1.5 |

was the standard, at fifteen gold doubloons.[28] Adult men and women had the same value in trade. Children between seven and eight years were valued at 40 percent to 45 percent of the adult price, six to seven doubloons. Elderly slaves, over thirty-six years old, fetched no more than 35 percent of the adult standard value, or five doubloons of gold. Once sales ended, the slaves were segregated in holding pens by sex.

The slave-trading activities of the Portuguese entrepôts peaked around the turn of the sixteenth century in response to a series of African political, social, and religious factors that influenced the internal trade routes. At the interregional level, the Arab and Berber merchants played the role of intermediaries between the Europeans and the Africans, and imposed on the Europeans a precise selection of the trade goods and finally demanded that slaves should be exchanged only for grain, because of a drought that affected the whole of North Africa and the Sahel in the early sixteenth century. The Portuguese themselves were dependent on Andalusia for the wheat needed by the metropolis and the Atlantic islands and could not supply the North African market. At the same time Portuguese military defeats in their fortified positions along Morocco's Atlantic coast (presidios at Agadir, Safi, Azemmour, Alcácer Ceguer, and Arzila) and the attacks of pirates from the Canaries against these Portuguese possessions weakened Portugal's commerce. The fall of Agadir in 1541 was a great blow to the Portugal.[29] During Gil Sardinha's governorship at Arguin (1545–49) nearly three hundred slaves were captured by Canary Islanders. To counter this trend the Portuguese sent two caravels in 1550 under the command of Francisco Luis Neto and Diogo Velho. Exports of slaves to the metropole fell drastically. Between June 1549 and November 1550, a period of nearly a year and a half, the governor of the fort sent fewer than six hundred instead of the two thousand each year in the 1520s. The trade of the whole region was nearly dead, and the role of Arguin declined, to be replaced by that of Santiago in the Cape Verde Islands, which turned to the "Southern Rivers" of the mainland coast (Guinea-Bissau and Conakry). Ouadane, one of the important Saharan cultural and commercial centers at the end of the fifteenth century, with some three thousand inhabitants, began to decline. According to Leo Africanus, who visited the town in the sixteenth century, the learned men and Muslim merchants had left the town en masse for Tombouctou and Gao, two towns on the Niger River, both of which fed the trans-Saharan trade eastwards to Tunis, Ghadames (Libya), and the Ottoman Empire, dominant in the eastern Mediterranean since the fall of Constantinople, in 1453. The Arab-Berber intermediaries turned away from the Portuguese centers and directed themselves toward the Maghreb and Agadir (in Mauritania), blending into a strong trade with Portuguese Jews established in the interior oases. At the same time Mande traders apparently migrated from Awkar (Mauritania) south toward the kingdom of Mali, where they founded the towns of Odienné and Boron (now in northern Côte d'Ivoire).[30]

In sub-Saharan Africa the expansion of Islam and of the Mande toward the bend of the Niger and into Senegambia ended in the fifteenth century with the creation of a vast integrated cultural and commercial region.[31] In the area of the Niger Bend, during the reign of Sunni Ali (1468–73), the Muslim kingdom of Songhai extended its rule north to Tombouctou and west to Jenne. The prosperity of the kingdom depended on the long-distance trade in salt and gold, and on warfare. Askia Muhammad (r. 1493–1528), who succeeded Sunni Ali, created a vast military empire that included part of present-day Mauritania, lower Senegal, Aïr in the west-central Sahara, and Bornu on the shores of Lake Chad to the east. Well versed in Islamic doctrine, he began a series of wars of conquest notably against the Mossi, in the highlands around which the Niger flowed, who resisted successfully. In December 1514 a young slave girl from Mandinga country was sold in Valencia. Her African name, Moro, indicates that she was probably Mossi and spoke the language of the region, Moré. The same year Leonor, age twenty-eight, reported that she had been captured by other Africans in Mandinga country and resold to whites, who brought her to Spain.[32]

On the Senegambian coast the Wolof kingdom of Kajoor, with which the Portuguese had been in contact since the middle of the fifteenth century, expanded as a result of the Atlantic trade. The revenues that the Damel, a Muslim king, derived from selling slaves for horses enabled him to domi-nate neighboring kingdoms, notably Bezeguiche, on the Lébou Peninsula on Cape Verde (Senegal), which had no similar dealings with Europeans. The Kajoor ruler dominated the Cape Verde Peninsula by 1515 and re-gained the Lébou Peninsula between 1480 and 1515.[33] The origins of many of the slaves who came to Arguin in Lébou is likely, if one can believe the Portuguese documents, which mention the activities of a military leader called Dama at the beginning of the sixteenth century as a chief on the coast, at the head of a considerable cavalry, the Narzigues, who devastated the villages on the Cape Verde Peninsula and supplied slaves to the Por-tuguese fort. Among the blacks in the kingdoms of Siin and Saalum, the dynasty, originally Malinke of Gelwaar, introduced new castes when it came to power in 1490 and allied with the great Wolof and Sereer families to establish centralized power based largely on the export of captives captured in wars.

At Arguin a "*jagarafe* of the blacks" presided over trade between Portuguese and Africans.[34] He served as an ambassador—a commercial intermediary between the Portuguese traders and the military chief, who collected trib-ute and looked after the economic interests of the king at the Portuguese post. The *jagarafe* spoke Portuguese and Arabic as well as the two local languages, Wolof and Peul. These Arab-Berber intermediaries were the link between Europeans and Africans at this margin of the desert and sub-Saharan Africa. Commercial exchanges and the interior trade networks between Senegambia and surrounding areas were controlled by the Dioula and Wangara, names applied by the Sudanese, Portuguese, and Arabs to Malinke and Soninke traders, as well as to Luso-Africans, who were par-ticularly mobile since they used family networks that crossed frontiers and relied on their knowledge of the area.[35] The cooperation between all these groups was considerable and presumably supposes the existence of a trade in girls and boys sold for domestic service, agricultural labor, or for use as artisans in the markets of Upper Guinea or in the African interior.

## SLAVE CHILDREN: FROM AFRICA TO PORTUGAL

Figure 1.1 shows a sample of 1,248 slaves arriving at Arguin. The records of the Portuguese factors show that the great majority were women and children. For raiders, women who were breast-feeding and small children were the easiest to capture. After days of walking across the desert in extreme conditions from one oasis or well to another, the caravans reached their termini along the coast of Mauritania and at the fort at Arguin, places where complex interests were at play. Once the slaves arrived at Arguin, they were carefully examined by the Portuguese and divided up according to age and sex: men (*homens*), women (*mulheres*), children (*moços* and *moças*), and babies at the breast (*crianças de mimo*). And since precise ages were not known, they were divided according to "life stages": children, (pubescent) youths, adults, and old people. This arbitrary classification was made on physical characteristics (for instance the presence of bodily hair on young men) that corresponded to the Christian schema of growth, maturity, and decline.[36] The two parties engaged in spirited negotiations at the time of the actual transaction. The slaves were bartered one by one against goods in wooden cases. The goods fell into three categories: textiles, harnesses and other tack for horses, and copper, leather, and brass utensils.

On the slaves' arrival in Lisbon, they were taken to the warehouses of the Casa da Mina e da Guiné, where they were counted and inspected by an *almoxarife* (assessor) who established their value in *reis* (the basic Portuguese currency unit of account). After half a day being paraded naked in single file through the streets of the town center, they were offered for sale at the Praça dos Escravos close to the present Campo das Cebolas, on the banks of the Tagus. The Portuguese brokers who specialized in the buying and reselling of slaves bought whole lots (some consisting of over a hundred individuals) whom they reexported by sea to Seville or Valencia, where they had branches, run by local agents overseen by trusted family members or fellow Portuguese nationals.

In October 1483, Bartolomé de Carries, a notable of the town of Valencia, and Juan Gallach acquired two small black children, Ali and Amet, ages eight and ten. In January 1491 little Zamba, then about fourteen, was bought by the trader Jerónimo Simó. The same year Gomba, age nine, came into the hands of a white master.[37] Ali, Amet, Zamba, and Gomba were four children among the hundreds of thousands of Africans brought to the Iberian Peninsula via North Africa or the Atlantic to be used in all sorts of work in the fields or in households, when they were not also forced to submit to the sexual desires of their owners. From their names we can deduce that two of the four children were born in Africa and appear in the documents as boçais, or recently arrived and not yet culturally assimilated, in contrast to the *ladinos,* those who had been latinized.

As their names show, two of the children were Muslim, or had been Islamized, and must have come through the trans-Saharan trade, which supplied the Mediterranean areas with such slaves. The Portuguese classed these four slaves as Jolofos—a term applied to a vast geographical area which included several ethnic groups. Zamba and Gomba were clearly African names. However, it is not clear that they represent the ethnic origins of the children. They might have named themselves, or these names might have been ones the Portuguese gathered from the African traders or through their interpreters. Alonso Franco Silva records the sale in Seville of many slaves called Zamba and Gomba in the 1490s, one of whom came from "Mandinga country."[38] According to Paul E. H. Hair, Gomba (and its derivatives Cunba, Conba, or Coba) came from Coumba, a very common feminine name in Senegambia, and Zamba was originally a Peule word designating a young boy.[39] It might have been either a given name or a surname. In 1566 a young Wolof slave appeared before the Tribunal of the Inquisition in Lisbon with three other slaves. He declared to the officials that his Wolof name was Zamba, that he had been captured by Moors during a war, and that he was then sold to Portuguese traders. Taken to Lisbon, he was bought by Bastião da Silva of Porto and then was taken to Coimbra to serve a new master.[40] Everything points to the fact that these Zamba children were already slaves or dependents while in Africa, that they belonged to "castes" regarded as inferior, and that they knew this from an early age. Perhaps they were prisoners of war consigned to domestic, agricultural, or artisanal labor. Whatever the case, children and women were the first victims of the regional trades among various political entities, which grew to completely new—and larger—scales once they developed connections with the Atlantic trade and Europe.

In Europe slave children adopted as parents the owners who fed and clothed them and looked after them when they were ill. If most slaves were treated roughly and cruelly,[41] some became parts of extended families (women, children, servants, clients) and might benefit from better treatment or were freed, or able to buy their freedom, and found their own families. Owners did not free their slaves until they were old and could no longer work for them. Even after they were freed, ties remained between former owners and their former slaves. Child slaves when educated, converted, and acculturated while very young were more easily integrated into Portuguese society than adults. Baptism turned slaves into Christians and, in theory, gave them certain rights previously denied them by their birth. Family origins were social givens; the slaves accepted that they came from elsewhere, remembering their African childhoods when they became adults, and the tragic moment that had changed their lives.[42] One must not minimize the violence inherent in their domination in Portuguese society, nor the trauma of having become a piece of merchandise, sold and resold. However, seen in the perspective of forced labor, past and present, the traffic in children is a story as old as human history itself.

## NOTES

1. Wife of Martim Leitão de Lodares, one of the most important *fidalgos* (faithful vassals) of the kingdom.

2. Leontina Ventura, "Testamentária nobiliárquica (século XIII)," *Revista de história das ideias* (Coimbra) (1998): 143.

3. Aurélia Martín Casares, *La esclavitud en la Granada del siglo XV* (Granada: Universidad de Granada, 2000).

4. Michel Fontenay, "L'esclavage en Méditerranée occidentale au XVIIe siècle," *La Méditerranée occidentale au XVIIe siècle* (Bulletin 14 de l'Association des Historiens Modernistes de l'Université, Paris, 1990), 11-50 ; Fontenay, "Le Maghreb barbaresque et l'esclavage méditerranéen aux XVIe et XVIIe siècles," *Cahiers de Tunisie* 45, nos. 157-58 (1993): 7-44.

5. Nuno Silva Campos, *D. Pedro de Meneses e a construção da Casa de Vila Real (1415–1437)* (Lisbon: Colibri, 2004), 96-104; David Lopes, *A expansão portuguesa em Marrocos* (1936; Lisbon: Teorema, 1989).

6. David Eltis, "The Volume and Structure of the Transatlantic Slave Trade: A Reassessment," *William and Mary Quarterly* 58, no. 1 (2001): 17-46; Ivana Elbl, "The Volume of the Early Atlantic Slave Trade, 1450-1521," *Journal of African History* 38, no. 1 (1997): 31-75; António de Almeida Mendes, "Traites ibériques entre Méditerranée et Atlantique: Le Noir au cœur des empires modernes et de la première mondialisation (ca. 1435-1550)," *Anais de história de além-mar* 6 (2005): 351-87.

7. A. C. de C. M. Saunders, *A Social History of Black Slaves and Freedmen in Portugal, 1441-1555* (Cambridge: Cambridge University Press, 1982); Maria do Rosário Pimentel, *Viagem ao fundo das consciências: A escravatura na época moderna* (Lisbon: Colibri, 1995); Didier Lahon, "Esclavage et confreries noires au Portugal durant l'Ancien Régime (1441-1830)" (doctoral thesis, EHESS, Paris, 2001). For Spain, see Alessandro Stella, *Histoires d'esclaves dans la Péninsule ibérique* (Paris: Éd. de l'EHESS, 2000); Bernard Vincent, "La schiavitù nella peninsola iberica," in *Schiavi, corsari, rinnegati*, ed. Giovanni Fiumi (Palermo: Edizioni Guida, 2001) (*Nuove effemeridi, rassegna trimestrale di cultura* 14, no. 54), 62-68.

8. Didier Lahon, *O negro no coração do Império: Uma memória a resgatar: Séculos XV–XIX* (Lisbon: Entreculturas, 1999).

9. *Cria* contains the notion of livestock farming.

10. María Cristina Navarrete, "Consideraciones en torno a la esclavitud de los Etíopes y la operatividad de la ley, siglos XVI y XVII," *Historia y espacio* (Colombia) 27 (2006): 2.

11. Instituto dos Arquivos Nacionais/Torre do Tombo (IAN/TT), Inquisition of Lisbon, *processo* against Maria Rodrigues, 16 April 1541.

12. António de Almeida Mendes, "Esclavages et traites modernes: Le temps des empires ibériques, entre Moyen Age et Modernité, entre Méditerranée et Atlantique (XVe-XVIIe siècles): Une histoire globale" (thesis defense, EHESS, 2007).

13. David Eltis and Ugo Nwokeji, "Characteristics of Captives Leaving the Cameroons for the Americas, 1822-1837," *Journal of African History* 43, no. 2 (2002): 191-210.

14. António de Almeida Mendes, "The Foundations of the System: A Reassessment of the Slave Trade to the Spanish Americas in the Sixteenth and Seventeenth Centuries," in *Extending the Frontiers: Essays on the New Transatlantic Slave Trade Database*, ed. David Eltis and David Richardson (New Haven: Yale University Press, 2008).

15. Didier Lahon, "Esclavage, confréries noires, sainteté noire et pureté de sang au Portugal (XVI-XVIIIe siècles)," *Lusitana Sacra* 15 (2003): 119-62.

16. Roger Botte, "Les habits neufs de l'esclavage: Métamorphoses de l'oppression au travail," *Cahiers d'études africaines* (special issue, "Esclavage moderne ou modernité de l'esclavage?") 45, nos. 3-4 (2005): 651-66.

17. Roger Botte, "Les rapports Nord-Sud, la traite négrière et le Fuuta Jaloo à la fin du XVIIIe siècle," *Annales ESC* 46, no. 6 (1991): 1411-36.

18. An oasis in Cyrenaica (Libya) that was the destination of the trans-Saharan caravans coming from the Niger River.

19. Henri Bresc, *Un monde méditerranéen: Économie et société en Sicile, 1300–1450*, 2 vols. (Rome: Ecole Française de Rome, 1986).

20. Manuel Lobo Cabrera, *La esclavitud en las Canarias orientales en el siglo XVI: Negros, moros y moriscos)* (Santa Cruz de Tenerife: Cabildo Insular de Gran Canaria, 1982).

21. Calculated from sources published in Vicenta Cortés Alonso, *La esclavitud en Valencia durante el reinado de los reyes católicos (1419–1516)* (Valencia: Excmo. Ayuntamiento, 1964), doc. 99, 232.

22. Yahya Ould Al Bara, "Fiqh, société et pouvoir: Étude des soucis et préoccupations socio-politiques des théologiens-légistes (fuqaha) à partir de leurs consultations juridiques (fatawa) du XVIIe au XXe siècle," 2 vols. (doctoral thesis, EHESS, Paris, 2000).

23. João Lúcio de Azevedo, *Épocas de Portugal económico* (Lisbon: Clássica Editora, 1988; first ed., 1928).

24. Duarte Pacheco Pereira, *Esmeraldo de situ orbis* (Lisbon: Academia Portuguesa da História, 1988), 39.

25. Translators, working in Arabic. One finds this term in Valentim Fernandes, *Description de la côte d'Afrique de Ceuta au Sénégal*, ed. Pierre de Cenival and Théodore Monod (Paris: Larose, 1938), 94-95. Also see Juan Antonio Frago Gracia, "Arabismos saharianos (*alforma, alformaje, alformar*) en el español de Canarias," *Revista de filología*

*española* (Consejo Superior de Investigaciones Científicas, Ciencia e Investigación, Madrid) 77, nos. 1-2 (1997): 149-52.

26. The *caïd* (judge) of Safi until 1500 had the authority to send a ship loaded with merchandise annually. Cited in Bernard Rosenberger, "Aspects du commerce portugais avec le Maroc (XVe-XVIe siècles)," in *Aquém e além da Taproban: Estudos luso-orientais à memória de Jean Aubin e Denys Lombard* (Lisbon: Centro de História de Além-Mar, 2002), 71-84.

27. A number of Jewish traders had left Spain and Portugal to establish themselves in North African markets; see Bernard Rosenberger, "Le rôle des Juifs hispaniques dans l'adaptation du Maroc à son temps (1493-1603)," in *Os Judeus sefarditas entre Portugal, Espanha e Marrocos*, ed. Carmen Ballesteros and Mery Ruah (Lisbon: Colibri, 2004), 126.

28. The doubloon was a double-faced Spanish coin weighing 0.225 troy ounces and one of the standards of value in the consolidating Mediterranean and early Atlantic economies of the era.

29. Joaquim de Abreu Figanier, *História de Santa Cruz do Cabo Gué (Agadir), 1505–1541* (Lisbon: Agência Geral das Colónias, 1945).

30. Andreas W. Massing, "The Wangara, an Old Soninke Diaspora in West Africa?" *Cahiers d'études africaines* 40, no. 2 (2000): 281-308.

31. Djibril Tamsir Niane, *Histoire des Mandingues de l'Ouest: Le royaume du Gabou* (Paris: Khartala-Arsan, 1989).

32. Cortés Alonso, *Esclavitud en Valencia*, 435, 461.

33. Jean Boulègue, *Le Grand Jolof (XIII–XVIe siècles)* (Blois: Éd. Façades, Diffusion Karthala, 1987).

34. André Álvares de Almada characterized the jagarafe as a *capitão geral* (in the ranks of Portuguese colonial system, the officer in charge); Luís Silveira, ed., *Tratado breve dos rios de Guiné* (Lisbon: Oficina Gráfica, 1945), 260, 267.

35. Boulègue, *Grand Jolof*, 92.

36. Jean-Claude Schmitt, "L'invention de l'anniversaire," *Annales histoire, Sciences sociales* 62, no. 4 (2007): 793-835.

37. Cortés Alonso, *Esclavitud en Valencia*, 223, 225, 235.

38. Alonso Franco Silva, *Regesto documental sobre la esclavitud sevillana (1453–1513)* (Seville: Publicaciones de la Universidad de Sevilla, 1979).

39. P. E. H. Hair, "Black African Slaves at Valencia, 1482-1516: An Onomastic Inquiry," *History in Africa* 7 (1980): 119-39.

40. IAN/TT, Inquisition of Lisbon, processo of Damião Mendes, 16 February 1656.

41. Lahon, "Esclavage, confréries noires."

42. The historian Alessandro Stella found a considerable number of statements by slaves in the archives of Cadiz that revealed the indelible scar of sale, years after the event. Stella, "La traite des enfants," *Cahiers des anneaux de la mémoire* 5 (2003): 197-205.

# 2

## CHILDREN AND EUROPEAN SLAVE TRADING IN THE INDIAN OCEAN DURING THE EIGHTEENTH AND EARLY NINETEENTH CENTURIES

RICHARD B. ALLEN

On 1 February 1835 slavery was formally abolished in the British colony of Mauritius in the southwestern Indian Ocean. The act of abolition stipulated that emancipated slaves had to serve their former masters as "apprentices" for no more than six years before finally being freed and that owners were to be compensated for the loss of all legally acquired slaves. Shortly thereafter, the Mauritian government set out to determine how many of the colony's new apprentices for whom compensation was being claimed had been imported illegally into the island.[1] Officials soon identified at least 3,384 former slaves deemed likely to have reached the colony illicitly.[2] Among the cases subsequently investigated by the compensation commissioners was one in which an apprentice named Victorine declared that she had been brought to the island as a child from Bali about a year before the cholera epidemic that struck Mauritius during 1819 and 1820.[3] Victorine, estimated to be twenty-five to thirty years old at the time of her deposition in 1836, was accordingly probably between seven and twelve years old when she reached Mauritius as part of a human cargo that included at least three other females (Charlotte, Charlotte's sister Clarisse, and Rose) who were also apparently children or adolescents.[4] These women were not the only former "Malay" slaves to report having been imported illegally into the colony as children during the early nineteenth century.[5] Another woman, Esther, informed the compensation commissioners that she too had reached the island from Bali, probably in 1816 as a young woman about fifteen years of age.[6]

The importation of children and adolescents such as Victorine, Charlotte, Clarisse, Rose, and Esther into Mauritius, its sister Mascarene Islands of Réunion and Rodrigues, and its lesser dependencies such as the Seychelles from the far reaches of the Indian Ocean was not an isolated occurrence. An 1817 Mauritian slave register provides evidence that significant numbers of Indian children reached these islands during the late eighteenth century. Fifty-one percent of 1,506 Indian slaves sampled from this register were between thirty and thirty-nine years old in 1817,[7] which would have made them between six and fifteen during the last great surge of slave trading from India to the Mascarenes between 1785 and 1793.[8] Colonial censuses reveal that children regularly comprised approximately one-fifth of a Mauritian slave population that grew steadily in size during the late eighteenth and early nineteenth centuries.[9] Low birth rates and high death rates among the Mauritian slave population indicate that the importation of large numbers of children rather than natural reproduction underpinned this increase in the number of child slaves on the island.[10]

The presence of substantial numbers of enslaved children in the Mascarenes comes as no surprise. Historians have long appreciated that European and other slave traders carried many African children far from their homes and families over the centuries. More than one million boys and girls under the age of fourteen were shipped across the Atlantic between 1600 and 1800. The proportion of children in transatlantic cargoes also increased dramatically—from 12.2 to 22.7 percent—between the late seventeenth and early nineteenth centuries and soared still further, to 40 percent or more of all slaves reaching the Americas, by the time the transatlantic trades came to an end during the 1860s.[11]

Although the recent publication of a number of important works on slavery and slave trading in the Indian Ocean attests to a growing scholarly interest in forced labor systems in this part of the world,[12] the region continues to be largely ignored in slavery studies. Almost thirty years ago, Hubert Gerbeau discussed the various problems that hamper attempts to reconstruct slave trading in the Indian Ocean, including a scarcity of archival sources, the scattered and often problematic nature of the sources that do exist, and the conceptual problems of dealing with a geographically huge and culturally diverse area.[13] The need to reconstruct the history of slave trading in the world of the Mare Indicum in as much detail as possible is underscored, however, by two simple facts: the Indian Ocean trades, along with those across the Sahara, were of far greater antiquity than those across the Atlantic, and the total number of African slaves transported across the Indian Ocean and Sahara probably exceeded that carried across the Atlantic.[14] Millions of men, women, and children are estimated to have been shipped by Arab and Muslim traders from eastern Africa across the Red Sea and the western Indian Ocean into the Middle East, the Persian Gulf, and South Asia during the last fourteen hundred years.[15] Arab, Muslim, and Indian merchants likewise transported slaves from the Indian subcontinent to the Persian Gulf and Southeast Asia,[16] where a regional trade in chattel labor also flourished.[17]

Europeans also trafficked in slaves following their arrival in the Indian Ocean at the end of the fifteenth century. The Portuguese shipped a small but steady stream of slaves from Mozambique to their possessions in India and as far east as Macau.[18] Beginning in the late eighteenth century, increasing numbers of Mozambican slaves were also transported to the Americas. In addition to searching for slaves along the East African coast, the Dutch exported increasing numbers of chattel laborers from the Indian subcontinent during the seventeenth century and became more heavily involved in trading slaves in Southeast Asia.[19] The seventeenth century also witnessed the arrival of British slave traders who continued to operate in this part of the world until the late 1780s and early 1790s, when the British East India Company formally banned the exportation of slaves from its Indian possessions.[20] French slave traders likewise reached the Indian Ocean during the seventeenth century, where they continued to conduct their business well into the nineteenth century.[21]

Despite our expanding knowledge about slave trading in the Indian Ocean and the impact of these trades on indigenous peoples and polities,[22] children remain more notable for their absence than their presence in these studies. Reconstructing their place in the Indian Ocean trades is important not only to a fuller understanding of the nature and dynamics of these trades, but also to assessing the ways and extent to which the movement of forced labor constituted an important sinew that bound together this huge and diverse world. The fact that Europeans transported significant numbers of enslaved children across the Mare Indicum at precisely the same time that the proportion of child slaves in transatlantic cargoes was increasing is, moreover, a potent reminder that European slave trading reached far beyond the confines of the Atlantic in ways that invite us to reconsider how we conceptualize the worlds of the Atlantic and the Indian Ocean and the relationship between these two entities.[23]

Histories of the charter companies that dominated European trade and commerce in the Indian Ocean during the seventeenth and eighteenth centuries frequently make little or no reference to slave ownership or slave trading by these companies or their personnel.[24] More specialized studies of European commerce and trade in southern Asia are equally reticent.[25] As noted earlier, this silence is due in part to a paucity of archival sources compared to those that exist for the Atlantic trades. The British East India Company archives, to cite a prominent example, contain only scattered and rather oblique references to the company's involvement in slave trading during the seventeenth and eighteenth centuries.[26] Important information about European slave trading in general, and the trafficking in children in particular, can nevertheless be gleaned from a careful examination of existing sources, especially when multiple archives are consulted.

How was a child defined in the Indian Ocean world? Unlike in the Atlantic trades, where height was often used to distinguish a child from an adult,[27] Europeans apparently relied on an individual's perceived age to classify the slaves they transported across the Indian Ocean. In the French-controlled Mascarenes, boys (négrillons) and girls (négrittes) were usually defined as fourteen years of age and younger. References also appear in the Mauritian archival record to male and female youths (caports and caporines, respectively) among slave cargoes bound for the islands. However, the age at which African, Indian, or Malay boys and girls became youths or when these youths became adults remains a subject of debate. One possible approach to this quandary may be to follow the lead of British officials in the Moluccas, who in 1804 defined children as being ten years of age and under.[28] Youths accordingly may have been regarded by many Europeans as being eleven to fourteen or fifteen, and possibly even sixteen.[29]

Evidence of European trafficking in children in the Indian Ocean during the sixteenth and seventeenth centuries is sparse. During the 1630s and 1640s, small numbers of children were among the slaves acquired by Dutch traders along the Arakanese coast in the Bay of Bengal.[30] Markus Vink reports that an adult-to-child ratio of five or six (or more) to one characterized most of the slave populations found in Dutch settlements scattered around the Indian Ocean during the late seventeenth century.[31] Five years after a 1683 report that "a great number" of slaves had been shipped yearly from the British East India Company's fort at Madras,[32] Governor Elihu Yale noted that this traffic had led to "great complaints and troubles" from the Mughal government about "the loss of their children and servants stolen from them."[33] As the sale of a twelve-year-old boy named François on the Île de Bourbon (Réunion) in 1687 attests, Indian children numbered among the earliest servile residents of the Mascarenes.[34]

The eighteenth century witnessed the continued shipment of children across the Indian Ocean by Europeans. In May 1758 the British East India Company's directors ordered the governor of Bombay to procure up to five hundred Mozambican or Malagasy (or both) men, women and child slaves for the company's factory at Bencoolen (Benkulen), on Sumatra's west coast.[35] Six years later the factory reported that sixty-one of the eighty-seven slaves Bombay had sent out on the *Neptune* had died from smallpox and scurvy; of the thirty-four men, twenty-one women, thirty-one boys, and one girl put on board the ship, twelve men, two women, seventeen boys, and the one girl had apparently died on the high seas.[36] The need for labor both on St. Helena, in the South Atlantic, and at Bencoolen prompted the company's directors in 1764 to order the *Royal George* to sail to the Angolan coast to purchase 250 slaves.[37] Two hundred thirty-six Angolans (125 men, forty-five women, thirty-eight boys, twenty-five girls, and three "children") subsequently reached St. Helena on board the *Royal George*, 150 of whom were then sent on to Bencoolen.[38] In 1767 two boys and a girl would be among the sixty-eight slaves, apparently from Madagascar, who reached Bencoolen on board the *Solebay* and the *Bukinham*.[39]

Much of the information currently available about Europeans trafficking in children during the eighteenth century involves the slave trade to the Mascarenes from Madagascar, the eastern African coast, India, and Southeast Asia. Eighteen boys were among the sixty-five slaves on board *Le Rubis* when the ship arrived at Mauritius on 8 December 1722 from Madagascar.[40] One hundred boys and girls from India's Coromandel Coast reached the island in 1729.[41] Eleven years later, Mauritius was home to at least seventy-four eleven-to-twelve-year-old Indian "apprentices."[42] More substantive data become available after 1770 when the presence of significant numbers of children in cargoes destined for the Mascarenes is attested to in various ways, including reports about slave mortality en route to the islands. Twenty of the sixty-four slaves who survived the voyage from Kilwa to Mauritius aboard *La Montaine* in 1784, for example, were identified as youths and children.[43] Six years later, eighty youths, fifty-four boys, and fourteen girls were listed among the 297 slaves who died on board *La Félicité* as it sailed to Mauritius from Kilwa.[44]

Detailed information on the composition of Mascarene-bound cargoes exists only for 1769 through 1775, and especially 1772 to 1775.[45] Boys and girls accounted for 30.2 percent of the 3,329 slaves in forty-two cargoes landed on Mauritius and Réunion during this period; male and female youths accounted for another 12.9 percent of these slaves. A striking feature of these data is the varying proportion of children in cargoes arriving from different catchment areas. More specifically, children made up approximately one-fifth of cargoes of Indian and Malagasy origin, a pattern generally consistent with that in the Atlantic at the same time.[46] However, children comprised almost 35 percent of cargoes that arrived from the Mozambican and Swahili coasts. Unfortunately, the extent to which this trend was maintained over time cannot be ascertained.[47] These data also suggest that youths may have constituted a larger proportion of cargoes arriving from India (24.6 percent) than from Madagascar (3.7 percent) and Mozambique (13.7 percent). Once again, the extent to which any such trend persisted beyond the mid-1770s cannot be determined.

Isolated reports suggest that the age and sex composition of Mascarene-bound cargoes after 1775 remained generally in line with the broad pattern then prevailing in the Atlantic—that is, males outnumbered females two to one, with children accounting for at least 20 percent of all slaves being transported. In 1792, for instance, the seventy male and female youths and forty-nine boys and girls landed at Port Louis from *Le Perier* accounted for 17 percent and 11.9 percent, respectively, of the 411 slaves who survived the voyage.[48] Sixteen years later, children and youths appear to have comprised at least 30 percent of the 350 to 355 slaves found on board the Portuguese brig *La Santa Delfina* when it was captured by a French privateer.[49] These percentages, when applied to recent projections about the volume of the Mascarene trade, suggest that a minimum of 26,200 to 30,300 children and youths reached the islands between 1770 and 1810 and that the number of such imports may very well have been as high as 39,300 to 45,500. When slave mortality rates on Mascarene-bound slavers are taken into consideration, there is reason to believe that a minimum of 32,100 children and youths were exported to the islands between 1770 and 1810 and that the number of such exports may have climbed as high as 56,000.[50]

As Victorine's and Esther's depositions attest, children and youths were also caught up in the illegal slave trade to the Mascarenes that flourished between 1811 and the early 1830s.[51] The Réunionnais notarial record confirms the arrival of Malay slaves, and Malay children and adolescents in particular, in the islands during the 1810s and 1820s,[52] as do other sources. Among the vessels calling at Diego Garcia in 1826, for example, was the forty-five-ton *Chicken*, bound for Réunion with a cargo of forty boys aged seven and eight purchased at Nias, an island off the west coast of Sumatra.[53] Nias was well known to British authorities not only as a source of slaves sold by Achinese and Chinese merchants in various Malayan and Indonesian ports,[54] but also as a place where it was "universally believed" that the French traded "to a considerable Extent" for slaves.[55] French merchants apparently continued to purchase Nias slaves for shipment to Réunion in the 1830s.[56]

Other sources provide some sense of the demographic structure of these illicit cargoes. Children accounted for 17.2 percent of the 1,822 slaves found on seventeen vessels seized by Mauritian authorities and the Royal Navy in the southwestern Indian Ocean between 1815 and 1821. On occasion, children comprised a substantial proportion of individual cargoes: twenty-six (26.8 percent) of the ninety-seven slaves found on *Les Deux Amis* in 1819; forty-seven (30.3 percent) of the 155 slaves seized on *La Neptune* in 1816; thirty-four (38.6 percent) of the eighty-eight slaves carried on *La Joséphine* in 1817; and twenty-seven (41.5 percent) of the sixty-five slaves found on *La Circonstance* in 1815.[57] One hundred seventy-one (24.1 percent) of the 710 Malagasy slaves liberated by Royal Navy and Mauritian cruisers between 1816 and 1821 whose age and sex are known were fourteen years of age or younger; of the 727 Mozambicans liberated during this same period, 18.2 percent were under the age of fifteen. Overall, individuals under fifteen accounted for 21.1 percent of these prize slaves, the overwhelming majority (91.4 percent) of whom were reported to be between ten and fourteen years old.[58] This percentage, when applied to estimates of the Mascarene trade's volume after 1810, suggests that 21,400 to 25,100 children were imported illegally into the islands between 1811 and 1848, mostly between 1811 and the early 1830s. The number of children exported from Madagascar, eastern Africa, and Southeast Asia to the islands during the same period may have ranged between 26,000 and 30,600.[59]

Children were enslaved in the Indian Ocean world by the same means (for example, slave raiding, kidnapping, sale by family members) and for the same reasons (their vulnerability and the ease with which they could be exploited) as they were elsewhere in the world. British East India Company officials noted that the practice of kidnapping children and selling them as slaves was a well-established tradition in some parts of the subcontinent. Such was the case in Malabar province, where W. G. Farmer reported in 1792, "It has long been a custom of the Moplas to steal Children of the Nair and other Gentoo Casts and carry them to the sea coast for sale."[60] The commissioners who subsequently investigated conditions in the province likewise noted the existence of a "nefarious traffick of kidnapping children" who were carried to the coast for sale to the captains and supercargoes of European vessels.[61] In other instances, children and youths were enticed on board ships where they were detained against their will. Such had been the case for Harroo (a ten-year-old beggar boy), Joomun (a fourteen-year-old day laborer), and four other persons of undetermined age rescued from the *Hero* by Calcutta police in October 1789.[62]

A common mechanism by which many children were enslaved in southern Asia was sale by their parents or other relatives. An 1812 account of Bali outlined the means by which slave traders bargained clandestinely with parents to purchase their children, who were then sent to the bazaar on some pretext where they could be carried off with relative ease.[63] Twelve years later, the report filed by Messrs. Burton and Ward after a trip among the Batak of Sumatra noted that destitute families were sometimes induced to sell their children to persons who promised to care for them and "in a manner adopt them." Burton and Ward also reported that Batak children orphaned at an early age whose relatives did not want to be bothered with the trouble and expense of rearing them were usually sold.[64]

Children in India could easily suffer the same fate. Two of the eight Bengali children recovered by Calcutta police from the house of a Mr. Borel, a Swiss officer in the service of the Dutch at Colombo, in 1789 reported that they had been sold by relatives, twelve-year-old Khirun by her brother and nine-year-old Flora (alias Minba) by her mother. Many of these eight children, who ranged from six to twelve years old, also noted that they had been sold two or three times during the several weeks between their abduction or initial sale and arrival at Borel's house.[65] Two years later, British authorities would remove seventeen girls and seven boys from the French-flagged *Stisam Low* as it passed Kedgeree, near the mouth of the Hugli River.[66] Three of the boys rescued from the ship were subsequently determined to have been sold by relatives: four-year-old Jack by his uncle, seven-year-old Juggoo by his father, and twelve-year-old Josa Sylrah by his grandmother following his mother's death.[67]

The famines that followed in the wake of the droughts, floods, and other natural disasters that periodically swept parts of the subcontinent generated many of the slaves exported from India during the seventeenth and eighteenth centuries. Reports on the famines that struck central Bengal in 1785 and the Northern Circars in the early 1790s underscore children's vulnerability in such circumstances as men and women struggled desperately to keep themselves alive. The British collector at Dacca reported that the 1785 famine forced many poor and lower-class individuals in the countryside around the city to sell their children, "many hundreds" of whom were shipped immediately to the "Foreign Settlements [near Calcutta] from whence . . . they are embarked in Vessels to different parts."[68] Many parents also sold their offspring during the famine that struck the Northern Circars during the early 1790s. Native merchants attempting to recover the children who had been seized from them by British authorities in March 1790 reported that north of Jaggernatporum "everyone disposed of their Children from want of food to live on."[69] As events in and around the French factory at Yanam in 1792 demonstrated, slave traders from the Mascarenes were among those exploiting local conditions to their own advantage.[70] The scale of such activity is suggested by a report from the port of Bimilipatnam where a raid by British authorities early in 1793 uncovered 565 "young persons" being held in a number of houses and warehouses awaiting exportation.[71] The seriousness with which British officials viewed this problem was underscored by the instructions issued by the governor at Madras on 12 November 1791 to feed people in Ganjam, Vizagapatam, and Masulipatam at company expense so they would not have to sell themselves or their dependents into slavery.[72] Several weeks later, officials at Vizagapatam reported that most of the poor being fed from company stores were children and announced plans to increase the number of children being fed in order to prevent "Parents privately exposing their Children to sale from their inability to Support them."[73]

Human life became exceedingly cheap during these periods of severe economic hardship. Judge W. T. Smith noted as much when he reported that the famine that racked four Bengali districts between June and October 1814 had aggravated the long-established practice of selling children. Local conditions were so bad, Smith observed, that slaves could be purchased in public markets "for a less sum than would purchase a Cat or a Dog."[74] The famines that ravaged Bengal and the Northern Circars undoubtedly had a similar effect on slave prices in general, and on those for children in particular.

Information about the price of child slaves in the Indian Ocean is sparse. On occasion children were clearly deemed to be as valuable as adults. Such was the case in 1736 at Mattatan on the Malagasy coast, where boys sold for as much in guns, gunpowder, and shot as adult men and women,[75] and again in 1769 at Foulpointe, where the boys loaded on board La Normande cost as much as some adult males.[76] In other instances, however, the price of boy and girl slaves along the Malagasy coast was determined by their age and height, as at Fort Dauphin in 1740[77] and several locations along the coast in 1750.[78]

The value of children and youths relative to adults also varied in the Mascarenes. Adult male slaves on Réunion were valued at 600 livres for customs purposes between 1770 and 1772 compared to 500 livres for adult women, 400 livres for male youths, and 300 livres for boys and girls.[79] However, as the sale of Mozambican slaves from the cargo of Le Thélémaque at

Port Louis in 1773 indicates, the price actually paid for slaves in various age categories could fluctuate considerably. Adult males from the ship's cargo sold for 500 to 700 livres while adult women sold for 300 to 380 livres, male youths for 363 to 710 livres, boys for 463 to 504 livres, and girls for 415 to 420 livres.[80] Sixteen years later, the *armateur* (outfitter) of *Le Chevalier d'Entrecasteaux* informed the ship's captain and supercargo that he expected the eighty twelve-to-eighteen-year-old male and female slaves that he wanted the captain to acquire in India to bring 1,000 livres each upon their arrival at Mauritius. To ensure that they would fetch this price, the captain received detailed instructions about the slaves he was to obtain: none was to be less than twelve or more than eighteen years old; all were to be in good condition and well fed; males were to be at least five feet two inches tall and females as tall as possible; and all were to have had smallpox before they were embarked on the ship.[81] Some thirty years later, children remained more valuable commodities than might otherwise be supposed. Adult male slaves landed clandestinely by *Le Succès* on Réunion in October 1820 sold for $150 to $200 (usually $200), compared to $140 to $170 for adult women, $130 to $180 for male youths, and $130 to $135 for children.[82] The value of young children on Mauritius is known to have increased between 1825 and 1827,[83] a trend consistent with the final demise of the illegal trade to the colony at this time.[84]

Children could also command relatively high prices in Southeast Asia depending on their age and gender as well as the circumstances of their sale. According to British officials, "middle aged" (that is, under fifty years old) Banda slaves in the Moluccas were worth fifty rix dollars in 1804, while children (defined specifically as ten years old and younger) and slaves more than fifty years of age were valued at twenty rix dollars each.[85] Eight years later, a Mr. Knops reported that a handsome young girl in Bali cost $60 to $80, while a young Balinese boy ten or fifteen years old cost $30 to $40. "Big" boys on the island fetched $12 to $15, and women above an unspecified age could be had for $20 to $25.[86]

Like their counterparts elsewhere in the world, European slave owners in the Indian Ocean valued child slaves for their labor and, in the case of girls and especially adolescent females, for their sexual and reproductive potential. Information on how children were used in European factories scattered throughout South and Southeast Asia remains elusive, but there is reason to believe that many, if not most, of these boys and girls were employed as domestic or personal servants. Several historians have argued that slavery in southern Asia was largely urban or domestic (or both) and that, at least in Southeast Asia, Europeans adopted the beliefs and practices associated with indigenous slave systems.[87] Such also appears to have been the case, at least to some extent, in India. Early in the 1770s, for example, several East India Company employees requested permission to take slave boys and girls, some of whom were identified explicitly as servants and native Indians, with them when they returned to England.[88] Some sixteen years later, Mr. Borel, the Swiss officer whose house had been raided by the Calcutta police, would state that he had purchased six of the eight children found on his premises as servants for himself and other officers.[89]

Information about the daily existence of child slaves in the Mascarenes during the eighteenth and early nineteenth centuries is also scanty. Many of these children probably led lives similar to those of their peers in the Americas. Aside from helping to care for younger children, child slaves in the New World frequently did little or no work per se before the age of eight. Those between eight and twelve years old assumed duties such as participating in food preparation, toting water, cleaning yards and engaging in light field work as members of the "third gang." By their early teens, most slave children could expect to be increasingly engaged in the kind of strenuous field work that would remain their lot for much of the rest of their lives.[90]

Our first opportunity to determine with some certainty how child slaves were used in the Mascarenes comes from the 1817 Mauritian slave register. The register distinguished between "personal" slaves, found mostly in and around the city of Port Louis, and "plantation" slaves who lived and worked on the island's rural estates. Almost two-thirds of a sample of 1,012 "personal" child slaves (that is, fourteen years of age and younger) were employed as household or personal servants; another 22.2 percent were described as a laborer of some kind, while 12.2 percent practiced a skilled craft or trade (such as blacksmith, carpenter, mason, seamstress, wigmaker), undoubtedly as an apprentice.[91] The information at our disposal about "plantation" slave children is more problematic, since it is often unclear whether the occupation ascribed to a child was actually that of his or her parents. Not surprisingly, an overwhelming majority (85.4 percent) of a sample of 434 "plantation" children were described as laborers, usually as *pioches* (field hands) or as members of the *petite bande* charged with lighter manual tasks.[92] Those not engaged in agricultural labor worked in various capacities, often as domestic servants and apprentices in the skilled crafts.

The demise of the illegal slave trade to the Mascarenes by the early 1830s marked the end of large-scale European trafficking in children within the confines of the Indian Ocean basin. The death of the Mascarene trade did not, of course, bring an end to the trafficking in child slaves in this part of the world; Arab, Indian, and other indigenous merchants continued to do so into the twentieth century in numbers that often can only be guessed at.[93] And, as the dramatic expansion of the Mozambican slave trade after 1811 demonstrates, Europeans would continue to export enslaved children from the southwestern Indian Ocean to the Americas for some time. An estimated 386,000 slaves were shipped from eastern Africa across the South Atlantic after 1811 to meet the Brazilian demand for chattel labor.[94] That 24 percent of the slave population in the province of Rio de Janeiro between 1789 and 1832 was under fifteen years of age underscores the fact that children comprised a sizable proportion of these cargoes.[95]

The significance of this Indian Ocean traffic in child slaves by Europeans extends, however, beyond simply permitting us to deepen our understanding of the character and dynamics of European slave trading or to finally begin to appreciate the truly global scale of this commerce.[96] As early as 1774, British officials in Bengal expressed their concern about the large numbers of unfortunate children who were being swept up in what they characterized as a "Savage Commerce."[97] As I have noted elsewhere, the persistent concern of British authorities in India between the mid-1780s and early 1790s about the exportation of large numbers of boy and girl slaves from the subcontinent raises an important but hitherto unasked question: to what extent did knowledge of an expanding trade in children in an era marked by the emergence of the modern concepts of the child and childhood shape the development of the abolitionist movement?[98] Addressing this question will require careful research that is truly imperial in scope and may ultimately require revising our understanding of how and why the slave trade came to an end. In so doing, we will also undoubtedly have to come to grips with the often unappreciated irony that the humanitarianism that sought to end this "nefarious traffick" in boys and girls actually made them even more desirable commodities as slave owners anticipated the slave trade's demise and took appropriate steps to protect their interests.[99] These steps would result in suffering, hardship, and death for even greater numbers of what Jeremiah Church described in 1787 as "those miserable and deserted Objects, whom the unequal hand of fortune has placed in bondage," the youngest of whom, he avowed, were subject to "every species of barbarity . . . that ungovernable rage and anger unprovoked, can suggest or invent."[100]

## NOTES

Research for this paper was made possible in part by an American Council of Learned Societies/Andrew W. Mellon Fellowship and by support from the Aapravasi Ghat Trust Fund, Mauritius.

## Abbreviations

BNA      British National Archives, Kew
CO       Colonial Office records, BNA
HCA      High Court of the Admiralty records, BNA
MNA      Mauritius National Archives
OIOC     Oriental and India Office Collections, British Library, London
PRO      Domestic Records of the Public Record Office, Gifts, Deposits, Notes, and
         Transcripts, BNA
T        Treasury records, BNA

1. The illegal importation of slaves into Mauritius began in 1811 and continued until about 1827. See Richard B. Allen, "Licentious and Unbridled Proceedings: The Illegal Slave Trade to Mauritius and the Seychelles during the Early Nineteenth Century," *Journal of African History* 42, no. 1 (2001): 91-116.

2. T 71/1520, Extracts from the Returns furnished by Slave Proprietors at the Census of 1826 by which it would appear from the ages then given that the undermentioned Individuals must have been illegally imported into the Colony, 1 May 1835. A second list compiled from these returns reports 3,423 such individuals.

3. On the Balinese trade, see A. van der Kraan, "Bali: Slavery and Slave Trade," in *Slavery, Bondage, and Dependency in Southeast Asia,* ed. Anthony Reid (New York: St. Martin's, 1983), 315-40.

4. T 71/1520, case 1334, Declaration by Rose, a free woman, before the Assistant Commissioners of Compensation, 19 April 1836; Declaration of the apprentice woman Charlotte before the Assistant Commissioners of Compensation, 18 April 1836.

5. Persons identified as Malay in contemporary documents came not only from Malaya and Indonesia but also from India and the Maldives. Hubert Gerbeau, "Des minorités mal-connues: Esclaves indiens et malais des Mascareignes au XIXe siècle," in *Migrations, minorités et échanges en océan indien, XIXe-XXe siècle,* IHPOM Études et Documents, no. 11 (Aix-en-Provence, 1978): 160-64.

6. T 71/1520, case 4000, Declaration by the Malay woman Esther before the Assistant Commissioners of Compensation, 28 June 1836.

7. T 71/566, Registry of Personal Slaves, 1817, pp. 1-647; T 71/571—Registry of Plantation Slaves, 1817, pp. 1-237.

8. Richard B. Allen, "A Traffic Repugnant to Humanity: Children, the Mascarene Slave Trade and British Abolitionism," *Slavery and Abolition* 27, no. 2 (2006): 223.

9. Ibid., 221.

10. CO 415/6/A.124, Returns of the number of Births and Deaths of Slaves in the [district/town] from the Year 1810 to 1826, inclusive; R. R. Kuczynski, *Demographic Survey of the British Colonial Empire,* 3 vols. (London: Oxford University Press, 1948-53), 2:852.

11. Paul E. Lovejoy, *Transformations in Slavery: A History of Slavery in Africa,* 2nd ed. (Cambridge: Cambridge University Press, 2000), 65-66. For recent work on children in the transatlantic trades, see Audra A. Diptee, "African Children in the British Slave Trade during the Late Eighteenth Century," *Slavery and Abolition* 27, no. 2 (2006): 183-96; Paul Lovejoy, "The Children of Slavery—the Transatlantic Phase," *Slavery and Abolition* 27, no. 2 (2006): 197-217.

12. See, for example, Shihan de S. Jayasuriya and Richard Pankhurst, eds., *The African Diaspora in the Indian Ocean* (Trenton, NJ: Africa World Press, 2003); Gwyn Campbell, ed., *The Structure of Slavery in Indian Ocean Africa and Asia* (London: Frank Cass, 2004); Edward Alpers, Gwyn Campbell, and Michael Salman, eds., *Slavery and Resistance in Africa and Asia* (London: Routledge, 2005); Gwyn Campbell, ed., *Abolition and Its Aftermath in Indian Ocean Africa and Asia* (London: Routledge, 2005).

13. Hubert Gerbeau, "The Slave Trade in the Indian Ocean: Problems Facing the Historian and Research to be Undertaken," in *The African Slave Trade from the Fifteenth to the Nineteenth Century* (Paris: UNESCO, 1979), 184-207. Recent overviews of the Indian Ocean trades include: Edward A. Alpers, "The African Diaspora in the Northwestern Indian Ocean: Reconsideration of an Old Problem, New Directions for Research," *Comparative Studies of South Asia, Africa and the Middle East* 17, no. 2 (1997): 62-81; Marina Carter, "Slavery and Unfree Labour in the Indian Ocean," *History Compass* 4, no. 5 (2006): 800-13; Gwyn Campbell, "Slavery and the Trans-Indian Ocean World Slave Trade: A Historical Outline," in *Cross Currents and Community Networks: The History of the Indian Ocean*, ed. Himanshu Prabha Ray and Edward A. Alpers (Oxford: Oxford University Press, 2007), 286-305.

14. Pier Larson, "African Diasporas and the Atlantic," in *The Atlantic in Global History, 1500-2000*, ed. Jorge Cañizares-Esguerra and Erik R. Seeman (Upper Saddle River, NJ: Pearson Education, 2007), 129-47.

15. Bernard Lewis, *Race and Slavery in the Middle East: An Historical Enquiry* (New York: Oxford University Press, 1990); Patrick Manning, *Slavery and African Life: Occidental, Oriental, and African Slave Trades* (Cambridge: Cambridge University Press, 1990); Lovejoy, *Transformations in Slavery*.

16. S. Arasaratnam, "Slave Trade in the Indian Ocean in the Seventeenth Century," in *Mariners, Merchants and Oceans: Studies in Maritime History*, ed. K. S. Mathews (Delhi: Manohar, 1995), 196-97.

17. Andrew Turton, "Thai Institutions of Slavery," in *Asian and African Systems of Slavery*, ed. James L. Watson (Berkeley: University of California Press, 1980), 251-92; H. S. Morris, "Slaves, Aristocrats and Export of Sago in Sarawak," in Watson, *Asian and African Systems*, 292-308; James Francis Warren, *The Sulu Zone, 1768-1898: The Dynamics of External Trade, Slavery, and Ethnicity in the Transformation of a Southeast Asian Maritime State* (Singapore: Singapore University Press, 1981); Reid, *Slavery, Bondage*; Andrew Turton, "Violent Capture of People for Exchange on Karen-Thai Borders in the 1830s," in Campbell, *Structure of Slavery*, 69-82; Peter Boomgaard, "Human Capital, Slavery and Low Rates of Economic and Population Growth in Indonesia, 1600-1900," in Campbell, *Structure of Slavery*, 83-96; James Francis Warren, "The Structure of Slavery in the Sulu Zone in the Late Eighteenth and Nineteenth Centuries," in Campbell, *Structure of Slavery*, 111-28; Karine Delaye, "Slavery and Colonial Representations in Indochina from the Second Half of the Nineteenth to the Early Twentieth Century," in Campbell, *Structure of Slavery*, 129-42.

18. Rudy Bauss, "The Portuguese Slave Trade from Mozambique to Portuguese India and Macau and Comments on Timor, 1750-1850: New Evidence from the Archives," *Camões Center Quarterly* 6-7, nos. 1-2 (1997): 21-26; Pedro Machado, "A Forgotten Corner of the Indian Ocean: Gujarati Merchants, Portuguese India and the Mozambique Slave-Trade, c. 1730-1830," in Campbell, *Structure of Slavery*, 17-32.

19. Robert Ross, "The Dutch on the Swahili Coast, 1776-1778: Two Slaving Journals, Part I," *International Journal of African Historical Studies* 19, no. 2 (1986): 305-60; Arasaratnam, "Slave Trade in the Indian Ocean"; Gerrit J. Knapp, "Slavery and the Dutch in Southeast Asia," in *Fifty Years Later: Antislavery, Capitalism and Modernity in the Dutch Orbit*, ed. Gert Oostindie (Pittsburgh: University of Pittsburgh Press, 1996), 193-206; Markus Vink, "'The World's Oldest Trade': Dutch Slavery in the Indian Ocean in the Seventeenth Century," *Journal of World History* 14, no. 2 (2003): 131-77.

20. Robert J. Young, "Slaves, Coolies and Bondsmen: A Study of Assisted Migration in Response to Emerging English Shipping Networks in the Indian Ocean, 1685-1765," *Indian Ocean Review* 2, no. 3 (1989): 23-26; Richard B. Allen, "Suppressing a Nefarious Traffic: The Mascarenes, Britain and the Abolition of Slave Trading in the Western Indian Ocean, 1770-1835," paper presented to "The bloody Writing is for ever torn," Conference on the Domestic and International Consequences of the First Governmental Efforts to Abolish the Atlantic Slave Trade, Accra and Elmina, Ghana, 8-12 August 2007.

21. G. S. P. Freeman-Grenville, *The French at Kilwa Island* (Oxford: Clarendon Press, 1965); G. A. Akinola, "The French on the Lindi Coast, 1785-1789," *Tanzania Notes and Records* 70 (1970): 13-20; Edward A. Alpers, "The French Slave Trade in East Africa (1721-1810)," *Cahiers d'études africaines* 37 (1970): 80-124; J.-M. Filliot, *La traite des esclaves vers les Mascareignes au XVIIIe siècle* (Paris: ORSTROM, 1974); Gerbeau, "Des minorités mal-connues"; Hubert Gerbeau, "Les esclaves asiatiques des Mascareignes: Enquêtes et hypothèses," *Annuaire des pays de l'océan indien* 7 (1980): 169-97; Marina Carter, "Indian Slaves in Mauritius (1729-1834)," *Indian Historical Review* 15, no. 1-2 (1988): 233-47; Teotino R. de Souza, "French Slave-Trading in Portuguese Goa (1773-1791)," in *Essays in Goan History*, ed. Teotonio R. de Souza (New Delhi: Concept, 1989), 123-26; Sudel Fuma, "La traite des esclaves dans le bassin du sud-ouest de l'océan indien et la France après 1848," in *La route des esclaves: Système servile et traite dans l'est malgache* (Paris: L'Harmattan, 2000), 247-61; Richard B. Allen, "Carrying Away the Unfortunate: The Exportation of Slaves from India during the Late Eighteenth Century," in *Le monde créole: Peuplement, sociétés et condition humaine, XVIIe-XXe siècles*, ed. Jacques Weber (Paris: Les Indes Savantes, 2005), 285-98; Marina Carter, "A Servile Minority in a Sugar Island: Malay and Chinese Slaves in Mauritius," in Weber, *Monde créole*, 257-71.

22. See, for example, Edward A. Alpers, *Ivory and Slaves in East Central Africa* (Berkeley: University of California Press, 1975); Abdul Sheriff, *Slaves, Spices and Ivory in Zanzibar: Integration of an East African Commercial Empire into the World Economy, 1770-1873* (London: James Currey, 1987); Pier Larson, *History and Memory in the Age of Enslavement: Becoming Merina in Highland Madagascar, 1770-1822* (Portsmouth, NH: Heinemann, 2000); José Capela, *O tráfico de escravos nos portos de Moçambique, 1773-1904* (Porto: Edições Afrontamento, 2002); Gwyn Campbell, *An Economic History of Imperial Madagascar, 1750-1895: The Rise and Fall of an Island Empire* (Cambridge: Cambridge University Press, 2005).

23. Richard B. Allen, "The Constant Demand of the French: The Mascarene Slave Trade and the Worlds of the Indian Ocean and Atlantic during the Eighteenth and Nineteenth Centuries," *Journal of African History* 49, no. 1 (2008): 43-72.

24. See, for example, C. R. Boxer, *The Dutch Seaborne Empire, 1600-1800* (New York: Knopf, 1965); Philippe Haudrère, *La compagnie française des Indes au XVIIIe siècle* (Paris:

Librairie de l'Inde, 1989); John Keay, *The Honourable Company: A History of the English East India Company* (London: HarperCollins, 1991); H. V. Bowen, *The Business of Empire: The East India Company and Imperial Britain, 1756–1833* (Cambridge: Cambridge University Press, 2006).

25. See, for example, Ashin Das Gupta, *Malabar in Asian Trade, 1740–1800* (Cambridge: Cambridge University Press, 1967); Sinnappah Arasaratnam, *Merchants, Companies and Commerce on the Coromandel Coast, 1650–1740* (Delhi: Oxford University Press, 1986); Om Prakash, *European Commercial Enterprise in Pre-Colonial India* (Cambridge: Cambridge University Press, 1998); Lakshmi Subramanian, ed., *The French East India Company and the Trade of the Indian Ocean: A Collection of Essay by Indrani Ray* (New Delhi: Munshiram Manoharlal, 1999); Arvind Sinha, *The Politics of Trade: Anglo-French Commerce on the Coromandel Coast, 1763–1793* (New Delhi: Manohar, 2002).

26. Jill Louise Geber, "The East India Company and Southern Africa: A Guide to the Archives of the East India Company and the Board of Control, 1600–1858" (Ph.D. diss., University College London, 1998), 101.

27. British slave traders often considered individuals under four feet four inches tall as children and those above four feet four inches as adults. Diptee, "African Children," 185.

28. OIOC: F/4/184/3719, p. 24, Cecil Smith and P. Bruce to Chief Secretary to Government, 15 December 1804.

29. In the Americas, slaves up to the age of twelve were generally considered to be children, while those between twelve and fifteen to eighteen years of age were considered to be youths. Gwyn Campbell, "Children and Slavery in the New World: A Review," *Slavery and Abolition* 27, no. 2 (2006): 261–62.

30. Sanjay Subrahmanyam, *Explorations in Connected History: From the Tagus to the Ganges* (New Delhi: Oxford University Press, 2005), 217, 222.

31. Vink, "World's Oldest Trade," 154–55.

32. Basanta Kumar Basu, "Notes on Slave Trade and Slavery in India during the Early Days of John Company," *Muslim Review* (Calcutta) 4, no. 4 (1930): 22.

33. OIOC: Mss. Eur. Mack General 55, pp. 46–47, The Diary & Consultation Book of the Hon^ble Elihu Yale Esq^re President Governour & Councill their proceedings & transactions for the affairs of the R^t. Hon^ble English East India Company in the Presidency of the Coast of Choromandell & the Bay of Bengala.

34. Jean-Marie Desport, *De la servitude à la liberté: Bourbon des origins à 1848* (Réunion: Océan Editions, 1989), 8.

35. OIOC: E/4/996, pp. 646–47, Court of Directors to President and Council of Bombay, 5 July 1758.

36. OIOC: G/35/72, p. 187, Public Consultation, Fort Marlboro', 20 August 1764.

37. OIOC: E/4/997, p. 561, Court of Directors to President and Council of Bombay, 12 December 1764.

38. OIOC: G/32/25, fol. 120v, Public Consultation, St. Helena, 27 May 1765. The *Royal George* delivered 149 slaves to company officials at Bencoolen on 9 September 1765. OIOC: L/MAR/B/17H, Ship's log of the *Royal George*—journey from England to Cabinda, St. Helena and to Bencoolen, 1764–65. Unfortunately, the age and sex of these arrivals was not reported.

39. OIOC: G/35/73, pp. 265, 279, Fort Marlborough Public Consultation, 11 June 1765.

40. Robert Chaudenson, "À propos de la genèse du créole mauricien: Le peuplement de l'Île de France de 1721 à 1735," *Etudes créoles* 1 (1979): 44.

41. Doojendraduth Napal, *Les indiens à l'Île de France* (Port Louis: Editions Nationales, 1965), 9.

42. Carter, "Indian Slaves," 243.

43. MNA: OB 23/102 bis, 18 décembre 1784.

44. MNA: OB 28/456, 3 août 1790.

45. Allen, "Constant Demand of the French," table 4.

46. Lovejoy, *Transformations in Slavery*, 65.

47. These figures may not be out of line with recent information on the composition of French transatlantic cargoes. See David Geggus, "The French Slave Trade: An Overview," *William and Mary Quarterly*, 3rd ser., 58, no. 1 (2001): 135.

48. MNA: JH 13–21 7$^{bre}$ 1792–Dépot de la livraison de la cargaison du N$^{re}$ le Perier consistant en 411 tetes d'esclaves a Durouzou[?].

49. MNA: GB 26/1054–17 June 1808; GB 116/4–Amirauté–Relevé du cargaison d'esclaves du navire portugais La Santa Delfina, 1808.

50. Based on figures reported in Richard B. Allen, "The Mascarene Slave-Trade and Labour Migration in the Indian Ocean during the Eighteenth and Nineteenth Centuries," in Campbell, *Structure of Slavery*, 33–50.

51. Following their capture by a British expeditionary force in 1810, the Mascarenes became subject to the 1807 Act of Parliament, which prohibited British subjects from trading in slaves. This ban remained in force in Mauritius and its dependencies following their formal inclusion in the British Empire in 1814. In 1818 the formal abolition of slave trading in the French empire was applied to Réunion, which had been returned to French control in 1814. On the illegal slave trade to the Mascarenes, see esp. Hubert Gerbeau, "Quelques aspects de la traite illégale des esclaves à l'Ile Bourbon au XIXe siècle," in *Mouvements de populations dans l'océan indien* (Paris: Librairie Honoré Champion, 1979), 273-308; Gerbeau, "L'océan indien n'est pas l'Atlantique: La traite illégale à Bourbon au XIXe siècle," *Revue outre-mers, revue d'histoire* 89 (2002): 79-108; Allen, "Licentious and Unbridled Proceedings."

52. Gerbeau, "Minorités mal-connues."

53. CO 415/7/A.164, Memorandum for Captain Ackland from Mr. Finniss [after 13 September 1826]. Only twenty-four of the boys reached Réunion alive.

54. OIOC: F/4/345/7981, p. 23, Extract of a Letter from Mr. Prince dated 22nd August 1808; F/4/659/18295, pp. 55, 58-59, John Prince and William Jack to Sir T. Stamford Raffles, 31 December 1820.

55. CO 415/1, p. 15, W. M. G. Colebrooke and W. Blair to Earl Bathurst, 25 October 1826.

56. A. Reid, "The French in Sumatra and the Malay World, 1760-1890," *Bijdragen tot de taal-, land- en volkenkunde* 129, parts 2-3 (1973), 210, n52.

57. HCA 30/974.

58. CO 167/43, Returns of Prize Negroes condemned by the Court of Vice Admiralty in the Colony, 1 June 1816 to 28 January 1818; CO 167/71, Detailed Statement

of Blacks Seized since the last Return dated 31$^{st}$ December 1820 on board different Vessels or on shore in the Island of Mauritius and Dependencies [dated 1 January 1822].

59. Based on figures in Allen, "Mascarene Slave-Trade."

60. OIOC: P/E/5, p. 399, letter from W. G. Farmer at Calicut, 17 May 1792.

61. [Jonathon Duncan, William Page, Charles Boddam, and Alexander Dow], *Reports of a Joint Commission from Bengal and Bombay, Appointed to Inspect into the State and Condition of the Province of Malabar in the Years 1792 and 1793* (Bombay: Courier, 179?), vol. 1, 165.

62. OIOC: P/3/48, pp. 500-501, Police Office, 28 October 1789.

63. OIOC: Mss. Eur. Mack Private 82, p. 84, Some particulars on the Island of Bali [by Mr. Knops, 1812].

64. OIOC: Eur. Mss. E 108, pp. 352-53, Report of a Journey into the Batak Country by Mess$^{rs}$ Burton and Ward, 1824.

65. OIOC: P/3/47, pp. 859-62, T. Motts and Edw$^d$ Maxwell to [Earl Cornwallis], 14 September 1789.

66. OIOC: P/165/53, pp. 441-43, W. N. W. Hewett to Earl Cornwallis, 14 April 1791.

67. OIOC: P/165/53, pp. 444-51, List of Children Disambarked from the Snow Stisam Low . . . on the 14$^{th}$ April 91 at 1 p.m.

68. OIOC: P/50/60, M. Day to William Cowper, 2 March 1785, following L. R. No. 311, W$^m$ Cowper to John Macpherson, 14 March 1785, in Fort William proceedings of 9 September 1785. The "foreign settlements" in question included the French factory at Chandernagore, which supplied slaves to the Mascarenes.

69. OIOC: P/241/17, p. 640, [Petition] To the Worshipfull James Taylor Esq$^{re}$ [by] Merchants &$^c$ of foreign Countries of Southward.

70. Allen, "Constant Demand of the French."

71. OIOC: P/241/38, p. 1235, John Chamier and John Snow to Sir Charles Oakeley, 12 March 1793.

72. OIOC: P/241/27, pp. 3009-10, Cha$^s$ Oakeley to Henry Crawford, 12 November 1791.

73. OIOC: P/241/27, p. 3323—John Chamier and John Snow to Major-General Medows, 29 November 1791.

74. OIOC: F/4/578/14078, pp. 23-24, [Report by W. T. Smith, 2nd Judge of the Court of Circuit of Moorshedabad, 5 July 1815].

75. OIOC: H/628, no. LXVIII, p. 508, Terms of Trade at Madagascar settled by Captain Jenkins in the *Harrington* in 1736.

76. MNA: HB 16/9, Compte des noirs particuliers embarqués par connaissance sur la Corvette *La Normande*—Année 1769. Adult males cost between 30 and 34 piastres, or Spanish dollars ($), compared to $29 to $34 for adult females, $32 for male youths, $28 to $32.50 for boys and $28.50 for girls.

77. OIOC: H/628, no. LXVIII, p. 506, [Terms of Trade at Madagascar settled] By Captain Cobham in the *Edgebaston* in 1740.

78. OIOC: H/628, no. LXVIII, pp. 510-11, [Terms of Trade at Madagascar settled] By Captain Bell in the Company's Ship *Swallow* in 1750.

79. MNA: OA 117/2, Domaine du Roi—Compte rendu par le Receveur du Domaine à Bourbon pour 1767-1772, No. 6.

80. MNA: OA 107/1, Conseil Supérieur–Extraits et expeditions des actes du Greffe, 1-2, 1773–No. 1–19 janvier 1773–vente de noirs provenant de la cargaison du N^re le thelemaque.

81. MNA: JH 10, Instructions, et conditions de M^r Bartro Capiteine du N^re le Ch^r Dentrecasteaux en avril 1789.

82. CO 167/92, Tableau de 220 Negres et Negresses de la Cargaison du Brick le succès de Nantes. The slaves in question probably came from the Swahili Coast.

83. Shirley Chenny, Pascal St-Amour, and Désiré Vencatachullum, "Slave Prices from Succession and Bankruptcy Sales in Mauritius, 1825-1827," *CIRANO Série Scientifique*, September 2002, 14.

84. Allen, "Licentious and Unbridled Proceedings."

85. OIOC: F/4/184/3719, pp. 23-26, Cecil Smith and P. Bruce to Chief Secretary to Government, 15 December 1804.

86. OIOC: Mss. Eur. Mack Private 82, p. 84, Some particulars on the Island of Bali [by Mr. Knops, 1812]. Knops did not elaborate on how old "big" boys were.

87. See, for example, Lionel Caplan, "Power and Status in South Asian Slavery," in Watson, *Asian and African Systems*, 170, 173, 182, 189; A. Reid, "Introduction: Slavery and Bondage in Southeast Asian History," in Reid, *Slavery, Bondage and Dependency*," 14-17, 24; Gerrit J. Knaap, "Slavery and the Dutch in Southeast Asia," in Oostinde, *Fifty Years Later*, 197.

88. OIOC: P/1/47, fol. 283 recto, J. Richard Lodge to John Cartier, 10 December 1770; P/1/49, p. 630, George Hadley to John Cartier, 1 November 1771; P/1/49, p. 631, John Deffell to John Cartier, 1 November 1771; P/2/3, p. 79, Mills [to John Stewart], 25 January 1773.

89. OIOC: P/3/47, pp. 859-60–T. Motts and Edw^d Maxwell to [Earl Cornwallis], 14 September 1789. Borel reported that the other two children belonged to Mr. Milliat from Chandernagore.

90. Eugene Genovese, *Roll, Jordan, Roll: The World the Slaves Made* (New York: Vintage Books, 1976), 502-03; Wilma King, *Stolen Childhood: Slave Youth in Nineteenth-Century America* (Bloomington: Indiana University Press, 1995); Bernard Moitt, *Women and Slavery in the French Antilles, 1635–1848* (Bloomington: Indiana University Press, 2001), 42-43; Peter Kolchin, *American Slavery, 1619–1877*, rev. ed. (New York: Hill and Wang, 2003), 141-42.

91. T 71/566, pp. 1-647.

92. T 71/571, pp. 1-152.

93. Suzanne Miers, *Slavery in the Twentieth Century: The Evolution of a Global Problem* (Walnut Creek, CA: Altamira Press, 2003).

94. Herbert S. Klein, *The Atlantic Slave Trade* (Cambridge: Cambridge University Press, 1999), 70-71. On the volume of the Mozambican trade, see also Edward A. Alpers, "'Mozambique and 'Mozambiques': Slave Trade and Diaspora on a Global Scale," in *Slave Routes and Oral Tradition in Southeastern Africa*, ed. Benigna Zimba, Edward Alpers, and Allen Isaacman (Maputo: Filsom Entertainment, 2005), 39-61.

95. Manolo Florentino, "Slave Trade between Mozambique and the Port of Rio de Janeiro, c. 1790-c. 1850, Demographic, Social and Economic Aspects," in Zimba, Alpers, and Isaacman, *Slave Routes*, 65.

96. On what has aptly been characterized as the "tyranny of the Atlantic" in slavery studies, see Alpers, "African Diaspora," 62.

97. OIOC: P/49/46, p. 1485, [Regulations to control slave trading in Bengal, 17 May 1774].

98. Allen, "Traffic Repugnant"; Allen, "Nefarious Traffic."

99. Lovejoy, *Transformations in Slavery*, 143; Allen, "Licentious and Unbridled Proceedings," 99-100, 115.

100. PRO 30/11/13, fol. 26 recto, Jere^h Church to Earl Cornwallis, 30 January 1787.

# 3

# SMALL CHANGE

*Children in the Nineteenth-Century East African Slave Trade*

FRED MORTON

During the nineteenth-century East African slave trade—in which long-distance caravans channeled slaves from the interior to coastal ports for transshipment to Zanzibar, Pemba, the Kenya coast, Arabia, the Persian Gulf, and India—prepubescent boys and girls were a significant portion of the traffic. Some children were in demand as servants in urban homes on the Indian Ocean littoral, where domestic slavery permeated the free societal culture. But children were especially valuable as an important component of an interior trade built on multiple transactions. In a system of collecting and supplying slaves to long-distance caravan routes, children commonly changed hands at least once or twice in the catchment areas, again along long-distance trade routes, and again at the coast, before embarking for their ultimate destination. To the slave traders, children served as small capital suited for negotiating deals, settling debts, or establishing credit. Most youngsters were easily controlled, impressionable, and teachable. As slave traders waited to sell or trade them, child slaves could be put readily to a variety of temporary, productive uses and usually appreciated in value.

Little has been published about children in the East African slave trade. Though references to children are common, as a rule children are lumped with adults in narrating and analyzing East Africa's slave trade and slavery. Edward Alpers alone has tried to summarize the experiences of children on trade routes, using some of their narratives, but he restricts discussion to the reasons for their entering the trade and their exchange en route to the coast.[1] His account of Swema, a female child enslaved in Yaoland and taken in a slave caravan to Kilwa, is limited to her individual experience and bypasses issues pertaining to children generally.[2] Otherwise, child slaves are mentioned in the literature only in passing.[3] The same may be said with regard to the fate of slave children after the final sale. The purpose intended for slave children must therefore be inferred. The vast majority of children appear to have been purchased by Muslim households, whether in East Africa or the northern Indian Ocean littoral. In this regard, the literature has assumed that East Africa was like the Saharan and Red Sea trade in that slave children were destined for domestic roles. Paul Lovejoy, for example, estimates that up to 30 percent of the slaves traded in these regions were thirteen or under and became eunuchs, domestics, and military trainees.[4] Abdul Sheriff's small sample of dhows seized in the Persian Gulf reflects similar proportions.[5] Studies of East African societies show that domestic slavery was a significant feature of coastal Muslim communities, and they allude to the same in Oman, a principal destination of East African slaves, but seldom distinguish between the roles of children and adults.[6] An exception is the study of child slaves and pawns on the Kenya coast, but as with Alpers's Swema, it is built on a single case.[7]

Fortunately, many child slave biographies, albeit mostly brief and sketchy, can help to narrow this gap in the literature. Accounts exist of at least forty persons enslaved as children in East Africa. Fourteen are published and well known.[8] The others can be found in mission correspondence of the Church Missionary Society.[9] ( James Mbotela's *Uhuru wa watumwa,* or *The Freeing of the Slaves in East Africa,* has been left out because it is a conflation of traditions he heard as a youngster and is full of embellishments.)[10] These accounts were set down after the subjects had been liberated and taken up residence on missionary stations. All but three of the thirty-nine are male, an imbalance not reflected in available references to slave gender. Other female accounts exist, but only for those pubescent at enslavement.[11] The preponderance of males in this collection may be explained by the fact that almost all the accounts were written by youngsters earmarked to form a Christian vanguard on East African terrain then under the sway of Muslim political and economic interests. Missionaries had in mind a male ministry literate in English. Most of the published biographies were issued by the Universities' Mission to Central Africa (UMCA) as a means of raising opposition to the slave trade and support for UMCA missions that had taken in liberated slaves and tried to convert them. Not surprisingly, physical abuse of slaves and violence associated with the trade are common features of the published accounts. Whether published or otherwise, they contain very little about child slavery in coastal communities, because almost all these children were liberated en route to market.

Yet, as a whole, the (auto)biographies contain uniform and revealing details about the slave trade and the place of children in it, not to mention some remarkable stories of slave children enmeshed for years in the trade. Twenty-nine of these children (74 percent) originated in the Lake Malawi (Lake Nyasa) region, the principal source of slaves in the nineteenth-century East African trade. Their stories help explain why so many children survived the long journey to the coast and the voyage across the Indian Ocean. Contrary to Mbotela's popularized account, in which youngsters are captured in the interior by Arabs and marched straight to the coast, children were enslaved by Africans, remained relatively near their original homes for extended periods, and changed hands repeatedly, inching their way coastward as the multiple-transfer process continued. Between enslavement and reaching their ultimate destination, months, even years, were likely to pass.

### CHILD ENSLAVEMENT IN THE EAST AFRICAN INTERIOR

Small and vulnerable, children were easy prey for adults involved either in slave trading or raiding. Some were simply lured away in their innocence by strangers. "Yao boy" recalled that "a man from another town" approached him and said, "Come along with me, and let us go for a walk. And I said nothing to my father or my mother, but went with him. That man was stealing me. I walked on for six hours, simply walking on and on. At last he sold me to some Arab traders."[12] Famine made strangers promising food into pied pipers: "A man came and said to me 'Come along to my house.' And I said 'Very well,' and went, because his house was near, and I thought I should go home again. . . . [He gave me some millet porridge] and I ate it. But really the man had deceived me; he had already stolen me."[13]

During wars or raids, surviving children could be led away with a promise of reuniting them with their families. "Gindo boy," his father, mother, three brothers, uncles, and cousins were attacked by Maviti (marauders, slave raiders) and, with the exception of himself, caught. Remarkably, he remained quietly in a thick stand of grass, where his father had hidden him, for a week.

> At the end of the seventh day, late in the evening, I gave a loud cry, and said "Father." But no one answered. Then I kept on calling, and I heard a voice answer me, "Eh!"[Yes!] Well, I thought it really was my father; but no! it was not he, it was someone else. The

man came and said, "I'm your father. Don't cry, my child." He took
me and put me on his back. And I said to him, "You are not my
father." And he said to me, "He is in the house. Don't cry." We
came to the house, and I asked him again, and he said, "Perhaps
he will not come home to-day; perhaps to-morrow you will see
him." I remained silent. In the morning I said to him again, "Where
is my father?" The people said, "You have no father. He has been
killed by the Maviti. We saw him yonder yesterday, a child and
your father and mother, and your father is dead." Well, they sold
me to some Yaos and Nyassas [Nyanja].[14]

Whether kidnapped, taken as war captives, or handed over by parents
or family to strangers, children lacked the means to resist. Fear kept them
close to their new masters. Strikingly rare in these accounts is the attempt
to run away, except in the seconds before capture. Once away from home
scampering was futile, as "Makua boy 3" understood. After his caravan
reached the coast for the ocean voyage, he recounted, "I ran away, and they
did not see me because it was quite in the evening and getting dark. Presently I stopped, and thought in my mind, and felt it was best to go back.
So I went back, and they put me on board with all haste, for fear I should
run away again."[15]

The only child daring enough to bolt was "Makua boy 1," doing so thrice,
but each time falling in with persons quick to sell him back into slavery.[16]
Resistance other than escape likewise was rare. Swema refused eating to the
point of being force-fed, but apparently she was reacting to the death of
her mother, who had accompanied her on the march. Unlike Swema, most
children had been separated from their parents by the time they had been
enslaved. They became dependent entirely on their new masters. Typically,
newly enslaved children complied with their masters' wishes and submitted
quietly to their surroundings.

Docility did not necessarily mean acceptance of one's fate. The trauma
of removal from parents and familiar surroundings, more often than not
amid violence, made a lasting impression. In the thirty-nine biographies,
thirty-six children recount how they were enslaved, and the longer accounts
show that life's memory was anchored in that place and moment. Such was
as true for children handed over by parents or relatives as it was for those
snatched from their homes.

The claim that slaves in the East African trade were preponderantly war
captives does not seem true for children. Of this sample, children pawned
or sold by families represent a third of the cases, and for children from the

Lake Malawi region they approach 40 percent.[17] Often children became enslaved because of a parent's or relative's debt. William Jones of Yaoland was seized by his stepfather's brother to force his stepfather to return his wife, whom the stepfather had seized to force his brother to settle a debt. When the stepfather delayed, the brother took Jones to Kilwa (a month's journey) and sold him. In similar fashion George David first saw his life flash before his eyes as a temporary pawn, later to be sold into slavery by his stepfather's brother-in-law. First, David was seized in retaliation against David's grandfather, who had seized a slave woman from a man to redeem an old debt. The grandfather then returned the woman to redeem David. However, the slave owner was David's stepfather's brother-in-law, who later conspired with others to lure the stepfather and his family to a spot where they could be captured. The stepfather escaped, leaving David, his mother, and younger brother behind to be taken. They were sold off separately. David and Jones lost their freedom after their full fathers had died, and their mothers could not prevent them from being pawned off or taken.

Jacob Wainwright was sold by his parents to slave traders, but it was much more likely that the death or absence of parents was decisive in rendering children unprotected. Some parents, while alive, understood this. "Zaramo boy" was warned by his mother, "When I die, your friends will make away with you." After her death, he was ransomed by his own grandfather.[18] Such was James Deimler's case in Makua country. After his father had been killed and his mother died, Deimler was sold by his elder brother. Without his mother knowing, Makua boy 1 was pawned by "my family" to redeem his elder brother who had been seized for compensation. Makua boy 1 did not mention his father. Abraham Periala (a.k.a. Akunsindja) of Yaoland lost his father and was left with a neighboring people by his mother during war in Yaoland, where she returned. He was sold.

Most children understood clearly what was happening to them. As "Bemba boy" recounted, when "the people came and caught me . . . I thought, 'This man will make me his slave.'"[19] Realization of separation was often emotional, if not terrifying. Zaramo boy recalled his late mother as he was about to be ransomed by his grandfather: "And then I thought how [she] had warned me, and cried bitterly."[20] "I cry very much indeed," wrote Paul Deimler, "and they put sand in my mouth [to prevent him from crying] and I want to run away to my father's house and they would not let me go."[21] At the point William Jones was pawned to his stepfather's brother, Jones recalled that he "sorryfully [sic] wished my mother and brothers a welcome (bid them farewell). I thought of seeing them again."[22] When George David, his mother, and younger brother watched his stepfather escape from his brother-in-law's trap to enslave them, "his tears for us, and ours for him, was all vain, there was no one here to pity us or say a word of consolation. And so all of us three, became slave in one day."[23]

## FROM ENSLAVEMENT TO SLAVERY

Judging from the accounts, few children enslaved in the distant interior left for the coast soon after their purchase or capture. Weeks, sometimes months or more, passed before children were taken to the coast. In the mean-time children customarily changed hands and became part of their masters' households or those of their friends. Martin Furahani of Bunyoro recalls being sold and resold nine times before reaching the coast at Bagamayo. Seldom did children end up in a stockade with other children or adults, unless at a collection point along one of the main Arab trade routes.

Between their enslavement and departure for the coast, child slaves served a variety of purposes in their holding locations. They became servants, assisted in child care, protected crops from birds and baboons, fetched wood and water, or tended goats and chickens. Throughout the waiting period, they remained easily exchangeable commodities and often were resold (some, like Tom Smith, were even repurchased), exchanged for goods, or used to reduce or cancel debts. Time was on the side of the owner, at least until children reached an age where they might become difficult to control. In the meantime the exchange value of boys especially was the more likely to increase with age. In 1842 in Zanzibar boys under ten years sold for $7 to $15, boys from ten to twenty, from $15 to $30, with prices for males tapering off after that.[24] Apart from financial, the gain in owning children was their gradual attachment to their masters. The smarter slave owners understood this, and it is not uncommon to read in these slave accounts references to masters as being "very fond of me." Cecil Mabruki (Blessed One) kept the Swahili surname given to him by the Arab to whom he was sold and who in turn eventually sold him before he reached the coast.

In East African child slave narratives, if length is a reliable measure, memories of life in slavery were stronger in the period immediately after capture than during the transfer process, which began with departure for the coast. In fact most narratives have little to relate about this long, cer-tainly arduous journey, perhaps because weariness and bewilderment made passing through unfamiliar territory too fleeting and strange to remember. The slave owners who handled these children prior to departure were Africans or Arabs living in the interior rather than members of long-distance cara-vans and more inclined to fit these children into their communities. This was true even when children changed hands fairly frequently, such as Lewis

Brenn of Makualand, in the Lake Malawi region, after his capture by slave raiders during a famine:

> They sold me to the strangers and they sent me to their land I live
> there one year and they sold me again, and I live one month, to
> mananthira[?] I live there two years and I travel with my master to
> Ukurwani. . . . I left my master at Ukurwani. I came down with
> them and they sold me to a king, and that king tied me with a rope
> round my neck and told his son to hold the rope and went with
> me at night time, and we reached his house after a few days . . .
> until we came to that king's friend and we live there many days
> and that man took us at night time through the country on the
> morning we went in another country and those men wanted to
> catch us but we ran away in the woods and we cross over mululi[?]
> and we came to the land called Oniwaruni on another day we
> came to the Arab's [sic] land and those men sold me to the Arabs
> and those Arabs took me to Ofusi.[25]

Some children lived in localities within a few week's journey of their point of capture and remained long enough to adopt local languages. Church Missionary Society (CMS) missionary Charles Isenberg noted after questioning ex-slave Ismael Semler: "Semler a Yao. Taken captive in a war between Yaos and Waniasa Sultan's. Father escaped. Ishmael captured and sold by Nyassa [Nyanja]. Sold back to Yao. Stayed a year with man who bought him. Man died. Man's people sold him to a Makuba. With him 3 years. Learned Kikuba. Treated well. Sold with 400 slaves to Matipan[?]"[26]

"Nyassa boy 1" was captured and sold to Yao, then resold to other Yao, taken across Lake Malawi and kept for two harvests (he chased pests from the maize fields) before being exchanged for a woman in a passing coast-bound caravan. In the meantime, he learned Yao and forgot his own Nyanja language. Chilekwa, from Bisaland, was captured by Nyanja and taken to Lake Nyasa (Malawi). After his owner died of smallpox, the deceased's friend kept Chilekwa for a year then sold him to Nakaona, a Yao man, who kept him in Yao country for another year.[27]

Ultimately, Chilekwa and the others were trekked overland to Kilwa or another port or sold to caravans bound in same direction. From the Lake Malawi region, children tended to leave for the coast in small groups, or alone with their masters. In contrast to the extended, detailed account of this journey offered by James Mbotela's conflated memories of the tales he was told in Frere Town, Mombasa, by his father and other ex-slaves from the Lake Malawi region, only a few of the accounts used in this chapter provide any insights into this watershed phase, when they departed familiar surroundings never to return.[28] Children taken relatively close to the coast might be exchanged several times in an easterly direction, keeping them unaware of their ultimate fate. Makua boy 1 was captured and sold to an Arab living in "Usilabani," an African town, then walked "on the road" for eight months, apparently moving in the area for purposes of trade. The boy (then eight or nine) ended up with agents of the Arab's trading creditors as security for debt payment, and was taken to an "Arab" town serving as a caravan-collecting point. There he became a servant of the resident Arabs before being taken to another town and sold to an Arab who likewise used him as a servant ("I was a great favorite at this place") before selling him again. He was then near the coast and was taken aboard a dhow by Comorians. Makua boy 2 had a similar experience: he was captured, transferred to relatives, and sold and resold again eastward, finally to an Arab dhow owner. Following each transfer, the boy resided for a brief period, including the coastal port "Msheliwa," and was tasked with one chore or another. Makua boy 3 repeated his pattern, with one variation. He was sold by his captor to a "sort of Arab, but black" who had many slaves. He lived with him before being taken on a "journey of many days" and then left with a couple to help them raise a crop. Eventually he was put in a caravan that soon reached the coast.

For children from distant areas, the journey coastward was more likely to have been a single one, in a caravan. For example Frejala from Yaoland walked with many other slaves in a caravan led by Arab traders and that took one month to reach Kilwa. Chilekwa's owner took him to Mwembe, a collecting point, and the two journeyed with a caravan to the coast at Mikindani, where his owner ("a kind man . . . he brought me up as his own child.") sold him.[29] Nyassa boy 1 and Yao boy alone among the children remember their journeys in any clear detail. They traveled with many slaves, many of whom died en route, and walked extended periods without rest days. Whereas older slaves were shackled with slave sticks (sticks forked at each end and attached to the necks of two bound slaves) or chains, children were left unhindered. Of course, it was up to children to keep up, and woe to infants who hindered their mothers: "If a woman had a little child, and the child kept on crying, an Arab would say to her 'Give me the child and let me carry it for you.' And the woman gives it to him, and when she has given it him, he dashes the child against a stone, and throws it aside dead."[30] Young Swema suffered the double tragedy of making a long caravan journey and watching her mother die en route. Losing the desire to survive, she stopped eating and arrived at Kilwa in a wasted condition, having been force-fed, beaten, and abused.

After reaching the coast, many children changed hands at least once before traveling to the main coastal markets. Like Swema, about half the children in this sample were put on board dhows immediately and sailed to Zanzibar, but the other half remained on the coast for extended periods. As in the interior, their value to traders apparently was derived through one-on-one exchanges. Easily controlled, maintained, and put to various tasks, they made ready servants for men dealing in the caravan slaves, shunted onto dhows or marched along the coast to other ports. At Kilwa, the major port for the Lake Malawi caravan trade, children could spend months. On arrival Nyassa boy 1 was sold to a resident Arab and sold mangoes on his behalf for a "great many days" in Kilwa before being sold to another Arab and boarded for Muscat. At Kilwa, "Bisa boy" was given as security on a debt and helped his creditor-master oversee another older slave selling oil. He ran away and was kidnapped by other Arabs. They used him to help lead a coastal caravan, even giving him a sword (in the 1870s, as British antislave naval patrols cracked down on sea trading, slaves were marched north along the coast to less-monitored ports).

Yao boy stayed in Kilwa and neighboring Kilwa Kivinje for a year and a half before being sold to another Arab and taken to Bagamoyo, where he was sold to a "Banyan" (Asian). During his new master's long absences, Yao boy became the trusted house servant of another Asian, put in charge of the keys, and made to oversee building projects. After his master returned, Yao boy was sold for export.

Another boy slave, Ismael Semler, was taken to Mozambique and "employed in ship work" (probably scraping dhow hulls) before being bought by a "Brahmin" (Hindu Asian), who sold him to a Muslim "merchant captain." He was taken to Inhambane ("Waniamban"), where he was used to tap coconut palms, returned to Mozambique, then put on board a dhow to Bombay.

Unquestionably the most remarkable experience of a child slave was that of William Jones. He originated in Yaoland, where he was enslaved, and was taken to Kilwa and shipped to Zanzibar. However, his owner could not find a buyer and took Jones back to the mainland on a journey through Zigua country and on to the eastern edge of Nyamwezi territory in central Tanzania. Though ready to sell Jones along the way, his owner found no takers and so returned with him to Zanzibar, where Jones remained four months before someone bought him and put him on a dhow bound for Muscat. In all, from the point of enslavement, Jones walked an estimated fifteen to sixteen hundred kilometers on the mainland.[31]

Once on board a vessel in Indian Ocean waters, children were taken to Zanzibar for the slave market or shipped to Madagascar, Pemba, the Comoros, the Mascarenes, Oman, or India. Journeys aboard long-distance dhows, which embarked between September and December to catch prevailing northeasterly winds and currents, lasted as long as three to five weeks. Of the accounts, only Chilekwa's provides any information about this longer journey, which was carried out in contravention of antislave trade treaties enforced by British naval patrols. Though brief, Chilekwa's retelling is vivid: "All the slaves were placed on the lower deck. We traveled all night and in the morning we found that we were in the midst of the sea and out of sight of land. We went on thus for many days over the sea. At first we had food twice a day . . . and for our relish we very often had fish, for our masters the Arabs caught a large number of fish with hooks and line. But because the journey was so long the food began to run short and so we were hungry, and also water was short and they began to mix it with salt water."[32]

Jones, Semler, George David, and Tom Smith of the CMS mission in India offer no account of their lengthy voyages. CMS schoolchildren at Frere Town, who wrote down their accounts in their 1880 school exams, were liberated by the naval patrol from the same dhow, which had been at sea only three days. None of the lads in the care of the UMCA in Zanzibar and whose autobiographies Madan published, made this journey, because they were liberated after reaching the island and before they could be transshipped.[33] A trip on the high seas, even the short one to Zanzibar, was nevertheless one of extreme hardship, as can be seen in the picture of emaciated children captured from a dhow by HMS *Daphne*.[34] An account of the seizure of a vessel carrying children turned over to the UMCA also provides a glimpse of life on board:

> In a space two feet high, in heat unimaginable, were literally packed like herrings 300 human beings, fifty of whom were children. The dhow, after sheltering at Zanzibar, started off for Arabia, when the wretched slaves heard shots fired, one of which came among them and wounded a little girl. For about ten minutes a desperate battle was fought, and then the Arabs left the ship and swam to land; the fresh air was let in, and the miserable slaves, who had only uncooked rice to eat, and who were wasted to skeletons, were put on board a British man-of-war, and liberated.[35]

Emaciated youngsters were observed in the Zanzibar market shortly after they had been brought over from the mainland.[36]

For child survivors who remained slaves, the sketchy information about their lives suggests that through the rest of their childhood and even later they remained in Muslim societies, much as they had been since enslavement in the East African interior. C. S. Nicholls has claimed that imported boys were given an Islamic education and taught a trade, but evidence from children's accounts tends to accord with Frederick Cooper and Sheriff, who have argued that domestics in Zanzibar were an unproductive slave element.[37] Gindo boy was the exception, working with a silversmith for a year, before being sold to an Asian who kept him as a servant until he was registered (as free). Enslaved children were held as ornaments of purchasing power and kept as servants or dependents. Nevertheless always they were dispensable. Dado became a page of Mombasa *liwali* (governor) Ali b. Nasur and given an Arabic name (Farusi), but he was treated harshly and given no privileges. Rather than groomed as productive property, children could be regarded as company, by female as well as male owners. "And when we came to Muscat," wrote George David, by then having reached young manhood, "I was given to a woman, of about 24 or 25 years of age; whether I was bought for her, or whether I was made present to her I do not know, but his one thing I know, that she loved me very much indeed. She quite made up her mind to keep me for herself. But God, who wished to reach me to better friends and better home, opposed her wishes, by striking me with severe sore eyes, which made her afraid of loosing [sic] me by death, and so she made up her mind to sell me if ever I should recover again."[38]

"Sagara boy," who ended up in coastal Pangani, not far from his highland home, worked in an Arab home cleaning and washing for his master. But when the master was away, his mistress had other duties in mind: "'Let us ___,' do something that was utterly bad and foolish, but I refused to be so bad, and so I said, 'I cannot, young woman; I don't understand you.' Then she said, 'I will tell your master to sell you if you refuse.'"[39] Sagara boy maintains he upheld his honor.

After 1873, when the sultan of Zanzibar decreed the prohibition of the sea trade, the long-distance trade to the coast dried up, though an internal trade in Nyamwezi-land continued to flourish.[40] Moreover, in Zanzibar and other western Indian Ocean islands, and on the Tanganyika, Kenya, and Somali coasts, slavery remained legal for decades. And during famines, such as the Mwachisenge (1884–85), many parents sold children into slavery to enable both to survive.[41] Batches of child slaves were being shipped to Oman as late as the early 1890s.[42] Little evidence is available to evaluate the experiences of children enslaved after 1873 or to assess slavery's effects on them. Recorders of this period seldom distinguished slaves by age, perhaps because children arriving on the coast were within a few years of becoming young adults. What is understood, however, is that on the East African coast and adjoining islands, few children were born into slavery.[43] "I was on the roof of the church in the old slave market, looking at the work, yesterday," commented UMCA bishop Edward Steere in 1878, "when a party of twenty women [free women attached to the UMCA Maweni mission] each with a baby, came up the street. Babies are so scarce in Zanzibar that all the masons and workmen ran to the side to look at them."[44] Children of concubines (*masuria*) were probably the exception. These children (*wazalia*) were known to rise to prominence as caravan leaders, governors, commanders, and other positions of responsibility. They stood in contrast to the children brought in as slaves, who, though perhaps serving as domestics in Arab households, likely were consigned to menial household duties or made into artisans. Little evidence, however, is available to support this point.

To date the only enslaved children whose lives may be traced into adulthood are those who became free persons in association with European missionaries. Although the UMCA assisted freed slaves in Zanzibar for a time, the largest record available pertains to the children raised in India and Kenya by the CMS to evangelize the East African mainland. The CMS had decades of experience in using freed slave converts from Sierra Leone to create a Christian foothold in Nigeria and other parts of West Africa. Since 1860, at its African Asylum in Sharanpur, Nasik, the CMS had cared for East African slave children liberated by British patrols in the Persian Gulf and the Bombay presidency. And in 1874, East African ex-slave children-become-adult converts were transferred from India to assist CMS missionaries establish the Frere Town settlement in Mombasa. These were the so-called Bombay Africans.[45] Soon more than one hundred children (*mateka*) captured by British patrols in East African were placed in the care of the Frere Town mission. From the Bombay Africans and mateka, the CMS derived almost all their African teachers and evangelists in the nineteenth century and used them to establish mission stations in the interior.

The short- and long-term effects of the slave trade on the children who became freed slaves on CMS missions are clear but open to interpretation. The trauma of being removed from family and home to distant points unknown have been charted above, but the end point was more than likely the most terrifying, particularly for those removed from Africa and sold in Muscat or in Bombay, where their languages and experiences left them entirely unequipped. In East Africa, all had moved about in a Bantu-speaking world; the ease of communication was a facilitator of enslavement and control. In India force and defilement dominated master-child slave relationships. As observed by Charles Isenberg, who helped open the African Asylum in 1860, soon after receiving his first charges,

> The orphanage, containing 51 children, required a constant supervision. There were, for instance, girls who had been stolen from different quarters by rope-dancers. The cruel treatment they received induced one of them to complain at the police office, in consequence of which the other two were set at liberty. . . . But what a wild set of vagabonds were these children! [After their arrival at the African Asylum,] Horrible words of abuse, violent quarrels, escapes by night, and other such things were of constant occurrence. Some had lived like brutes; and a large scar on the neck of one of them betrayed that she had once been devoted to death.[46]

Though it is true that, before being freed, some may have ended up in more agreeable circumstances than the children above, the consequences of living without something akin to a home life or social acceptance took its toll. For what is striking about these children is that as adults (Bombay Africans) few were able to form stable relationships or have children themselves. Marriages were promoted by the missionaries, but in India none of the Bombay Africans married outside their group, and after returning to East Africa only a few did so. The stigma of enslavement, amplified by their Christian identities (Christianity was adopted by very few indigenous free Africans before the twentieth century), Western names, and dress, kept them isolated from others and dependent on the mission. By the same token, the "Bombays" in particular rankled under European missionary rule and many found ways of relocating away from the CMS, principally in Zanzibar, where they could obtain wage work from Europeans.

Yet, just as the CMS in West Africa had its Samuel Crowther, the CMS in East Africa had its own African priest who operated independently. William Henry Jones—Yao, Bombay African, evangelist, ordained a priest in 1895, and head of the Rabai CMS mission among the Miji Kenda (in the hills immediately west of Mombasa)—placed a unique stamp on what it meant to be an African Christian in East Africa during the era of slavery. Whereas the CMS policy strictly forbade assisting slaves who fled to the mission from surrounding plantations and towns, Jones harbored runaways by the hundreds, hoodwinking his European superiors in Frere Town, and fought alongside them when the Rabai mission was attacked by Arab slave owners. Jones was also popular among the surrounding non-Christian Arabai population. He was an enthusiastic protagonist for African assertion well in advance of anticolonial politics, and in this regard he is not unlike several other Bombay Africans, notably Tom Smith, George David, Matthew Wellington, Jacob Wainwright, and Charles Isenberg, who in spite of their English names and customary suits and cravats, regarded themselves as Africans.

Interestingly, what they shared in common as enslaved children is that all but Isenberg were pawned or sold by parents or relatives, rather than captured or kidnapped. It is tempting to assume that for children who ended up in slavery through a self-acknowledged family tragedy understood that what lay ahead was in some manner necessary for the well-being of all and that the children's role was to accept their circumstances and do as best they could. Perhaps they understood their absence as easing the family's burden. In contrast, children who were wrested from parents through violence and death probably felt that the future offered only errant responsibilities.

## NOTES

Thanks to the Loras College Redactors for their comments.

### Abbreviations

CA       Central Africa (Church Missionary Society archives reference)
CI       (Church Missionary Society Western India Mission correspondence/archives reference)
CMS      Church Missionary Society
UMCA     Universities' Mission to Central Africa

1. Edward A. Alpers, *Ivory and Slaves: Changing Pattern of International Trade in East Central Africa to the Later Nineteenth Century* (Berkeley: University of California Press, 1975), 240-42.

2. Edward A. Alpers, "The Story of Swema: Female Vulnerability in Nineteenth-Century East Africa," in *Women and Slavery in Africa*, ed. Claire C. Robertson and Martin A. Klein (Madison: University of Wisconsin Press, 1983), 185-99.

3. Richard Gray, *The British in Mombasa, 1824–1826* (London: Macmillan, 1957), 66, 77-78, 164, 168, 170; Roland Oliver, *The Missionary Factor in East Africa* (London: Longmans, Green, 1965), 100; Reginald Coupland, *The Exploitation of East Africa, 1856–1890: The Slave Trade and the Scramble* (London: Faber and Faber, 1968), 139, 143-44, 163; Christine S. Nicholls, *The Swahili Coast: Politics, Diplomacy and Trade on the East African Littoral: 1798–1856* (London: Allen and Unwin, 1971), 210, 288; Richard W. Beachey, *The Slave Trade of Eastern Africa* (London: Rex Collings, 1976), 39, 62-63, 85-87; John Iliffe, *A Modern History of Tanganyika* (Cambridge: Cambridge University Press, 1979), 50; Marguerite Ylvisaker, *Lamu in the Nineteenth Century: Land, Trade, and Politics* (Boston: African Studies Center Boston University, 1979), 91; Burton Benedict, "Slavery and Indenture in Mauri-

tius and Seychelles," in *Asian and African Systems of Slavery*, ed. John L. Watson (Berkeley: University of California Press, 1980), 155–56; Fred Morton, *Children of Ham: Freed Slaves and Fugitive Slaves on the Kenya Coast, 1873–1907* (Boulder: Westview, 1990), 52, 61.

4. Paul Lovejoy, *Transformations in Slavery: A History of Slavery in Africa* (Cambridge: Cambridge University Press, 1983), 16, 59, 62-63, 149; Frederick Cooper, *Plantation Slavery on the East Coast of Africa* (New Haven: Yale University Press, 1977), 221.

5. Abdul Sheriff, "Localisation and Social Composition of the East African Slave Trade, 1858-1873," in *The Economics of the Indian Ocean Slave Trade in the Nineteenth Century*, ed. William G. Clarence-Smith (London: Frank Cass, 1989), 139; R. W. Beachey, *A Collection of Documents on the Slave Trade of Eastern Africa* (London: Rex Collings, 1976), 86-102.

6. Nicholls, *Swahili Coast*; Cooper, *Plantation Slavery*; Margaret Strobel, *Muslim Women in Mombasa, 1890-1975* (New Haven: Yale University Press, 1979); Strobel, "Slavery and Reproductive Labor in Mombasa," in Robertson and Klein, *Women and Slavery*, 111-29; Abdul Sheriff, *Slaves, Spices, and Ivory in Zanzibar: Integration of an East African Commercial Empire into the World Economy, 1770-1873* (London: James Currey, 1987); Jonathan Glassman, *Feasts and Riot: Revelry, Rebellion, and Popular Consciousness on the Swahili Coast, 1856-1888* (Portsmouth: Heinemann, 1994).

7. Fred Morton, "Pawning and Slavery on the Kenya Coast: The Miji Kenda Case," in *Pawnship, Slavery, and Colonialism in Africa*, ed. Paul E. Lovejoy and Toyin Falola (Trenton: Africa World Press, 2003), 239-54.

8. Twelve accounts are found in Arthur C. Madan, *Kiungani; or, Story and History from Central Africa* (London: George Bell and Sons, 1887); another in Alpers, "Story of Swema." Two lengthy autobiographies are Percy L. Jones-Bateman, ed., *The Autobiography of an African Slave Boy* (London: Universities' Mission to Central Africa, 1891); Petro Kilekwa, *Slave Boy to Priest: The Autobiography of Padre Petro Kilekwa* (Westminster: UMCA, 1937). See also W. Yates, *Dado; or, Stories of Native Life in East Africa* (London: Andrew Crombie, 1886).

9. East Africa Mission correspondence (CA5, G3A5), microfilm, Center for Research Libraries, Chicago; Western India Mission correspondence (CI3), Church Missionary Archives, London.

10. James Mbotela, *Uhuru wa Watumwa*, 2nd ed. (Nairobi: East African Literature Bureau, 1967); Mbotela, *The Freeing of the Slaves in East Africa* (Aylesbury: Hazell Watson and Viney, 1956).

11. Philip H. Colomb, *Slave-Catching in the Indian Ocean: A Record of Naval Experiences*, 2nd ed. (London: Dawsons of Pall Mall, 1868), 28-30; Elizabeth W. Wakefield, *Koona Koocha; or, Dawn upon the Dark Continent* (London: Andrew Crombie, 1892), 13-14.

12. Madan, *Kiungani*, 56.

13. Ibid., 51.

14. Ibid., 75.

15. Ibid., 52.

16. Ibid., 42.

17. For child pawns, see Lovejoy and Falola, *Pawnship, Slavery*; for war captives in the Lake Malawi region, see Alpers, *Ivory and Slaves*, 240.

18. Madan, *Kiungani*, 61.

19. Ibid., 34.

20. Ibid., 61.

21. School exam, 1880, CA 5/011, CMS.

22. Jones's encl., Isenberg report, July 1861, CI 3/048, CMS.

23. David to CMS, 29 November 1876, CA 5/06, CMS.

24. Nicholls, *Swahili Coast*, 210. Prices in Maria Theresa dollars. Sheriff's figures do not differentiate by gender. They tend to place higher values on slave "juveniles" than on children. Sheriff, *Slaves, Spices*, table 2.6.

25. School Exam, 1880, CA 5/011, CMS.

26. Isenberg report, July 1861, CI 3/048, CMS.

27. Kilekwa, *Slave Boy*, 9-13.

28. Mbotela, *Freeing of the Slaves*.

29. Kilekwa, *Slave Boy*, 13-14.

30. Madan, *Kiungani*, 56.

31. Encl., Isenberg report, July 1861, CI 3/048, CMS.

32. Kilekwa, *Slave Boy*, 14.

33. Madan, *Kiungani*.

34. G. L. Sulivan, *Dhow Chasing in Zanzibar Waters and on the Eastern Coast of Africa* (London: Samson Low, Marston and Searle, 1873), frontis.

35. A. E. M. Anderson-Morshead, *The History of the Universities' Mission to Central Africa, 1859-1909* (London: UMCA, 1909), 49-50.

36. Beachey, *Documents*, 13-14.

37. Nicholls, *Swahili Coast*, 288; Cooper, *Plantation Slavery*, 34, 37; Sheriff, *Slaves, Spices*, 37-38, 60.

38. David to CMS, 29 November 1876, CA 5/06, CMS.

39. Madan, *Kiungani*, 70-71.

40. Jan-Georg Deutsch, pers. comm.

41. Morton, *Children of Ham*, 40, 160-68; Cooper, *Plantation Slavery*, 122-30.

42. A. B. Grenfell report, 11 April 1893, in Beachey, *Documents*, 100.

43. Cooper, *Plantation Slavery*, 220; Sheriff, *Slaves, Spices*, 59.

44. Letter, 13 August 1878, in E. Steere, *Central African Mission, Occasional Paper* X (London: UMCA, 1879), 15.

45. Morton, *Children of Ham*, 52-76.

46. Isenberg letter, 8 November 1860, in H. Gundert, *Biography of the Rev. Charles Isenberg, Missionary of the Church Missionary Society to Abyssinia and Western India from 1832 to 1864* (London: CMS, 1885), 73.

# 4

## THE BRIEF LIFE OF 'ALI, THE ORPHAN OF KORDOFAN

*The Egyptian Slave Trade in the Sudan, 1820–35*

GEORGE MICHAEL LA RUE

The D'gellab was now introduced with his young charge, certainly a noble little fellow, though only three years old; he was a native of Cordofan, and of a very dark brown colour, with short, frizzly hair, and the negro cast of countenance; but evidently one of a very handsome tribe.

Phrenologically speaking, he had a very fine head, inasmuch as the animal propensities were but little developed, and the intellectual organs were larger than we generally see in the African. I examined him thoroughly; he bore marks of the small-pox on his body, and was in perfect health. Indeed, I was so pleased with the child, that I purchased him for twenty-five dollars, thinking that, being so young, I could train him up in my own way; and as he could have nothing to unlearn, no prejudices to overcome, and few, if any recollections of his home, that a very fair opportunity would be afforded of ascertaining what could be done in the way of education.[1]

'Ali was one of the few child slaves from the nineteenth-century Sudan to be described by more than one European writer.[2] His life is recounted by Dr. William Holt Yates, a member of the British Royal College of Physicians and an abolitionist, and in part by Edmond de Cadalvène and

J. de Breuvery, two scholarly French travelers who briefly accompanied Yates up the Nile in 1834.[3] Yates purchased 'Ali in Wadi Halfa (then in Upper Egypt), intending to release him from slavery. These accounts depict the forces that brought 'Ali into slavery, the market where he was purchased, the implicit ideology of his liberator, and his fate as a freed slave in Egypt and England. 'Ali's brief biography is best understood in the contexts of the trans-Saharan slave trade and the abolitionist movement of the era.

## "THE D'GELLAB WAS NOW INTRODUCED WITH HIS YOUNG CHARGE . . ."

In 1834 the slave trade between the Sudan and Egypt already had a very long history.[4] After the Egyptian invasion of the Sudan in 1820-21, Muhammad 'Ali Pasha, the ruler of Egypt, sought to monopolize the slave trade into Egypt and used Egyptian troops to conduct slave raids. By the early 1830s the troops were primarily Sudanese male slaves. Their pay was usually in arrears and cash was in short supply, so the soldiers were often paid in slaves. The raiding parties took the slaves they captured to collecting points such as El Obeid in Kordofan. The soldiers quickly sold them to Sudanese merchants who traded at the retail level in the Sudan, and moved some slaves to major markets such as Wadi Halfa, near the Egypt-Sudan frontier, where trans-Saharan merchants bought the more desirable slaves for transport to Egypt. There, slaves were sold both privately and—until about 1840—publicly in large market buildings in major cities, notably Cairo and Alexandria.

After Yates questioned the local Egyptian governor about the slave trade, he arranged for a Sudanese *jallab* (a merchant in long-distance trade) to meet him.[5] This merchant dealt openly in slaves in Wadi Halfa and had close ties to the governor. According to Cadalvène and de Breuvery, the three European travelers went to the jallab's home:

> we followed him to his house. Women occupied the first room, if one can even give this name to the small space surrounded by straw partitions, where they had been enclosed. They were there, mixed together pell-mell. . . . We saw seven or eight of them stretched out on the ground, some completely naked, the others still covered with a few shreds of cloth. When they saw us they drew close to each other, while looking at us with astonishment and fear.
>
> We went from there into a dark and unhealthy hovel where the boys were kept. One child of six years, elegantly formed, drew the

attention of Mr. Holt Yates, and the bargain was soon struck for about sixty francs.[6]

Why did Dr. Yates want such a young slave?

## ". . . THOUGH ONLY THREE YEARS OLD . . ."

The two Frenchmen immediately declared 'Ali to be six years old. But Yates put his age at three and called him a little fellow. Given his medical training, perhaps Yates estimated 'Ali's age by the proportion of his limbs and head, or by developmental criteria. In Egypt, slaves were measured in terms of hand spans, from ankle to ear. The smallest slaves sold in Cairo were three hand spans, and a child of five hand spans was under ten or eleven years old.[7] 'Ali quickly learned some English and later to read and write. He was very bright, verbally and socially precocious.

'Ali was thrilled to receive new clothing (including a fez and skullcap) when Yates "procured him a red tarboosch [fez] and takeeyah [skullcap] for his head, a pair of shoes, and some blue linen, which the wife of the Reis [Nile boat captain] made into shirts for him. It was amusing to witness his delight when these things were produced; he carried his shoes about, and shewed them to every body."[8]

'Ali's delight at his change of fortune (and clothing) does not indicate his age within the credible range of three to six years old. 'Ali's cuteness suggests the younger end, and his capabilities, the older end.

## ". . . GUARANTEEING US THAT HE WAS FREE FROM ALL VICES AND FLAWS . . ."

Purchasers have long been advised to consider a slave's health.[9] Some medieval treatises in Arabic suggest the proper way to inspect a slave, slave narratives mention rudimentary tests of physical fitness being performed, and medical manuals exist for potential slave owners in the New World.[10] While the three European travelers probably had no direct acquaintance with this literature, they could have learned in Egypt to consider a slave's health before purchase. Dr. Louis Frank's *Mémoire sur le commerce des nègres au Kaire et sur les maladies auxquelles ils sont sujets en y arrivant* treated the health of the slaves in the some detail.[11] Later, European and North African travelers addressed the health issues in sub-Saharan Africa and Egypt; for example, J. L. Burckhardt and Muhammad ibn Umar al-Tunisi each discuss health, medicine, and medical issues.[12] Other medically trained writers also wrote about health and slavery in Egypt and the Sudan.[13]

Egyptian law permitted the inspection of male slaves "above the navel and below the knees" but "only the face and hands" of females. In practice inspections were much more thorough. Manuals for prospective slave own-ers detailed "how to ascertain the health of a slave, his prospects for long life and innate beauty and character." In the inspection, the head and neck were given particular emphasis.[14]

Arabic sources and Frank's work emphasize the right of the buyer to return the slave if any "defects" were discovered within a certain period (often three days) after purchase. A buyer could return a slave for snoring, wetting the bed, or a recurrent symptom such as fever or itching. For female slaves, pregnancy was added to the list.[15] In his sales pitch to Yates, the jallab declared 'Ali "free from all vices and flaws."

## "PHRENOLOGICALLY SPEAKING . . ."

Dr. Yates, who was familiar with the new and popular nineteenth-century "science" of phrenology, expressed his approval of 'Ali: "Phrenologically speaking, he had a very fine head, inasmuch as the animal propensities were but little developed, and the intellectual organs were larger than we generally see in the African."[16] Today, phrenology is generally condemned as racist for assuming that certain physical attributes such as head shape de-termine character, and for idealizing Caucasian head shapes. Some scholars see phrenology as a step toward craniometry, a practice more clearly racist in its classifications of humans.[17] Yates's acceptance of phrenology is not surprising for his day.

Phrenology is more complex than some other attempts to compare races. Stephen Gould notes, "Phrenologists celebrated the theory of richly multiple and independent intelligences. . . . By reading each bump on the skull as a measure of 'domesticity,' or 'amativeness,' or 'sublimity,' or 'causality,' the phrenologists divided mental functioning into a rich congeries of largely independent attributes."[18]

In 1833, the year before Yates purchased 'Ali, a popular article provided a phrenological chart, including three views of a human head (front, side, back), with an explanation of the importance of each of the various la-beled sections.[19] Under "Animal Propensities" it explained such terms as *alimentiveness, destructiveness, philoprogenitiveness, inhabitiveness, combativeness, secretiveness,* and *acquisitiveness*—all thought to relate to the shape of specific portions of the occipital region. Based on the back of 'Ali's head, Yates said that the "animal propensities were but little developed." By contrast, "the intellectual organs" were generally considered to be in the frontal region, or forehead, and included such characteristics as "individuality, configura-tion, size, weight, coloring, locality, order, calculation, eventuality, time, tune and language." Yates judged 'Ali positively in this region.

Arabic manuals for slave buyers similarly argued that head shape reveals an individual's character. Terence Walz summarizes a medieval Arab manual for slave owners:

> A slave's character was revealed by almost every part of the face, head and neck. Soft hair . . . is an indication of cowardice, while a small-sized head meant the slave had a "weak brain and a constitution which will result in stubbornness, quick temper and indecision." Eyes especially, offered abundant clues to personal character. Depending on their size, steadiness or position, and individual could be "insolent and lazy, intriguing, cunning, imbecilic and given to lusts, cunning and envious," "given to evil deeds" or stupid. Droopy eyelids, apparently, forecast a "cunning, stupid and lying nature," while hairy eyebrows suggest an anxious and melancholic disposition and a laconic personality.

In the same vein, the manual discussed the shape of the ears, nose, lips and cheeks, gums, face, and the size of the neck.[20]

Phrenological terms may have been a cover for the more overtly racist terminology of an earlier day. For example, Frank commented on one group of African slaves in Cairo: "The Negroes who are brought from the kingdom of Darfur are most definitely black and are Negroes in the full sense of the word. Generally, they have a wide flat nose, thick upturned lips, and in sum a physiognomy displeasing to Europeans. Their moral qualities seemed to me to be in perfect accord with their physiognomy."[21] Another francophone observer in Cairo in 1835 bluntly described a female slave as having "thick protruding lips, a receding forehead, the ugliest type among the black races."[22] Such descriptions of African slaves in Egypt and the Sudan are common.[23]

Yates's positive phrenological appreciation of 'Ali's head can be seen as part of the broader effort by abolitionists to appeal to the European public. The early abolitionist movement highlighted intelligent, articulate individuals (such as Olaudah Equiano and Ottobah Cuguano), recounting their suffering while they were slaves. Later, abolitionists portrayed individual young enslaved Africans as phrenologically exceptional. For example, Captain Frederick Forbes brought Sarah Forbes Bonnetta from Dahomey to England in 1850. Writing to Queen Victoria, he described her as an "intelligent and good tempered (I need hardly add Black) girl about six or seven years of age." Specifically interested in her capacity for further education, he lauded her as "so excellent a phrenological specimen."[24]

Some phrenologists were actually egalitarian in their thinking. Friedrich Tiedemann argued in 1836 that notions of African inferiority (and physical ugliness) arose from studying "a few skulls of Negroes living on the coasts, who, according to credible travelers, are the lowest and most demoralized of all the Negro tribes; the miserable remains of an enslaved people, bodily and spiritually lowered and degraded by slavery and ill treatment."[25] To judge Africans properly, it would be best to find individuals with little or no experience of slavery: "The original and good character of the Negro tribes on the Western Coast of Africa has been corrupted and ruined by the horrors of the slave trade, since they have unfortunately become acquainted with Europeans."[26] Yates wanted to find a young Sudanese boy who had barely been touched by the slave trade to separate the effects of nature and nurture on the character and intelligence of Africans.[27] 'Ali became a specimen in a dispassionate and scientific experiment aimed—on the very eve of the political success of the British abolitionist movement in the Caribbean—to disprove the innate inferiority of Africans.[28]

## ". . . HE BORE MARKS OF THE SMALL-POX ON HIS BODY, AND WAS IN PERFECT HEALTH"

In 1802, Dr. Frank had emphasized smallpox:

> This disease is often disastrous for the Negroes and [jallaba]. It seems to be less widespread in the Sudan than in Egypt, but it is always deadly. The [jallaba] maintain that smallpox never breaks out in their land except when the germ of infectious disease is brought there. This assertion seems to be borne out . . . among the Negroes brought to Cairo, often two-thirds are found to have not yet suffered from this disease. . . .
>     Smallpox is generally widespread among the Negroes. . . . It is likely that the [jallaba] would lose fewer Negroes if they attended to them a little, and especially if they were willing to consult a European doctor. But either they cannot grasp this reality or they are not in the least disposed to allow for any such expense.[29]

Buyers in Cairo, fully aware of the dangers involved, paid a premium of about one-third for slaves who had already contracted smallpox.[30] As Cadalvène and de Breuvery commented in 1834: "The principle malady which the jallabs have to fear for the slaves is small pox; thus their prices increase considerably when they have recovered from it. It's by the color of their tongues that one recognizes their greater or lesser healthiness."[31] Like Frank, Cadalvène and de Breuvery were aware of the benefits of inoculation—as was Doctor A. B. Clot, a French surgeon who had become head of the Egyptian health system and who in 1837 initiated a local program of inoculating both Egyptians and African slaves in order to reduce "the introduction of small-pox into Egypt, by vaccinating all the Negroes that are transported there as the caravans arrive at Aswan." Clot argued that "the time necessary to observe the eruption of the vaccine" would also allow the slaves to rest after the arduous trans-Saharan journey.[32] Clot advocated extending the same measures to the Sudan to 'prevent the loss from small pox of a large number of individuals who die en route.'[33] Dr. Yates selected young 'Ali because he was healthy and immune to smallpox because he had already had it.

### "... FEW, IF ANY RECOLLECTIONS OF HIS HOME ..."

Although the silences of slaves in the African diaspora into Muslim lands have received ample comment, sometimes even a few words and the accompanying nonverbal evidence can speak volumes about slavery.[34] Yates's description of 'Ali's past shows this well:

> I found he had no recollection of his parents;—he said that his mother was "mat" dead—and when I mentioned his father, he broke out vehemently against him—calling him "battalla"—a bad man. This surprised me—but I discovered that he had been taught to call the slave-dealer his father, and that he had no other. This I was not sorry for, as, having previously been ill-treated, he was more likely to devote himself to me, and it was clear that there would be no pining after parents and kindred lost. All I could make out was, that they lived in pointed huts built of mud and straw.[35]

If 'Ali was really three and a half years old, these few facts about his past are especially interesting.

First, the two words directly from 'Ali are about his "parents" and are in Arabic. If he was captured in a slave raid, he was separated from his father then, or on the march to a collection point in Kordofan. 'Ali states that his mother is dead. Perhaps she died before or during the raid, but she was probably captured with 'Ali. Typically, the captured slaves were divided by Egyptian soldiers after the raids by size and sex:

> In one division were placed the old and infirm women, the pregnant females and young girls; in a second, boys about the age of 8 to 12 years; in a third, children from 4 to 8 years old;

and in a fourth, infants from one and a half to 4 years old. . . .
Upon receiving the slaves, the officers and soldiers immediately
conducted their property to their habitations, and whilst one of
the former was leaving the court my attention was attracted to
an infant two years and a half old, who rushed towards a female
(whom I afterwards learned was its mother) and seizing her, clung
with the most filial affection, imploring her to resume that parental protection which it so highly valued, until a Turkish soldier,
aroused from a state of apathy by the cries of the child, tore it
from its fondest hopes, and instantly separated it for ever from
her who alone could afford it comfort and consolation.[36]

One child from Kordofan ended up as the pay of his own elder brother,
who had earlier been pressed into service as a slave soldier.[37]

'Ali's mother would have helped him to keep up with the *qafila* (slave
coffle, or caravan), like the one described by a contemporary observer:
"Children from six years, and even from four years of age, were obliged to
run. But they could seldom bear the fatiguing march, and were obliged to
be carried by their mothers and sisters. I even saw mothers with a sucking
babe in one arm, a child of two years of age in the other, and at last an
exhausted boy on their backs, sink under this threefold burden."[38] 'Ali's
mother may have perished en route to Wadi Halfa.

'Ali referred to his father as *battala*—a bad man. This surprised Yates
until he realized that it was common practice in the nineteenth-century
Sudan (as elsewhere in Muslim Africa) for a slave to call his current master
"father."[39] The two words *mat* and *battala* cut through the text. Neither
word matches the gender of the person described. These errors could be
ascribed to 'Ali's tender age or to the possibility that Arabic was not his
native language. Four African boys between twelve and eighteen years old,
purchased by the Duke of Bavaria in Cairo and Alexandria and later studied by the Tutschek brothers,

had been stolen from their homes and been sold on the Nile as
slaves. Necessity had forced them, in order to make themselves mutu-
ally understood, to learn the vulgar dialect of the Arabian [language],
though but very imperfectly. When the Duke obtained them, three
of them had not been longer than a year from their homes, and
therefore, being old enough and endowed with excellent capacities,
they were not only able to give information concerning their languages, but also to describe the circumstances of the countries.[40]

'Ali was younger, and might have learned Arabic after capture. Or perhaps 'Ali's statements were misreported by Yates due to Yates's imperfect knowledge of Arabic. Yates said 'Ali had no other father, but there is no evidence either that he had died or that 'Ali was illegitimate.

### ". . . HE COULD HAVE NOTHING TO UNLEARN . . ."

After Yates purchased 'Ali, the local sailors on his Nile boat teased him, saying that he would be eaten by Yates and the crew. Then 'Ali "became very indignant and uttered some horrible imprecations and sayings of a most obscene nature, the meaning of which he could not possibly understand—and he could only have picked up such expressions whilst crossing the desert. I soon put a stop to this, by not allowing him to communicate with these men."[41]

Where did 'Ali learn to use such strong language? He may have spoken Arabic in his own home, or heard it nearby. Yates suggests that 'Ali learned these choice phrases in transit with the slave qafila. It is easy to imagine obscene language in frequent use by a raiding party of enslaved Sudanese soldiers in the Egyptian army, or by the jallaba, who reportedly abused their charges physically and sexually.[42]

Yates's desire to purchase young 'Ali because he was assumed to be a "blank slate" mirrors those of Egyptian slave purchasers: "Buyers in Cairo showed a strong preference for young, newly-imported slaves in the belief that their morals had not yet been corrupted or that only those raised in the owner's family could be trusted. There was an unwillingness to buy slaves who had been brought up in someone else's house for fear that such slaves would have picked up 'cunning tricks and bad habits.'"[43] Yates needed a young, freshly captured child for his experiment on nature versus nurture.

Yates paid a high price for 'Ali when he purchased him in Wadi Halfa. The price of black slave boys in Alexandria and Damietta in Lower Egypt ranged from twelve to twenty-five dollars.[44] A few years later, a child of five or six was worth about five dollars at Khartoum.[45] As a European, Yates paid a premium for 'Ali. 'Ali was healthy and Yates openly displayed his keenness to redeem him. In all events, the sale was unusual. It benefited the seller financially and as a means to dispose of illegal merchandise.

### ". . . MARKS . . ."

The nonverbal evidence of 'Ali's past was reflected in his actions and inscribed on his physical body: "He suffered the D'gellab to depart with the greatest indifference; doubtless he had been transferred more than once before, as he bore on his legs and back, marks which had been burnt in by the persons through whose hands he had passed. He was quite naked, and swarming with vermin."[46] Yates "read" the story of 'Ali's bad treatment by the jallab in the marks left by beatings or whippings inflicted along the road to keep the child moving.[47] Despite his young age, 'Ali's nakedness was humiliating. He was "swarming with vermin," undoubtedly lice. 'Ali had recently arrived at Wadi Halfa. Over a longer time, his beating marks would have faded, and he had not yet washed and rubbed himself with *dilka*, or oil, as most slaves were required to do when put on sale in the market.[48]

Yates is the sole source for some details, but the Frenchmen confirm 'Ali's recent arrival: "The last caravan from Kordofal [Kordofan] had left in Wadi Halfa, some slaves of the two sexes, who were too exhausted to take to Egypt, without a danger of seeing them perish en route."[49] The jallaba realized that some of the women and young children like 'Ali would not survive the trip. The two accounts differ slightly on chronology. Yates reports having 'Ali washed: "I gave him in charge to Mohammed [the captain of the Nile boat] for the night, and after he had taken a basin of bread and milk, the poor child fell into a sound sleep upon the bare boards. The first thing the next morning I had him well lathered from head to foot; I then set him to work to anoint his body."[50] By contrast, the French travelers say it happened at the jallaba's house: "After the child had been well washed up in our presence, while guaranteeing us that he was free from all vices and flaws, we prepared to take him away."[51] 'Ali's need for a bath was more important than its timing.

There is a silence in the two European sources: neither indicated that 'Ali had been castrated although that was the fate of about two to three hundred male slaves per year in El Obeid, Kordofan:

> Melik Tamar, brother to the late sultan of Dar Fur . . . enjoyed an exclusive monopoly of this brutal practice, but, as his success was great, other persons, finding they could realize a larger profit by making their captives eunuchs than by selling them as ordinary slaves, adopted a similar profession. . . . He emasculates from 100 to 150 slaves annually, and the same number are mutilated by the other operators in Kordofan. . . . The subjects selected for emasculation are boys from 7 to 11 years old. All the organs are removed, and the operation rarely proves fatal to more than five percent.[52]

Most contemporary estimates of mortality due to castration run rather higher than 5 percent.[53] Yates, Cadalvène, and de Breuvery knew of this practice in Kordofan and condemned it.[54] Their silence indicates that 'Ali was not a eunuch. Perhaps he did not pass through El Obeid because his home village was closer to the Nile, or because he was younger than seven. Or perhaps he was disqualified in other regards—as a Muslim, as an Arabic speaker, as the child of someone of relatively high social standing.

### ". . . HE . . . TOOK THE HAND OF EACH OF HIS COMPANIONS . . ."

'Ali's behavior as he was leaving his fellow slaves was quite remarkable: "he, undoubtedly not foreseeing the happy fate that awaited him, took the hand of each of his companions and brought it to his mouth and forehead, while speaking a few words to each one in turn. This was undoubtedly his adieus, the adieus of a slave, this last and touching speech addressed to friendly ears, between the memory of his native soil, and an unknown future."[55] Cadalvène and de Breuvery are the more objective and credible observers—they had little time to form an emotional attachment and judged 'Ali to be about six. Perhaps Yates did not witness this farewell scene or found it unremarkable. 'Ali's actions mark him as a very polite and well-brought-up child who has learned his manners not in a slave coffle or a "pagan" village, but in the home of educated, religious, and economically comfortable Muslims, where such exquisite manners were valued. One can speculate that he was not only saying good-bye but also blessing his young slave companions. In a Muslim society, a bright child might do this at the age of six or even younger.[56]

What are the implications of this behavior? 'Ali probably spoke Arabic at home, was raised by Muslim parents who had the upbringing and leisure to teach him the finest manners, and was illegally enslaved. Muslims are forbidden to enslave other Muslims; but this unfortunately was quite common in times of war and by unscrupulous slave kidnappers driven by profit. The illegally enslaved could seek to regain their freedom in Muslim courts. Selling an enslaved Muslim child to a European traveler solved the jallab's problem: how to dispose of "hot" merchandise. The complicity of Egyptian officials in the Sudan facilitated this circumvention of Muslim morality: it was the Egyptian governor at Aswan, "Mohammed Agah," who introduced Yates and the two French travelers to the slave dealer.

The governor portrayed 'Ali as unusual before the three travelers ever met him: "a little Negro child, who was remarkable for his talents and sagacity— 'not a common slave . . . but, as I understand, the son of one of the native chiefs.'"[57] His words, intended to tempt the travelers, match the nonverbal evidence that 'Ali was from the home of an Arabic-speaking Muslim "chief" from Kordofan. The governor was assisting the jallaba to avoid difficulties by facilitating a sale to foreigners unaware of 'Ali's legal status.

After Yates purchased the boy at Wadi Halfa, Cadalvène and de Breuvery watched sadly as the Nile boat turned down river to carry the doctor and 'Ali to Cairo. While Yates went on to Syria, he planned to send 'Ali "direct to England, in the charge of Capt. Riches and his wife, who fortunately were at Alexandria with *The Bristol* waiting for a cargo of cotton."[58] However, the pair had a few more adventures before they actually parted:

> We were just stepping into one of the shore boats, when a tall athletic Negro touched me on the shoulder, and asked for my *teskereh*, at the same time demanding a tax for *the slave*: I resented both, but having in my hurry, *given up the teskereh to the guides at Rosetta*, I was under the necessity of going, feverish and excited as I was, to the custom-house, where I deposited my baggage, and then proceeded with Ali to the British Consulate: the poor child was so fatigued that, in two minutes, he was in a sound sleep.[59]

The teskereh was generally an official receipt for the purchase of a slave that specified the physical attributes of the merchandise purchased. A slave owner had to present it when a slave was manumitted or transferred to another owner.[60] Here it meant a manumission document, required for the export of a slave or former slave from Egypt by a European. With this bureaucratic difficulty resolved, Yates sent 'Ali off to England:

> I entered my little boy as a passenger on board "the Bristol" in the name of Ali Hassanyn, to which I added the surname of *Felix,* in consideration of his happy condition.
> The captain and his wife were both very fond of him, and had him baptized at Liverpool. I did not [see] the child again for fifteen months: he would then often speak of Momma Riches, and I had no reason to regret having placed him under her care.[61]

'Ali was enrolled in a school in England. At the age of "six and a half" (over three years after Yates purchased him), he fell ill with "[w]hooping cough" and died of the complications. In recounting 'Ali's death, Yates's emotions pour out:

> A finer prospect, I am sure, never offered itself. He was everything I could wish him to be,—quick, ardent, generous, and truly affectionate. He loved me as if I had been his own father. I seldom had occasion to correct him,—and then, a word was

enough: for he would cry so bitterly, that to hear him was painful in the extreme. In all his actions he was graceful; he was full of intelligence, and evinced a most extraordinary predilection for religion; being never so happy as when he could get any one to read the bible to him; at school, he was the life of the little party, and nothing could be done without "dear Ali"—his companions left everything to his direction, and whenever he was absent, their games were dull and spiritless. He was open and sincere, and beloved and admired by all who knew him. Persons would frequently stop to talk about him in the street, and (forgetting that he understood English) would ask if he was not the son of some Prince, so impressed were they with his figure and demeanour. Love of admiration appeared to be his only fault. The ladies with whom he was placed were so fond of him, that they watched him narrowly;—possessing a large share of good sense, and being unaffectedly pious, they instilled into his mind the fundamental principles of Christianity, and I was very sanguine that as he grew up, his little vanities would be subdued, and that the seed which had been sown with such care; would be productive of good fruit—but all my hopes were blighted; it pleased the Almighty Disposer of events to call him hence. He resided in this country two years during which he never felt the cold, and I think had not a day's illness: but he was attacked at last with [w]hooping cough, one very inclement spring, during the prevalence of a severe epidemic *catarrh*, and he died in convulsions, at the age of six years and a half—a period when children twine themselves about us, and steal away our hearts. I was grieved, deeply grieved for the loss of my poor boy, though I felt it my duty to believe that it was for the best. It is impossible to tell what the result might have been, had he lived to become a man, and he is assuredly far happier than I could make him, were he now here. I bless God that he was removed during childhood—since it was to be, and I resign him cheerfully to his Saviour![62]

The grieving Yates was scarcely a dispassionate observer, though the man of science regretted losing an opportunity for his experiment on nature versus nurture.

The biography of this young boy reveals much about the places and times he lived in. Kordofan was particularly dangerous between 1821 and the 1840s—subject to invasion, to slave raids, and to kidnappings. Even young

'Ali from a "native chief's" home and a Muslim background was caught up by the violence of the era. He was torn from his home, lost his father, marched in a coffle to a major slave market, whipped to force him to keep up with the adults, hearing horrible curses, and seeing children and women (including perhaps his own mother) fall along the way. He was poorly fed, ill dressed, "covered with vermin" and thrown into a dark hut with other enslaved boys. He avoided castration in El Obeid through some fortunate combination of timing, geography, religion, stature, age, and luck.

Through it all, 'Ali maintained a sense of self. He demonstrated his social graces in bidding farewell to his slave companions, in sharing his pleasure at receiving new clothing, and by becoming the ringleader among his schoolmates in England. He showed his intelligence by using strong words to defend his dignity when under verbal attack, by learning English rapidly, and by learning to read and write. The Sudanese, Egyptians, and Europeans he met saw him as both a person and a very special commodity. For the jallab and the governor at Wadi Halfa, he was a problem. He should not have been enslaved by fellow Muslims; as an Arabic speaker he might have been able to launch an appeal, and as a chief's son he might have been able to find someone to help him in the Sudan. By collaborating, the jallab and the pasha avoided the repercussions of dealing in "hot" slaves and convinced Yates to purchase 'Ali.

For Yates, Cadalvène, and de Breuvery, 'Ali was also unusual. Each had an academic interest in slavery and the slave trade in Egypt and the Sudan. They perceived 'Ali's vitality, intelligence, and personal grace. But that perception conflicted with their received images of slaves and his status as a slave child for sale. For Yates, a doctor and abolitionist, 'Ali represented an untainted child, a blank slate, perhaps even a noble savage. Yates bought 'Ali, removed him from his "negative" environment, and provided him with a British education, to determine the impact of "proper nurturing" on 'Ali's innate nature.

'Ali's treatment by Yates was initially similar to that of other slaves. Yates used phrenology to judge 'Ali's head shape. On that basis he thought 'Ali was a worthy subject for his educational experiment. Yates also appraised 'Ali's general physical health, noting his previous exposure to smallpox. Sudanese or Egyptian purchasers also thought head shape revealed character and evaluated slaves' health, looking for evidence of smallpox.

'Ali died at a young age in England, but an early death was not uncommon for Sudanese nor for children in Britain at the time. Childhood diseases must have killed many of his age mates in the Sudan, while others died in slave raids, or along the slave-trade routes. If 'Ali had been sold to an Egyptian master, he might have died in the plague epidemic of 1834–35, which killed about fifteen thousand black slaves in Cairo and Alexandria.[63]

'Ali's story provides a glimpse of the trans-Saharan slave trade, the medical situation in the Sudan, and the mentality of European travelers in the Sudan and Egypt before 1835. Although abolitionist sentiment still considered New World slavery harsher than slavery in Muslim countries, travelers such as Cadalvène and de Breuvery began to see similarities and to understand the horrors of slave raids and the slave trade. The making of eunuchs appalled all who learned about it. Yates did not fully comprehend 'Ali's experiences, even as he heard and repeated *mat* and *battala*, and saw the whiplashes and the lice that covered him.

### NOTES

1. William Holt Yates, *The Modern History and Condition of Egypt*, 2 vols. (London: Smith, Elder and Co., 1843), 2:475-76.

2. See P. E. H. Hair, "The Brothers Tutschek and Their Sudanese Informants," *Sudan Notes and Records* 50 (1969), 53-62; for the place of origin of one of them, see Janet J. Ewald, *Soldiers, Traders, and Slaves: State Formation and Economic Transformation in the Greater Nile Valley, 1700-1885* (Madison: University of Wisconsin Press, 1990), 3, 179, 188.

3. Edmond de Cadalvène and J. de Breuvery, *L'Égypte et la Turquie de 1829 à 1836*, 2 vols. (Paris: Arthus Bertrand, 1836), 2:105-6.

4. Robert O. Collins, "Slavery in the Sudan in History," *Slavery and Abolition* 20, no. 3 (1999), 69-95. The benchmark study is Gabriel Baer, "Slavery in Nineteenth Century Egypt," *Journal of African History* 8, no. 3 (1967): 417-41; also see Baer, "Slavery and Its Abolition" in *Studies in the Social History of Modern Egypt* (Chicago: University of Chicago Press, 1969), 161-89.

5. Yates, *Modern History*, 2:474.

6. Cadalvène and de Breuvery, *Égypte*, 2:105-6.

7. Terence Walz, *The Trade between Egypt and Bilad as-Sudan, 1700-1820* (Cairo: Institut Français d'Archéologie Orientale du Caire, 1978), 184.

8. Yates, *Modern History*, 2:477.

9. The quote in the heading for this section is from Cadalvène and de Breuvery, *Égypte*, 2:106.

10. For a reference to a medieval manual, see John Hunwick, "Black Slaves in the Mediterranean World: Introduction to a Neglected Aspect of the African Diaspora," in *The Human Commodity*, ed. Elizabeth Savage (London: Frank Cass, 1992), 34n34. A treatise by Muhammad al-Ghazzali, *Counsel for the Novice on Examining Slaves*, is cited by Walz, *Trade*, 174-75. Compare G. I. Jones, "Olaudah Equiano of the Niger Ibo," in *Africa Remembered*, ed. Philip D. Curtin (Madison: University of Wisconsin Press, 1967), 92.

11. Vivant Denon, "Mémoire sur le commerce des Nègres au Kaire et sur les maladies auxquelles il sont sujets en y arrivant," appendix in *Voyage dans la basse et la haute Égypte* (Paris : Didot l'Aîné, 1802), 2:235-248. See also Michel Le Gall, "Translation of Louis Frank's *Mémoire sur le commerce de nègres au Kaire, et sur les maladies auxquelles ils sont sujets en y arrivant* (1802)," in *Slavery in the Islamic Middle East*, ed. Shaun E. Marmon (Princeton: Markus Wiener, 1999), 69-88.

12. J. L. Burckhardt, *Travels in Nubia*, (London: John Murray, 1822); Mohammed ebn-Omar El-Tounsy, *Voyage au Darfour* (Paris: Benjamin Duprat, 1845); El-Tounsy, *Voyage au Ouaday* (Paris: A. Bertrand, Franck, Renouard et Gide, 1851).

13. George Michael La Rue, "A Generation of African Slave Women in Egypt, from ca. 1820 to the Plague Epidemic of 1834-1835," in *Women and Slavery: Volume One– Africa and the Western Indian Ocean Islands*, ed. Gwyn Campbell, Suzanne Miers, and Joseph C. Miller (Athens: Ohio University Press, 2007) .

14. Walz, *Trade*, 181-83.

15. Le Gall, "Translation," 76, 80; Walz, *Trade*, 186, 193-95.

16. Yates, *Modern History*, 2:476.

17. Stephen Jay Gould, *The Mismeasure of Man* (New York: Norton, 1981), 129-41.

18. Ibid, 22.

19. "Hints about Phrenology," *Ladies Magazine* 6 (1833). http://chnm.gmu/lostmuseum/ lm/95/, accessed 13 February 2004.

20. Walz, *Trade*, 182.

21. LeGall, "Translation," 77.

22. Suzanne Voilquin, *Souvenirs d'une fille du peuple* (Paris: Maspero, 1978), 288-89.

23. John Lloyd Stephens, *Incidents of Travel in Egypt, Arabia Petraea and the Holy Land*, ed. Victor Wolfgang von Hagen (Norman: University of Oklahoma, 1970), 27-28, 62; James Ewing Cooley, javascript:open_window(%22http://lms01.harvard .edu:80/F/JSBBRBQE9Q3H4V5UP9JAC7FVLIN3F9X93JDMCAN1Y8YNVES197 -50086?func=service&doc_number=002195072&line_number=0011&service _type=TAG%22); (New York: D. Appleton and Co., 1842), 406.

24. "The London String of Pearls." http://www.obv.org.uk/sop/buckingham.htm, accessed 22 February 2004. See also http://www.nextag.com/Books~Walter+Dean +Myersz200000zozB10zmainz5-htm, *At Her Majesty's Request: An African Princess in Victorian England* (New York: Scholastic, 1999).

25. Stephen Jay Gould, "The Great Physiologist of Heidelberg" in *I Have Landed: The End of a Beginning in Natural History* (New York: Three Rivers, 2003), 372.

26. Ibid., 375.

27. Cf. Robin Law, "Dahomey and the Slave Trade: Reflections on the Historiography of the Rise of Dahomey," *Journal of African History* 27, no. 2 (1986): 237-67.

28. Hair, "Brothers Tutschek," 53-62; Gould, "Great Physiologist," 382-83.

29. Le Gall, "Translation," 82-83. I replaced his "Ghellabis" with *jallaba*, a term for merchants trading from Egypt to sub-Saharan Africa, and by extension, slave dealers.

30. Walz, *Trade*, 201, citing Burckhardt, *Nubia*, 290.

31. Cadalvène and Breuvery, *Égypte*, 2:105n.

32. Walz, *Trade*, 201. For other references to inoculation, see La Rue, "Generation."

33. A. B. Clot, *Compte rendu des travaux de l'École de Medécine d'Abou Zabel 1825 à 1832* (Marseille: Feissal Ainé et Demouchy, 1832), 92-94.

34. For some recovered voices of slaves, see La Rue, "The Capture of a Slave Caravan: the Incident at Asyut (Egypt) in 1880," *African Economic History* 30 (2002): 83-108. For discussion of silences, see Eve M. Troutt Powell, "The Silence of the Slaves," in *The African Diaspora in the Mediterranean Lands of Islam*, ed. John Hunwick and Eve M. Troutt Powell (Princeton: Markus Wiener, 2002), xxv-xxxvii.

35. Yates, *Modern History*, 2:478.

36. John Bowring, *Report on Egypt and Candia*, Parliamentary Papers, Reports from Commissioners, 11 (1840), 84.

37. Ibid.
38. Hunwick and Powell, *African Diaspora*, 67-69.
39. Cadalvène and Breuvery, *Égypte*, 2:122.
40. Hair, "Brothers Tutschek," 54-55.
41. Yates, *Modern History*, 2:477.
42. Edward William Lane, *The Manners and Customs of the Modern Egyptians*, 2 vols. (London: J. M. Dent, 1944), 1:257.
43. Walz, *Trade*, 184-85. See also Le Gall, "Memoirs," 81.
44. Yates, *Modern History*, 1:462
45. Bowring, *Report on Egypt*, 84.
46. Yates, *Modern History*, 2:477.
47. Le Gall, "Translation," 73.
48. See Cadalvène and de Breuvery, *Égypte*, 2:299; Le Gall, "Translation," 77.
49. Cadalvène and de Breuvery, *Égypte*, 2:105.
50. Yates, *Modern History*, 2:477.
51. Cadalvène and de Breuvery, *L'Égypte*, 106.
52. Arthur T. Holroyd, "Notes on a Journey to Kordofan in 1836-7," *Journal of the Royal Geographical Society* 9 (1839): 177-78.
53. The editorial footnote in Holroyd suggests a higher mortality is commonly reported. For a modern analysis, see Jan Hogendorn, "The Hideous Trade: Economic Aspects of the 'Manufacture' and Sale of Eunuchs," *Paideuma* 45 (1999): 137-60; Hogendorn, "The Location of the "Manufacture" of Eunuchs," in *Slave Elites in the Middle East and Africa*, ed. Miura Toru and John Edward Philips (London: Kegan Paul International, 2000), 41-68.
54. Yates, *Modern History*, 1:464.
55. Cadalvène and de Breuvery, *Égypte*, 2:106.
56. See Humphrey Fisher, *Slavery in the History of Muslim Black Africa* (New York: New York University Press, 2001), 18-32. For Egypt and the Sudan, see Walz, *Trade*, 226. The term *hami* (lit. warm) was used by jallaba en route to Dar Fur from Wadai in 1874 to describe slaves "whose legal status was open to question." Gustav Nachtigal, *Sahara and Sudan*, 4 vols. (London: C. Hurst, 1971), 4:231. See also Paul E. Lovejoy, "Slavery, the *Bilad al-Sudan*, and the Frontiers of the African Diaspora," in *Slavery on the Frontiers of Islam*, ed. Lovejoy (Princeton: Markus Wiener, 2003), esp. 10-18.
57. Yates, *Modern History*, 2:474.
58. Ibid., 2:589.
59. Ibid., 591; emphasis in original.
60. René Cattaui, *Le règne de Mohammed Aly d'après les archives russes en Égypte*, 3 vols. (Cairo: Cairo University Press, 1931), 1:230.
61. Yates, *Modern History*, 2:596.
62. Ibid., 2:476-77n.
63. Félix Mengin, *Histoire sommaire de l'Égypte sous le gouvernement de Mohammed-Aly ou récit des principaux événements qui on eu lieu de l'an 1823 à l'an 1838* (Paris: Didot Frères, 1839), 472n1.

# 5

## TRADED BABIES

*Enslaved Children in America's Domestic Migration, 1820–60*

SUSAN EVA O'DONOVAN

Sometime in 1843, a young Hawkins Wilson went on the block at a sheriff's sale. A quarter century later, Wilson, who had been born in Caroline County, Virginia, wrote from Galveston, Texas, eager to set back to rights what had been nearly demolished by a lifetime in slavery. "Dear Sir," Wilson opened his letter to a Freedmen's Bureau official from whom he sought assistance, "I am anxious to learn about my sisters, from whom I have been separated many years—I have never heard from them since I left Virginia twenty four years ago—I am in hopes that they are still living and I am anxious to hear how they are getting on." Tapping into a domestic and affective lineage that he had kept alive all those years in his mind, Wilson provided what clues he knew of his loved ones' coordinates:

> One of my sisters belonged to Peter Coleman in Caroline County and her name was Jane—Her husband's name was Charles and he belonged to Buck Haskin and lived near John Wright's store in the same county—She had three children, Robert, Charles and Julia, when I left—Sister Martha belonged to Dr Jefferson, who lived two miles above Wright's store—Sister Matilda belonged to Mrs. Botts, in the same county—My dear uncle Jim had a wife at Jack Langley's and his wife was named Adie and his oldest son was named Buck and they all belonged to Jack Langley—These are all my own dearest relatives and I wish to correspond with them with a view to visit them as soon as I can hear from them—My

name is Hawkins Wilson and I am their brother, who was sold at
Sheriff's sale and used to belong to Jackson Tally and was bought
by M. Wright of Boydtown C.H. [Virginia].[1]

Hawkins Wilson stands out for his remarkable letters, the light they
shed on a child's life in slavery, and the effort he made to reconnect with a
faraway family. In most other respects, however, Wilson stands in for many.
His story was a common story, one shared by hundreds of thousands of
black youngsters. Neither marginal to nor by-products of an agricultural
revolution that swept the United States between 1800 and 1861, enslaved
children played integral roles in a process that would define and nearly
destroy a young nation. Except for the absolute youngest, they performed a
wide range of agricultural, industrial, and domestic tasks. Their potential as
workers and parents underwrote the reproduction of a slaveholding class.
Their bodies represented half-liquid capital, forms that in the heady years
of national expansion were easily converted by slaveholders to cash. But
perhaps most important, slaveholders and planters saw in black children's
youth and inexperience a homegrown means to dilute the collective and
troubling power of their elders, that savvy and largely native born population of adult slaves whose labor and lives underwrote both regional and
national power.

Between 1820 and 1860, better than four million slaves traded hands
and homes in the United States. Nearly a fourth of those were carried
across state lines. Two million more were relocated more locally: bought,
sold, or moved within the boundaries of state lines. An even larger number
found themselves shuttled from place to place by owners who hired slaves'
labor out by the job, the week, the month, or the year. It was a migration
that dwarfed the two-hundred-year-long transatlantic traffic between Africa
and British mainland North America. It tipped the locus of American
slaveholding from southern Virginia to the Deep South. It decimated enslaved families and communities that had been generations in the making,
stripping away those considered the most fit and more fertile for the express
purpose of recreating slaveholding society on the western frontier. The
antebellum migration was also, however, a process of national economic
and political expansion that preyed hard on enslaved children, for though
the majority of forced migrants fell somewhere between the ages of fifteen
and twenty-five, smaller boys and girls accounted for better than 30 percent
of all those who were sold into the interstate trade.[2] Many more were sold
or traded locally. As Steven Deyle recently observed, "Young children were
always present" and often wholly alone. Across the South overall, at least

10 percent of slaves' children were sold apart from their parents. In some pockets, particularly the upcountry and piedmont regions of the mountain South—that band of territory that stretched south from western Maryland to northern Alabama and Georgia—the rate at which children entered the trade and its corollary, migration, crept even higher. According to Wilma Dunaway, "nearly two-thirds of all Appalachian slave sales separated children from their families—70 percent of these forced migrations occurring when they were younger than fifteen." With sound fiscal reason, for "the younger the child, the greater the mark up" in price if sold apart from his or her mother.[3]

Slaveholders and their allies liked to pretend that they did otherwise. Engaged in a pursuit of slave-made profits even as the outcry against one human's possession of another gained ground domestically and in Europe, planters were particularly keen to distance themselves from what abolitionists considered one of the most objectionable aspects of an institution they loathed generally: the destruction of black people's families.[4] Much of this effort was directed toward the more critical part of the North's population, a population slaveholders wanted very much to impress. Maine native Joseph Holt Ingraham, who went south in 1835, certainly came away with a very carefully scripted message, one doled out by planters and traders alike as he toured the estates that lined the banks of the Mississippi. "It is a rule seldom deviated from," he explained to friends in dispatches that would later be published for public consumption, "to sell families and relations together, if practicable, and if not, at least to masters" who live in the same neighborhoods. Lest his audience miss the salient point, Holt added, "A negro trader, in my presence refused to sell a negro girl, for whom a planter offered a high price, because he would not also purchase her sister—'for,' said the trader, 'they are much attached to each other, and when their mother died I promised her I would not part them.'"[5] Ever attentive to a volatile Northern public opinion, several Savannah citizens went to considerable lengths to assure another Northerner, Nehemiah Adams, that slaveholders rarely traded in small children. "We are very sorry that you happened to see it," they told Adams after he had witnessed the sale of a two-year-old girl during an 1854 visit. "Nothing of the kind ever took place before to our knowledge, and we all feared that it would make an unhappy impression upon you."[6]

White Southerners did make scattered attempts to bring realities in line with their rhetoric. Louisiana legislators, for instance, dropped their share of the interstate traffic in Virginia's youngest slaves from 13.5 to 3.7 percent when, in 1829, they banned traders and slaveholders from selling anyone under the age of ten into the state unless they could prove such people were orphans or they came in the custody of mothers. Alabama legislators attempted something of the same when in 1852 they outlawed the separation by sale of children under the age of five from their mothers. A few years later, citizens' groups in North Carolina and Virginia pressed their general assemblies to do the same, asking that they protect the integrity of slave families by mandating that children remain with their parents and husbands with their wives.[7]

But with the exception of Louisiana, such efforts generally had minimal or no effect. In Alabama legislative loopholes allowed slaveholders facing fiscal restraints to sell small children apart from their mothers, and in Virginia lawmakers decreed in 1838 that any slave, no matter his or her age, could be put on the market legally—a position that did not bode well for 103 Hancock County petitioners whose 1852 request to maintain mother and child bonds was last seen awaiting attention from the Committee for Courts of Justice, to which the general assembly had referred it. Indeed, many slaveholding states not only did nothing to prevent enslaved children from tumbling willy-nilly into the interstate market, they also exempted those who bought and sold children across state lines from many of the administrative requirements attached to the importation of older slaves, making it easier, for example, for slaveholders and traders in South Carolina and Mississippi to import slaves under the age of fifteen without having to present official certificates attesting to those slaves' good character and orderly behavior in their previous homes.[8]

Yet if each slaveholding state had followed Louisiana's lead and instituted strict controls on the ages of those who were imported for sale, little would have changed in the aggregate, for the interregional market accounted for only a part—and perhaps a minority part—of those millions of children who were made to change hands and homes between 1820 and 1860. Infants, toddlers, children under ten, and preteens remained vulnerable to other forms of exchange and forced migration. Besides being uprooted regularly by owners bound for fresh plantations, children as young as one or two years (and sometimes younger) were also commonly exchanged on local and intrastate markets. These were transactions that by the most recent assessments accounted for at least two-thirds (or 1,334,000) of the two million slaves estimated to have been bought and sold between 1820 and 1860. They were also transactions that commonly involved those children who doubled as security on slaveholders' debts and who, due to their relatively low asking prices, were easy to move in an often volatile market.[9] As a result, the most youthful of slaves were often the first to be sold when an owner "broke down," defaulted on a loan, or needed extra cash to "build a new house."[10] Nelson Moorer, guardian of John Crum, the minor heir of an Alabama estate, put fourteen-year-old Levi and eight- or nine-year-old Mary up for sale in order to invest the proceeds "in bonds, notes, or bill of Exchange."[11] Elizabeth Keckley's owner sold one of her childhood companions to cover the price of some pigs, while James Pitman traded away three little boys in order to finance his ward's education. One of the boys, an infant named Governor Daniel, was sold along with his mother; his brothers, Benjamin Franklin and Oliver Cromwell, went to two different owners; in all they netted their young master $2,623.[12] Most frequently, though, slaveholders seemed programmed to turn immediately toward the smallest of their slaves when the time arrived to satisfy creditors' claims, or "fi.fas." It was a practice that filled local newspapers with advertisements of court-ordered sales and put countless children like Crawford County, Georgia's, six-year-old Elbert and two-year-old Jane into the hands of a sheriff whose job it was to sell them at public outcry.[13]

While inter- and intrastate sales shifted millions from home to home, slave hiring may have dislocated many times more. Promoted by slaveholders for both pragmatic and political reasons, and appreciated by those of moderate means who wished to benefit from slave labor but who did not have the resources to purchase their own, slave hiring played an important role in the antebellum South's political economy. Hire allowed masters to keep otherwise idle or surplus hands safely employed. Hire allowed non-slaveholders to enjoy the privileges of mastery on an interim basis. Hire also dispersed slaves on a much larger scale than did the auction block or the slave trader's coffle. So pervasive was the practice that in a world in which few slaves went to their graves without having been sold at least once, most could expect to be hired out two or three or more times in their lives. Where the antebellum economy favored a fluid over a fixed work force—the mountain South, the upper South, and the urban South—as many as half of all resident slaves labored under some form of hire agreement. But even in the heart of the plantation South, the chief order of business on the first day of each year was not the buying but the hiring of slaves.[14]

Virtually any slave of any age stood at risk of being unilaterally hired away by his or her owner. Children, however, were often judged by their owners to be the most "natural candidates" for that sort of arrangement. Unlike the elderly and infirm, individuals whose peak productive and reproductive years lay in the past, children's lay in the future, making it sensible from an owner's perspective not only to retain them if at all possible, but to convince someone else to pick up the tab for their feeding, clothing, raising, and occasionally training.[15] Thus while boom years convinced a good many slaveholders to stock their estates with young slaves, lean times could prompt masters to economize by releasing black children into one form or another of term agreements, selling labor apart from the laborer. Most waited at least until those children had grown strong enough to perform some sort of useful service: minding white people's children, picking up trash (broken tree limbs and the like) from the fields, scaring birds away from ripening corn, feeding livestock, serving passengers aboard steamships, assisting stonemasons or blacksmiths, or hauling firewood, which was Henry Clay Bruce's job as a nine-year-old hired slave in Missouri.[16] Nevertheless, just as owners regularly put little children up for sale, they also frequently sent the smallest of slaves to live on someone else's estate, hiring them out if need be for nothing more lucrative than their "victuals & clothes."[17] Some did so repeatedly, eager to pass on the expense of rearing the next generation of labor. Henry Atkinson, for example, "never saw his owner, but when I was a little boy," having been hired out every year "by an agent." Neither much did North Carolina's Moses Grandy, whose master put him into the fields, "hir[ing him] out by the year, by auction" as soon as the child "became old enough to be" safely removed from his mother. Grandy was treated this way until his twenty-first birthday.[18]

Children, like their parents, also moved by non-market means. Gifts and inheritance especially dislodged and dislocated black people's families, separating husbands from wives, children from parents. In life, slaveholders often marked the departure of their own offspring from home by making them presents of one or more slaves, many of whom like eight-year old Jack, whose owner gave him away to his nephews, and the "negro about three years old" whom Thomas Graves bestowed on his daughter, Elizabeth, were scarcely old enough to fend for themselves.[19] In death, slaveholders accomplished much of the same, having made prior arrangement for the posthumous division of their property. To be sure, some owners attempted to keep enslaved families intact, stipulating as Frank Smith did when he supervised the disposal of Sarah O. Smith's Alabama estate that mothers should remain with their children. Most, however, showed no respect for slaves' personal and domestic connections. Prices, not people, were what mattered when the time arrived to reallocate a dead slaveholder's possessions. According to calculations that privileged white children over black, the court-appointed commissioners of Abel Hagerty's estate "fairly and impartially" sorted sixty-two slaves—men, women, and children—into six equal shares, basing their decisions solely on each slave's appraised market value.[20] The same kind of arithmetic reduced twelve-year-old Rueben's family to shambles ("We were all separated," he remembered, "—no two went together") and put six hundred miles between Charles Thompson and his mother after a court-ordered division cast him and two sisters "into one lot, [his] mother into another, and [his] father into another, and the rest of the family in the other lots." "I felt bereaved, forlorn, forsaken, [and] lost," Charles would recall later of the day a document dismembered his family.[21]

Fortunate were those children who suffered such pangs only once. But few did. Pushed and pulled across the slaveholding South by what amounted to a constantly revolving cast of owners, agents, and traders—all of whom found advantages in buying, selling, hiring out, or giving away the youngest of their slaves—bondage rendered black children nomads nearly from birth. Take, for example, Henry Goings. Born a slave in Virginia, he exchanged homes and occasionally owners at a dizzying rate. Three of those transactions took place in the space of seventeen months and carried the forcibly orphaned Henry away from his birthplace in what appears to have been New Kent County to the outskirts of Williamsburg, and from there to Halifax, North Carolina, where his then owner—Pearson Pricket (or Picket)—hired the youngster to the proprietor of a local hotel. According to Henry, Pricket was no fiscal wizard and, falling onto hard times shortly after arriving in North Carolina, he "converted" Henry "to money" by selling him to a Mr. Hives for $500. Four months later, it was Hives's turn to sell young Henry, this time to a man named Joseph Smith. Smith, whose restless character "exceed[ed] even the national propensity to change," proceeded to carry Henry along on what amounted to a grand tour of cotton's kingdom, transporting a child he purchased to serve as a groom from Halifax to Raleigh, North Carolina, to Humphries County, Tennessee, south into northern Alabama, east to Georgia, then back once more to northern Alabama via northern Georgia and western Tennessee—all of which took place before Henry reached sixteen.[22]

Other boys and girls followed similarly tangled routes as they grew up on the move through slavery. Henry Howlan, who after freedom opened an account with the Vicksburg, Mississippi, branch of the Freedmen Savings and Trust Company, explained how following his birth in Randolph County, Virginia, he had been transported "to S.C. when a small boy then to Ala—then to Miss," a series of shifts that cost him all contact with his father, mother, and two sisters.[23] Philip Younger, who landed in the hands of a "military man," was "born in Virginia, went, at ten, to Tennessee, at twelve, to Alabama."[24] John Brown landed in the hands of a slave trader who conveyed a child who had already known at least two owners out of Virginia through North Carolina and eventually into the hands of a Georgia slaveholder.[25] Eliza Jones arrived in Georgia from Virginia via Tennessee; James got to North Carolina from Virginia via Florida; Vina Micken, who was taken away from Kentucky—and her parents—"when small," arrived in Lee County, Georgia, the year she turned thirteen.[26] Henry Clay moved so many times that he, like Vina, simply quit keeping track. He had been raised "everywhere," the Virginia-born ex-slave would later explain when asked, after freedom "where [he had] been brought up."[27]

All slaves suffered as settlers cascaded across the Appalachians and down the Mississippi, eager to grow wealthy on the nation's new staple crops. Migration and trade gutted communities, toppled long-standing institutions, stripped black people of hard-won access to resources and time, and forced both those left behind and those made to move to adjust their lives and gender ideals to new demographic conditions. These were traumas that affected women and men, the youngest and the oldest. Still, some recovered faster than others. Adults, in particular, entered into what has become known (if misleadingly) as the Second Middle Passage relatively well equipped to rebuild their lives on the Southern frontier. Almost wholly native born, they shared a common language, a common culture, and above all, a common and keen understanding of the landscape under their feet and the people who lived on it. Many, particularly those who had been born and raised on the Virginia peninsula or in low-country South Carolina also traveled, having come of age in the shadow of Gabriel Prosser, Denmark Vesey, Nat Turner, and the thousands of other slaves who had seized freedom during the American Revolution. These were experiences that would enable the adult portion of a population that Ira Berlin has dubbed the Migration Generation, to begin restoring coherence to their lives even as they trudged toward their new homes. They were also experiences that would facilitate adult slaves' efforts to forge themselves into potentially powerful new communities after their arrival in the Deep South.[28]

These were not, however, experiences and attributes generally available to slavery's most youthful forced migrants. It takes time, as well as opportunity, to accumulate comparable bodies of social, political, and geographical knowledge and those sold or transported as youngsters rarely had either, especially those whose work assignments kept them confined "mostly [to] the [slave] quarters until twelve or thirteen."[29] Denied personal and direct contact with the world that lay beyond their home plantations—access that came most easily to those who drove slaveholders' wagons, rowed their boats, and herded their cows, the kind of work Henry Box Brown attributed to his early education—most of the information that came slave children's way came indirectly: through eavesdropping on visitors' conversations or listening to stories related by their parents or other resident slaves.[30] Charles Ball received much of his early lessons at his grandfather's knee.[31] Hire arrangements could hurry the process along. Indeed, Henry Bibb, whose owner hired him out as a child "eight or ten years in succession," concluded long after freedom that "it was no disadvantage to be passed [as a youth] through the hands of so many families, as the only source of information that I had to enlighten my mind, consisted in what I could see and hear from others."[32] But for those who were sequestered on their owners' estates, especially the youngsters who had not yet attained the necessary size and strength to work side by side with their elders, such information trickled their way slowly, if at all. Such children entered into the stream of black migrants knowing little about "how [their] brethren fared in other places" and even less about how to protect themselves individually or collectively from a slaveholder's abuses.[33] They also lacked the most basic understanding of local and regional geography, a phenomenon that created badly distorted maps even in the minds of those who attempted to attend to the direction and distance of their journeys. Thus it was that the 560-mile trip Henry Goings made with his master and nearly five hundred slaves from Raleigh, North Carolina, to Clarksville, Tennessee, loomed in his memory as a "formidable one" in which the party covered a thousand miles, much of it through unbroken forest.[34] As Frederick Douglass—who described in considerable detail the disorienting days that followed his twelve-mile move as a boy to Colonel Lloyd's plantation—knew from personal experience that only time could erase the multiple handicaps that dogged the heels of slavery's youngest migrants.[35]

Which was all perfectly fine from the standpoint of America's slaveholders. Since the late 1820s unease had been creeping through their ranks. To the north and abroad, antislavery forces had been gathering what was to slaveholders an ominously radical momentum.[36] Even worse, activists' cries for immediate abolition had begun to reach Southern audiences, appearing in freshly minted antislavery newspapers and between the covers of David Walker's fiery *Appeal*, copies of which had been discovered in slaves' hands.[37] These developments, along with Vesey's and Turner's revolts, had prompted slaveholders and their allies to crack down on their slaves in new ways. But despite exhaustive legislative efforts to restrict the congregation of unsupervised slaves; to limit slaves' contact with Northerners, foreigners, and sailors; to halt the circulation of abolitionist papers; to forbid the education of slaves; and in some locations to disarm free people of color, slaveholders failed to get things their way.[38] Accounts of uprisings, both real and imagined, continued to agitate slaveholders and white society right up to the eve of the war.[39] So too did a rising tide of black fugitives, a population composed primarily of men who, like Charles Ball and a man named Fountain, and other enslaved runaways, knew, or believed they knew, the way to their respective destinations. Indeed, snorted his Georgia-based owner, Fountain was "well acquainted with the road to Alabama. I carried the boy last spring to Texas with me . . . and he was well pleased with Mobile and N. Orleans, & may make in that direction."[40]

Slaveholders continued to experiment in their effort to retain sovereignty over a population of slaves that would approach four million by 1860. Grand juries urged patrollers to greater efforts, called on citizens to keep their slaves closer to home, and railed endlessly against peddlers and liquor dealers who traded with slaves. The latter class, grumbled a group of white Virginians in 1860, "corrupt[ed] the habits and morals of slaves" and instilled in their minds "the spirit of insubordination."[41] Others fixed their attention on free people of color, and from Maryland to Arkansas legislators pondered and in several cases enacted laws to expel them from their states, convinced that as a group free black people exercised undue and subversive influence over slaves.[42] While in Tennessee, after three cotton gins burned in quick succession in 1855—crimes immediately attributed to slaves—more than one hundred citizens issued a call for much stiffer punishments. The allowable limit of "thirty-nine lashes" was not enough.[43] Even clergymen weighed in as white Southerners and slaveholders struggled to keep control of their slaves, arguing that if states extended to slaves the right to an education and offered to protect their marriages, they might develop in black people a much-needed "affection and confidence" in their owners.[44]

Evidence suggests that slaveholders also turned their gaze toward the slave quarters, seeing in the slight and "inexperienced" bodies of enslaved children the means to impose order on their plantations.[45] They did so with reason. In a post-1808 nation, black children most closely replicated those first generations of culturally and linguistically heterogeneous "saltwater slaves," a people who had frequently arrived on North American shores as foreign to one another as they were to their new owners, qualities that made them vulnerable, at least for a time, to extraordinary levels of raw exploitation.[46] Unsure of their surroundings, inexperienced in elder slaves' well-honed strategies of self- and collective preservation—and, in the case of the youngest, remanded to a stranger's care—enslaved children shared many of the same characteristics that colonial planters had prized in their early Atlantic acquisitions. They appeared, in other words, ripe for learning the art of submission. Indeed, observes Marie Schwartz, it was the prospect of raising black babies up right that induced free Southerners to invest in slaves whose most fruitful years lay in the future.[47] Always a significant part of the market, the demand for black children spiked in flush times, those periods when capital and cash reserves fattened white people's pockets. Take nine-year-old Lucy, for example. Appraised on 19 January 1827, for $300, she sold at auction thirteen days later to William Lawrence for $401.50, a markup of one-third. A volatile trade always, one that like the trade in adults fluctuated with the prices and prospects of agricultural staples, the net commerce in kids nonetheless crept gradually upward, as children slowly edged their elders out of a part of the market.[48] By the eve of the Civil War and with what had been scattered talk about the reopening of the transatlantic slave trade dying away, slaves under the age of nineteen had come to account for more than 40 percent of the interstate trade, highly prized commodities to those who hoped to anchor their world with the bodies of black toddlers, teens, and infants, sending them, one enslaved mother wept as she explained their loss to her husband, "I don't k[n]ow whare."[49]

Hawkins Wilson never reconnected with his Virginia kin after freedom. Nor did America's planters soon lose their taste for child labor. Though prevented by Union victory from paying their debts in black babies, and no longer able to secure their own family futures by dismembering the families of slaves, many planters would continue nonetheless to exploit black people's children for political as well as productive gain. In the weeks following the Confederate surrender, they would attempt to contain the revolutionary potential of emancipation by assembling a free-labor system on a not-so-free basis. White Marylanders would act first, scooping up under apprenticeship codes leftover from slavery and reworked in freedom thousands of recently freed children. But they would not act on their own. Planters from throughout the former Confederacy soon followed in Marylanders' footsteps, seizing control of freedom—at least for a time—by seizing control once again of the "best of the children." As former slaveholder Thomas Willingham would explain when petitioning a senior government official to assist him in stocking a south Georgia plantation with "25 to 200 boys & girls Between the ages of 10 & 14," the diminutive part of the nation's ex-slaves made excellent workers. After all, the planter continued, children lacked the "run away & fortune-making natures of men."[50]

## NOTES

1. Ira Berlin and Leslie S. Rowland, eds., *Families and Freedom: A Documentary History of African-American Kinship in the Civil War Era* (New York: New Press, 1997), 17–18. "C.H." refers to "court house," or the seat of counties in Virginia.

2. Michael Tadman, *Speculators and Slaves: Masters, Traders and Slaves in the Old South* (Madison: University of Wisconsin Press, 1989), 26.

3. Steven Deyle, *Carry Me Back: The Domestic Slave Trade in American Life* (New York: Oxford University Press, 2005), 248; Tadman, *Speculators and Slaves*, 25; Wilma Dunaway, *The African-American Family in Slavery and Emancipation* (Cambridge: Cambridge University Press, 2003), 67-68.

4. Robert H. Gudmestad, *A Troublesome Commerce: The Transformation of the Interstate Slave Trade* (Baton Rouge: Louisiana State University Press, 2003); Marie Jenkins Schwartz, *Born in Bondage: Growing Up Enslaved in the Antebellum South* (Cambridge, MA: Harvard University Press, 2000), 89.

5. Joseph H. Ingraham, *The South-West, by a Yankee*, 2 vols. (New York: Harper & Brothers, 1835), 2:203-4.

6. Nehemiah Adams, *A South-Side View of Slavery: or Three Months at the South, in 1854* (Boston: T. R. Marvin, 1854), 65.

7. Schwartz, *Born in Bondage*, 89-90; Judith Kelleher Schafer, *Slavery, the Civil Law, and the Supreme Court of Louisiana* (Baton Rouge: Louisiana State University Press, 1994), 165-68; Thomas Elder et al. to the General Assembly, 27 February 1856, PAR no. 11685603, Race & Slavery Petitions Project, ser. 1, Legislative Petitions, University of North Carolina, Greensboro (hereafter RSSP, ser. 1); Kimberly R. Kellison, "Toward Humanitarian Ends? Protestants and Slave Reform in South Carolina, 1830-1865," *South Carolina Historical Magazine* 103, no. 3 (July 2002): 215.

8. Schwartz, *Born in Bondage*, 90; V. E. Howard and A. Hutchinson, comp., *The Statutes of the State of Mississippi of a Public and General Nature* (New Orleans: E. Johns and Co., 1840), 155; David J. McCord, ed., *The Statutes at Large of South Carolina* (Columbia, 1841), 10: 527; Thomas Elder et al. to the General Assembly, 27 February 1856, PAR no. 11685603, RSSP, ser. 1.

9. For a thoughtful discussion about the local or intrastate trade, its scope, and its youthfulness see Deyle, *Carry Me Back*, 157-73, 249, 291-96.

10. John Brown, *Slave Life in Georgia: A Narrative of the Life, Sufferings, and Escape of John Brown, A Fugitive Slave, now in England*, ed. Louis A. Chamerovzow (London: W. M. Watts, 1855), 13, http://docsouth.unc.edu/neh/jbrown/jbrown.html (accessed 28 April 2007); Henry Goings, *Ramblings of a Runaway from Southern Slavery* (Stratford, CT: J. M. Robb, 1869), 7, University of Virginia Library, Charlottesville; Benjamin Drew, *A North-Side View of Slavery. The Refugee: Or, The Narratives of Fugitive Slaves in Canada. Related by Themselves, with an Account of the History and Condition of the Colored Population of Upper Canada* (Boston: J. P. Jewett and Co., 1856), 198, http://docsouth.unc.edu/neh/drew/menu.html (accessed 28 April 2007).

11. Nelson J. Moorer to the Hon. E. H. Cook, Judge of Probate in Lowndes County, 10 January 1860, PAR no. 20186025, Race & Slavery Petitions Project, ser. 2, County Court Petitions, University of North Carolina, Greensboro (hereafter RSSP, ser. 2).

12. Elizabeth Keckley, *Behind the Scenes; or, Thirty Years a Slave in the White House* (New York: Oxford University Press, 1988), 28-29; John Bostock to [Chancery Court, Tallapoosa County, Alabama], 23 May 1853, PAR no. 20185317, RSSP, ser. 2.

13. *Georgia Journal* (Milledgeville), 3 September 1827.

14. Greensboro, Ala., *Beacon*, reprinted in the *Clarke County Democrat*, Grove Hill, Ala., 20 January 1859, box 40, U. B. Phillips Papers, Manuscripts and Archives, Yale University Library; Lewis Cecil Gray, *The History of Agriculture in the Southern United States to 1860* (Gloucester, MA: Peter Smith, 1958) 2:667-68; Jonathan D. Martin,

*Divided Mastery: Slave Hiring in the American South* (Cambridge, MA: Harvard University Press, 2004), 8, 192–93; Randolph B. Campbell, *An Empire for Slavery: The Peculiar Institution in Texas, 1821–1865* (Baton Rouge: Louisiana State University Press, 1989), 82–92; Wilma A. Dunaway, *The African-American Family in Slavery and Emancipation* (Cambridge: Cambridge University Press, 2003), 38–41; Christopher Morris, *Becoming Southern: The Evolution of a Way of Life, Warren County and Vicksburg, Mississippi, 1770–1860* (New York: Oxford University Press, 1995), 27–28, 66–67, 195–98; Midori Takagi, *"Rearing Wolves to Our Own Destruction": Slavery in Richmond, Virginia, 1782–1865* (Charlottesville: University Press of Virginia, 1999), 71–95; Suzanne Schnittman, "Black Workers in Antebellum Richmond," in Gary M. Fink and Merl E. Reed, eds., *Race, Class, and Community in Southern Labor History* (Tuscaloosa: University of Alabama Press, 1994), 72–86; John C. Inscoe, *Mountain Masters: Slavery and the Sectional Crisis in Western North Carolina* (Knoxville: University of Tennessee Press, 1989) 76–81.

15. Scott Walcott Howlett, "'My Child, Him is Mine': Plantation Slave Children in the Old South" (PhD diss., University of California, Irvine, 1993), 97.

16. Henry Clay Bruce, *The New Man: Twenty-Nine Years a Slave, Twenty-Nine Years a Free Man* (York, PA: P. Anstadt, 1895), 20, http://docsouth.unc.edu/fpn/bruce/bruce .html (accessed 23 April 2007); John Andrew Jackson, *The Experience of a Slave in South Carolina* (London: Passmore and Alabaster, 1862), 21–22, http://docsouth.unc.edu/ fpn/jackson/jackson.html (accessed 21 June 2007); Drew, *North-Side View*, 97, 107, 256; James W. C. Pennington, *The Fugitive Blacksmith; or, Events in the History of James W. C. Pennington, Pastor of a Presbyterian Church, New York, Formerly a Slave in the State of Maryland, United States* (London: Charles Gilpin, 1849), 4, http://docsouth.unc .edu/neh/penning49/penning49.html (accessed 29 June 2007); Bank of Alabama to the Honorable Anderson Crenshaw Chancellor of the First District of the Southern Chancery Division of [Alabama], 27 September 1854, PAR no. 20184515, RSSP, ser. 2; on the work children performed for slaveholders, see also Schwartz, *Born in Bondage*, 91–92, 108–9, 131–54; Wilma King, *Stolen Childhood: Slave Youth in Nineteenth-Century America* (Bloomington: Indiana University Press, 1997), 21–41.

17. Joseph R. Young to the Honorable Judge of the Probate Court of Yazoo County, 26 November 1855, PAR no. 21085537, RSSP, ser. 2.

18. Drew, *North-Side View*, 78–79; Moses Grandy, *Narrative of the Life of Moses Grandy, Late a Slave in the United States of America* (London: C. Gilpin, 1843), 9, http:// docsouth.unc.edu/fpn/grandy/grandy.html (accessed 3 July 2007).

19. King, *Stolen Childhood*, 103; Dunaway, *African-American Family*, 54, 59–60; William L. Owens et al. to the Honorable Charles Scott Chancellor of the State of Mississippi, 15 February 1855, PAR no. 21085516, RSSP, ser. 2; Dolly Ann Graves to the Hon. James W. Graham, of the [Lowndes County, Ala., Probate Court], 30 November 1863, PAR no. 20186315, RSSP, ser. 2.

20. A. J. Terrell to the Honorable H. W. Watson, Judge of Probate in and for the County of Montgomery, in the State of Alabama, 30 December 1854, PAR no. 20185402, RSSP, ser. 2.

21. Drew, *North-Side View*, 274; Charles Thompson, *A Preacher of the United Brethren Church, while a Slave in the South, Together with Startling Occurrences Incidental to Slave Life* (Dayton: United Brethren Publishing House, 1875), 17–19, 21, http://docsouth.unc .edu/neh/thompsch/thompsch.html (accessed 6 July 2007).

22. Goings, *Ramblings of a Runaway*, 5-15.

23. Entry of Henry Howlan, 20 August 1868, no. 1208, M816r15.

24. Drew, *North-Side View*, 248-49.

25. Brown, *Slave Life in Georgia*, 5-21, http://docsouth.unc.edu/neh/jbrown/jbrown.html (accessed 28 April 2007).

26. Entries of Eliza Jones, 16 November 1867, no. 254 and James Givens, 1 February 1868, no. 350, both in M816r5; entry of Vina Micken, 27 May 1870, no. 476, M816r6.

27. Entry of Henry Clay, 22 August 1871, no. 877, M186r3.

28. Ira Berlin, *Generations of Captivity: A History of African-American Slaves* (Cambridge, MA: Belknap, 2003), chap. 4; Johnson, *Soul by Soul: Inside the Antebellum Slave Market* (Cambridge, MA, Harvard University Press, 1999), 63-77; Susan Eva O'Donovan, *Becoming Free in the Cotton South* (Cambridge, MA: Harvard University Press, 2007), chap. 1; Joseph P. Reidy, "Obligation and Right: Patterns of Labor, Subsistence, and Exchange in the Cotton Belt of Georgia, 1790-1860," in *Cultivation and Culture: Labor and the Shaping of Slave Life in the Americas*, ed. Ira Berlin and Philip D. Morgan (Charlottesville: University Press of Virginia, 1993), 138-54; Steven F. Miller, "Plantation Labor Organization and Slave Life on the Cotton Frontier: The Alabama-Mississippi Black Belt, 1815-1840," in Berlin and Morgan, *Cultivation and Culture*, 155-69; Edward E. Baptist, *Creating an Old South: Middle Florida's Plantation Frontier before the Civil War* (Chapel Hill: University of North Carolina Press, 2002), 7.

29. Drew, *North-Side View*, 105.

30. Henry Box Brown, *Narrative of the Life of Henry Box Brown*, ed. Richard Newman (New York: Oxford University Press, 2002), 20-25.

31. Charles Ball, *Fifty Years in Chains* (Mineola, NY: Dover, 1970), 6-8.

32. Henry Bibb, *The Life and Adventures of Henry Bibb* (Madison: University of Wisconsin Press, 2001), 14-15.

33. Brown, *Narrative of the Life of Henry Box Brown*, 24.

34. Goings, *Ramblings of a Runaway*, 10; Drew, *North-Side View*, 274, 276.

35. Frederick Douglass, *My Bondage, My Freedom* (New York: Miller, Orton, and Mulligan, 1855), 45-50, http://docsouth.unc.edu/neh/douglass55/douglass55.html (accessed 26 July 2007).

36. Richard S. Newman, *The Transformation of American Abolitionism: Fighting Slavery in the Early Republic* (Chapel Hill: University of North Carolina Press, 2002).

37. Marshall Rachleff, "David Walker's Southern Agent," *Journal of Negro History* 62, no. 1 (January 1977): 100-103; Peter P. Hinks, *To Awaken My Afflicted Brethren: David Walker and the Problem of Antebellum Slave Resistance* (University Park: Penn State University Press, 1997), chap. 5; David Cecelski, *The Waterman's Song: Slavery and Freedom in Maritime North Carolina* (Chapel Hill: University of North Carolina Press, 2001), 183.

38. Heather Andrea Williams, *Self-Taught: African American Education in Slavery and Freedom* (Chapel Hill: University of North Carolina Press, 2005), chap. 1; W. Jeffrey Bolster, *Black Jacks: African American Seamen in the Age of Sail* (Cambridge, MA: Harvard University Press, 1997), 172, 199-200, 202-5; *Georgia Journal* (Milledgeville), 16 February 1832. For examples of the new laws of slavery, see John G. Aiken, comp., *A Digest of the Laws of the State of Alabama: Containing all the Statues of a Public and General Nature, in Force at the close of the Session of the General Assembly, in January, 1833* (Philadelphia: Alexander Towar, 1833), 389-98; Howard and Hutchinson, *The Statutes of the State of Mississippi*, 153-81.

39. Herbert Aptheker, *American Negro Slave Revolts*, 6th ed. (New York: International Publishers, 1993), chap. 14; William L. Link, *Roots of Secession: Slavery and Politics in Antebellum Virginia* (Chapel Hill: University of North Carolina Press, 2003), 43–61; Winthrop D. Jordan, *Tumult and Silence at Second Creek: An Inquiry into a Civil War Slave Conspiracy* (Baton Rouge: Louisiana State University Press, 1993); Steven Hahn, *A Nation Under Our Feet: Black Political Struggles in the Rural South from Slavery to the Great Migration* (Cambridge, MA: Belknap Press, 2003), 58–61.

40. John Hope Franklin and Loren Schweninger, *Runaway Slaves: Rebels on the Plantation* (New York: Oxford University Press, 1999), 96, 210–13; Ball, *Fifty Years in Chains*, 24, 79–80, 163, 228–30, 233, 249–96; *Georgia Journal* (Milledgeville), 26 January 1836.

41. Loren Schweninger, ed., *The Southern Debate over Slavery*, vol. 1, *Petitions to Southern Legislatures, 1778–1864* (Urbana: University of Illinois Press, 2001), 244–45.

42. Ira Berlin, *Slaves without Masters: The Free Negro in the Antebellum South* (New York: Oxford University Press, 1974), 360–64, 371–75.

43. Schweninger, *Southern Debate*, 228.

44. Kellison, "Humanitarian Ends?" 221.

45. Schweninger, *Southern Debate*, 234–35.

46. Stephanie Smallwood, *Saltwater Slavery: A Middle Passage from Africa to American Diaspora* (Cambridge, MA: Harvard University Press, 2006), chap. 4; Philip D. Morgan, "Cultural Implications of the Atlantic Slave Trade: African Regional Origins, American Destinations and New World Developments," *Slavery and Abolition* 18, no. 1 (April 1997): 122–45; Morgan, *Slave Counterpoint: Black Culture in the Eighteenth-Century Chesapeake and Lowcountry* (Chapel Hill: University of North Carolina Press, 1998), 441–63; Ira Berlin, *Many Thousands Gone: The First Two Centuries of Slavery in North America* (Cambridge, MA: Belknap, 1998), 109–19; William S. Pollitzer, *The Gullah People and Their African Heritage* (Athens: University of Georgia Press, 1999), chaps. 2–3; Allan Kulikoff, *Tobacco and Slaves: The Development of Southern Cultures in the Chesapeake, 1680–1800* (Chapel Hill: University of North Carolina Press, 1986), 320–27.

47. Schwartz, *Born in Bondage*, 89.

48. Robert William Fogel and Stanley L. Engerman, *Time on the Cross: The Economics of American Negro Slavery* (New York: Norton, 1974), 103–6; Tadman, *Speculators and Slaves*, 105–8, 289–91.

49. Marie Perkins to Richard Perkins, 7 October 1852, folder 47, box 3, U.B. Phillips Papers, Manuscripts and Archives, Yale University Library; King, *Stolen Childhood*, 102.

50. Rebecca Scott, "The Battle Over the Child: Child Apprenticeship and the Freedmen's Bureau in North Carolina," *Prologue* 10, no. 1 (Summer 1978): 101–13; Richard Paul Fuke, "Planters, Apprenticeship, and Forced Labor: The Black Family under Pressure in Post-Emancipation Maryland," *Agricultural History* 62, no. 4 (Fall 1988): 57–74; Berlin and Rowland, eds., *Families and Freedom*, 17–20, 193–24; Dunaway, *African-American Family*, 224, 265–67; Karin L. Zipf, *The Labor of Innocents: Forced Apprenticeship in North Carolina, 1715–1919* (Baton Rouge: Louisiana State University Press, 2005), chaps. 2–3; O'Donovan, *Becoming Free*, 155–56.

# SECTION II

# THE TREATMENT AND USES OF SLAVE CHILDREN THROUGH THE AGES

## Part A

*Children Acquired for Social, Political, and Domestic Roles*

# 6

## SINGING SLAVE GIRLS (*QIYAN*) OF THE 'ABBASID COURT IN THE NINTH AND TENTH CENTURIES

KRISTINA RICHARDSON

The category of slave in the Middle East encompassed a number of different duties and positions: eunuch, chattel, domestic servant, sexual subject, infantryman, concubine, entertainer, laborer, and sometimes a trusted and valued member of the household. As Shaun Marmon has noted, "there can be no single model for the study of slavery in Islamic societies,"[1] and to parse the statement further, especially not for intersections of slavery, gender, and childhood. Even so, there is some use in reading aspects of female slavery against Hegel's model of the master-slave dialectic and Orlando Patterson's elaboration of that theory. I have selected them because Patterson's model does try to accommodate Islamicate slave systems, though it does not take gender and childhood into account as an important aspect of it.[2] Patterson argues in *Slavery and Social Death* that all slave systems—from dynastic Mesopotamia to early medieval Iceland to modern Sudan—dominate the subject's body and mind. A slave's physical movement is controlled, her labor forced, and in many instances she is made to submit sexually to the master. The psychological domination starts in the first days of ownership with the alienation of a slave from her native surroundings. Or if she remains with her family, she recognizes that her master has authoritative power over her. In Hegel's formulation of master-slave relationships, the slave validates the master's existence because she exists only to fulfill the master's will. As a result, the slave's identity is wholly tied to that of her master. The slave dies unto herself and is reborn, so to speak, as an extension of the master's ego and will and a physical confirmation of his personal esteem. This alienation of the slave from a community (other than that of her master) negates her social existence, engendering "social death."[3]

## ELITE FEMALE SLAVERY IN ISLAMICATE LANDS

This theoretical model certainly has wide application but does not account for the many nuanced master-slave relationships in the medieval Islamicate world, where domination of master over slave was not fixed and absolute. Understanding this, Patterson devotes a later chapter of his book to slave systems that are not wholly explained by the "Hegelian-Pattersonian" model of degradation, slave dependency, and social death. He examines elite male slavery in the late-medieval Mamluk Empire (1250–1517 CE), where male slave soldiers (mamluks) were sultans, and he also analyzes the early-modern Ottoman Empire (1299–1922) where harem eunuchs, military officers, and guardians of the treasury formed part of the elite slave corps. He terms these men "ultimate slaves" because the definition of a slave as a powerless servant does not apply to them. There is even debate as to the appropriateness of calling these individuals slaves, seeing as "irony . . . the conception of slavery in Islamic contexts, for in practice the least respected individuals came to be entrusted with the most strategic posts of the empire."[4] These slaves' servitude was not entirely self-denying, as they gained prestige, political prominence, and important allies. Patterson does not account for women in this scheme of elite slavery, though female slaves also had some opportunities to command comparable political power in Islamicate society. In the Ottoman royal harem, for example, Kösem Sultan, a concubine who bore two future sultans, collaborated with Süleyman Agha, the chief black eunuch, to insulate herself and her sons from palace intrigues and tensions. These two slaves—a concubine and a eunuch—worked together to protect themselves and promote their agendas. Ultimately, however, Kösem Sultan was double-crossed and murdered by Süleyman Agha himself.[5] In this chapter I argue that, like the Ottoman concubines of the sultan's royal harem, the female slave entertainers of caliphs and other wealthy patrons of the 'Abbasid period (750–1258) exploited their sexuality and their proximity to the politically powerful for personal gain.

The 'Abbasid slave singers were well known for their beauty and sex appeal, and, as will be shown, their reputation as entrancingly beautiful women was widely acknowledged in Arabic literature of the period. By currying favor with the master, one could reap distinct social benefits. For example, a slave could enter into his inner circle of companions, even becoming one of his favored sexual partners and bearing him children. The nature of a slave's service allowed for informal relationships to develop between the slave and master, as shown in a story recorded by the 'Abbasid literary historian Abu al-Faraj al-Isbahani (d. 967): "An old woman who had been one of (the caliph) Wāthiq's slavegirls said: I was one of the girls that (the caliph) al-Muqtadir liked and took pleasure in. He was one of God's most accomplished creatures when it came to playing the lute and he had a most moving voice, though did his best to keep it secret. He would only play and sing when he was alone with his slavegirls (*jawarihi*), his intimate companions, and with me."[6] This anecdote attests to the familiarity and informality that could flourish between a patron and his slave girl(s). The power that a slave girl could acquire was subtle, and her scope of influence was not wide, quite unlike the power of the elite male slaves. The unique position of the female slave entertainers allowed them to use their sexuality and proximity to the master to secure personal benefits. In this way, the slave girls could assume greater control of their private lives and escape the traditional domination of a master over every aspect of a slave's life.

On the whole, gendered examinations of slavery are essential components of general slave studies, but are particularly needed in the field of Near Eastern history. Islamicate society is very gender conscious and maintains precise laws governing the conduct of men and women, and the intersection of two complex systems like gender and slavery provides a dynamic new framework within which to conceptualize one or both systems.[7] In the Islamicate world the relationship between a slave girl and her master could take many forms. She could be his abject servant, his concubine, or the mother of his child (or all three). According to Islamic law, concubinage is licit and a slave owner can have sexual relations with his slave girl. While sexual relations commonly occurred between male masters and their male or female slaves, the possibility of pregnancy with slave women added a new dimension to the traditionally imagined male-male, master-slave power dynamic. A slave girl who bore the child of her Muslim master acquired the new legal status of *umm walad* (lit., mother of a child; pl., *ummahat awlad*). This new standing conferred three guaranteed legal benefits on the mother and opened the possibility of still more. It was certain that the woman could never be sold, that she would be freed upon the death of her master, and that her child would be born free. Other possible benefits stemmed from the personal intimacy that often developed between parents of a child. In many instances, bearing a master's child strengthened the emotional bonds between slave and master to such a degree that the master emancipated his child's mother.

The legal consequences of a slave bearing her master's child favored the mother and child over the master. In theory a concubine or other female slave could use a sexual relationship with her master to secure her and her child's future. Male slave owners, of course, were well aware of the possible economic, legal, and emotional consequences of impregnating slave girls. Not being able to sell a slave required the owner to care for her throughout her lifetime, even if she became incapacitated by illness or old age. Of course, if an umm walad became too great a financial burden, the master could always manumit her, but he would have lost the opportunity to sell her at a profit. Another adverse economic consequence of a pregnant slave girl was the added financial responsibility of a new child in the household. For these reasons men were cautious about impregnating their slaves. Hadith collections (collections of sayings of the Prophet) record several instances of Muslim men asking the Prophet Muhammad about avoiding the insemination of slave girls. One such hadith reads: "A man came to the Prophet and said, 'I have a slave-girl, and we need her as a servant and around the palm groves. I have sex with her, but I am afraid of her becoming pregnant.'"[8] The man is reluctant to sacrifice his slave's labor for the time that she would carry, deliver, nurse, and raise the child. His objection to her pregnancy stems purely from economic concerns. In another hadith, a man asks about the permissibility of coitus interruptus. "There is another person who has a slave-girl and he has a sexual intercourse with her, but he does not like her to have conception so that she may not become Umm Walad."[9] The speaker does not explicitly state why a slave owner would not want his slave to become umm walad, but one can assume that because the arrangement had little benefit for the master and gave the slave mother more power over her and her child's lives, this status was undesirable to him.

## MANIPULATING THE BOUNDARIES OF SLAVERY

The possible strategic uses of motherhood to better a slave woman's position, as well as the intersection of female slavery and sexual power, warrant further study. Here I examine the interplay of sexuality, child bearing, and power among a particular class of elite female singing slaves known as the qiyan (sing., qayna).[10] In the 'Abbasid period (750–1258 CE) these women performed in wealthy households and at the caliphal courts in Baghdad and Samarra. They formed part of Arab court retinues and worked as popular entertainers from pre-Islamic times until the abolition of slavery, in the twentieth century.[11] The qiyan were viewed as elite because they were not strictly consigned to labor or concubinage. Evidence of their elite status and desirability is found in the high prices of a qayna relative to that of an untrained slave girl. This price differential was due to the qayna's revered musical and literary gifts, which were greatly appreciated in wealthy circles. Typically purchased as children, qiyan received rigorous, expensive training in poetry, music, and the Arabic language in preparation for careers in performance and lyrical composition. In Baghdad and its environs slave girls were educated at establishments set up to train them in the art of becoming qiyan.[12] Singing girls owned by nobles, as opposed to those owned by caliphs, were hired out as performers and sometimes as prostitutes. But a fine line was drawn between performers and prostitutes, and one group was often associated with the other. For example, the ninth-century litterateur Ahmad ibn al-Tayyib al-Sarahsi (d. 899) wrote of a bandore player named al-Zubaydi, who heard a woman named Sabah singing. "Az-Zubaydi heard her voice and recognized her talent. He taught her and put much effort into training her. . . . She made her debut as a songstress [and] began to associate freely with men. She was kind and the young men were crazy about her." The story continues with Sabah taking a lover, marrying him, and bearing his child. Her husband soon divorces her. She moves into a friend's home and takes one of their black servants for a lover. Here, Ahmad ibn al-Tayyib notes that "she did not disdain or refrain from anyone, from the oldest to the youngest."[13] Many stories such as this that position female performers as profligate and indiscriminately sexual abound in medieval Arabic literature.

In Baghdad, the seat of the 'Abbasid caliphate and its hub of literary and musical activity, the qiyan were on the one hand praised for their contributions to Arabic literature and music and on the other vilified as unprincipled women. Viewed with admiration and suspicion, the qiyan occupied an intermediate position in Islamicate society between the secluded sphere of women and the visible sphere of male belletrists. The qiyan were not fully accepted as members of either group. They held liminal positions as "privileged" slave women who did not command the same respect as free entertainers and men of letters.

### INVESTIGATING THE LIVES OF THE SINGING SLAVE GIRLS

The evidence in local literary and historical sources of the period is particularly useful for properly situating the qiyan within their social milieus and performance environments and for better understanding the details of their training and professional lives. Unfortunately many sources about the qiyan are not available to the modern reader, but thanks to the *Fihrist al-Nadim,* a tenth-century catalog of all Arabic-language writings known to the compiler Ibn al-Nadim, modern scholars can at least know the titles of works produced in that time. Al-Nadim notes that the author Ishaq ibn

Ibrahim ibn Mahan ibn Bahman ibn Nusk wrote books entitled *Qiyan al-Hijaz* and *Al-Qiyan*. Yunus al-Katib, a Persian slave, also wrote a book called *Al-Qiyan*. Lastly, Abu Ayyub al-Madini wrote *Qiyan al-Hijaz* and *Qiyan Makkah*.[14] Singing slave girls were evidently popular literary subjects. Even without the benefit of reading these works, one can see that the frequent occurrence of the qiyan theme attests to their prominence in the consciousness of the learned classes.[15] Indeed, the intricacy of their training and the otherness of their origins likely enhanced their mystique, encouraging public curiosity about them.

Various means of acquiring slaves existed in the Islamicate world. Young girls could be captured in slave raids against nonbelievers or taken as prisoners of war. According to Islamic law, only non-Muslims can be enslaved, and this caveat brought girls from many ethnic groups into the central Islamicate lands. Hijazi, Ethiopian, Indian, Persian, and Roman girls served as qiyan at court and in wealthy households.[16] Precise biographical information is not available for these girls, so there is no way to know at what stage of childhood they were purchased and trained. Offspring of slave parents could also be trained as performers, and of course girls could be purchased outright from slave dealers. Once a slave girl had been acquired, her owner commenced with lessons in song, lute playing, and Arabic.

In the 'Abbasid period two prominent figures dominated the musical scene: Ibrahim ibn al-Mahdi (d. 838) and Ishaq al-Mawsili (d. 839). Al-Mahdi was a singer-musician for the caliphs al-Rashid and al-Amin and was himself the son of a caliph, and al-Mawsili was likewise an accomplished musician. Both men trained many qiyan, and studying under them was widely considered a great honor. A qayna's linguistic training was often just as integral to her professional success as was the musical instruction, since many of these girls did not speak Arabic natively. Quite exceptionally, there were cases of qiyan who received extensive educations. One reads in *Alf layla wa layla* (A Thousand and One Nights) of Tawaddud, a qayna of the caliph Harun al-Rashid (r. 786–809), who had studied grammar, poetry, law, philosophy, the Qur'an, mathematics, Arabic folklore, medicine, music, logic, rhetoric and composition.[17] It is no coincidence that a caliph owned Tawaddud, for an education of that caliber would have been too expensive for most *muqayyinun* (owners of qiyan). Although the rearing of a qayna by a muqayyin was an expensive venture, the returns on the investment were generally high. The best possible outcome was the sale of a qayna to an aristocrat or a caliph. The qiyan routinely fetched higher prices than untrained slaves, however some contemporary observers did not believe that their artistic talents determined the price. Al-Jahiz (d. 868 or 869), a respected Baghdadi litterateur, mused that "the degree of estimation whereby singing-girls fetch high prices is due to infatuation. If purchases [of them] were made on the same basis as the purchase of ordinary slaves, not one of them would run up to more than the price of a commonplace slave. But most of those who bid a high price for a girl do so because of passion."[18] The "infatuation" of which al-Jahiz speaks was complex, and if literary sources are to be believed, was also difficult to express. To wit, the ʿAbbasid poet Ibn al-Rumi (d. 896) addressed in his poem "Wahid the Singing Slave Girl of Amhamah" the entrancing power of a qayna's seduction: "O my two friends, Wahid has enslaved me. . . . The free-born are enslaved by her."[19] Her physical beauty is complex, and when asked to describe it, the speaker responds, "that is easy and difficult, all at once. / It's easy to say she's the most beautiful of creatures, without exception, / But it is difficult to define her beauty." Ibn al-Rumi also links her beauty to the grace of her musical performance. Her attractiveness is easily recognizable, but not readily articulated, and seems to be composed of many elements. Her poetry, skills as a singer, and beauty infatuate her audience.

Qiyan were hired out to customers for private performances, typically with the understanding that the girls would perform sexual favors. Although the Qur'an explicitly forbids this practice (verse 24:33 commands Muslims to "compel not your slave-girls to prostitution"), the sexual exploitation of qiyan was sufficiently common in the ʿAbbasid era for these singers to be readily identified with promiscuity and licentiousness. The poet ʿAbbas ibn al-Ahnaf (d. after 808) wrote a forty-seven-line poem describing an orgy with sing-ing slave girls.[20] Ibn Qutaybah (d. 889), another ʿAbbasid literary notable, included the following verse in his literary compendium *ʿUyun al-akhbar*: "Were it not for the uses of rue [an herbal contraceptive], the children of the singer-prostitutes [*mughanniyat*] would have covered the earth."[21]

The association of qiyan with sexual promiscuity was by no means uni-versally assumed. Singing slave girls who entertained royalty were held in higher esteem than their counterparts who performed for civilian audi-ences. Al-Jahiz strongly disapproved of this double standard of morality. "When they [qiyan] are in the dwelling of a man of the common folk, one may disapprove of them; but when they move up into kings' palaces, there is no excuse at all. But the cause and reason for the phenomenon is one and the same."[22] As al-Jahiz remarked, a qayna is always a qayna and should be condemned or accepted categorically, not based on her profes-sional associations. However, the reality was not so clear cut. The ambiguity surrounding the morality of a qayna's behavior formed just one part of a general vagueness that characterized their existence. The qiyan associated freely with men and women, slave and free, commoners and nobles, and the debauched and virtuous alike. And fittingly many qiyan existed simultaneously in competing social categories or oscillated between them. As shall be seen, slave girls at the 'Abbasid court were made to cross-dress and entertain as boys, slave women became free women, and slave children of unknown lineage and background gained fame (though perhaps not honor) as palace entertainers. The qiyan seemed to remain on the border of some sort of category, be it social, moral, gendered, or otherwise. The liminality that shaped their lives also manifested itself in the form of ambiguous power vis-à-vis their masters.

## LIMINAL EXISTENCES

In actuality, a qayna's sex appeal was an integral aspect of her enslavement. A qayna's first duty was to serve her master, which typically meant entertaining him and serving as an object of sexual desire. Her identity was not wholly tied to her master's, which in Patterson's model of slavery was the primary factor that engendered social death. The qayna effectively escaped this social alienation. The world she inhabited was not as insular and closed as those of certain other slaves because she received an education and was exposed to various cultural and literary elements of society. The nature of a qayna's service gave her opportunities for artistic creation and a public forum of expression. Although this fact provided a certain degree of psychological separation between master and slave, it was still true that her master derived sexual and nonsexual pleasure from a qayna's body and art. Unlike the free women in the palace, the caliph's qiyan were unveiled, even when performing before male audiences. Their unveiling spoke both to the social distinctions between free noblewomen and slave women and to the expectation of sex appeal in their performances. The significance of their unveiling is better understood in light of the centrality of the veil to Muslim social and moral attitudes about women. The Qur'anic verses commanding the Prophet's wives to veil were interpreted as a command for all Muslim women. Qur'anic verse 33:33 commands the Prophet's wives to "stay in your houses and display not your beauty like the displaying of the ignorance of yore." Verse 33:53 tells Muslim men that when speaking to the Prophet's wives, "ask of them from behind a curtain [hijab]." The verse was later interpreted to apply to all women, and so the hijab developed into a symbol of women's piety and a social marker distinguishing rich women from poor women, who often went unveiled for reasons of practicality. A veil could be cumbersome for a woman who labored inside or outside the home. The hijab was also thought to prevent fitna, or the undisciplined release of sexual energy in public spaces. In the Qur'an the term *fitna* is used to mean trial, but in ninth-century hadith collections it also takes on this meaning of dangerous female sexuality.[23] Whether or not fitna was more imaginary than real, it was believed that fitna originated with women who projected sexual energy onto men. From this perspective, the hijab was mandated not only to encourage female modesty, but also to protect men from the sources of fitna. Medieval Muslim jurists argued that slave girls were not required "to cover their hair, face or arms because they live an active economic life that requires mobility, and because by nature and custom slave-girls do not ordinarily cover these parts of their bodies."[24]

So a qayna was seen as socially and morally distinct from other women in the household by the prominence of her unveiling, which represented slave status, impiety, and the propagation of fitna. The association of the qiyan with seduction is certainly borne out in al-Jahiz's remark that "association between men and singing-girls is liable to lead to misbehavior, in view of the way in which he who indulges in such association is exposed to a sexual urge which compulsively drives one on to the commission of sexual indecency, and most of those who resort to singing-girls' houses do so for that purpose and not for mere listening to music or with the intention of purchasing them."[25] Most patrons of qiyan's performances attended for sexual arousal, not from a sense of musical appreciation. The slave girl was at once bound up with her audience's and master's desires but able to maintain a psychological separation from their expectations as patrons and owners. By manipulating their emotions, a qayna was well positioned to bring about any desired outcomes. The only power she had over a man, and consequently over her own life, grew out of her only connection to him—musical performance and sex—so, she had to overcome him with her artistic prowess, her body, or both. If the seduction was successful, the rewards could be great. Of course, not all singing slave girls were able to maintain an independent sense of self. The following anecdote illustrates one qayna's strong sense of obligation to her master. "Ar-Rashid, after he had killed the Barmecides, called for Danânîr, their slave girl. He ordered her to sing, but she said: O Prince of Believers, I have taken an oath not to sing any more, since my master is dead. Ar-Rashid became angry and ordered her face slapped."[26] Such accounts of a qayna's devotion to her master are not rare, but one reads more often of reversed roles, where masters are slaves to the beauty of their qiyan, as in the Ibn al-Rumi poem.

The qiyan were not the only musicians who performed at court. Free male and female musicians, along with male slave singers, performed for al-Rashid.[27] The actual structure of performances varied. The qiyan could sing and play an instrument as a solo act, perform in ensemble recitals that combined instrumentalism, song, and dance, or even participate in competitions between highly rated singers.[28] The most famous slave singer to have ever resided at the Baghdad court was 'Arib (d. 890), a woman renowned for her beauty, self-possession, and skill as a lutenist, poet, and singer.[29] 'Arib lived to the age of ninety-six, after having served at the courts of five caliphs. She began her career under Caliph al-Amin (r. 809–13), and if the lone mention in al-Shabushti's (d. 998) *Kitab al-Diyarat* is to be believed, she initially performed as a *ghulamiya* (pl., *ghulamiyat*), or female transvestite performer. 'Arib's stint as a ghulamiya is perhaps better understood in light of Caliph al-Amin's sexual interest in male youths. For him a girl dressed as a young boy would likely have had abundant sex appeal. In fact, his mother first came up with the idea of having slave girls entertain as transvestites in order to entice her son to bear an heir. The ghulamiya phenomenon is noteworthy because it serves as another example of slave girls' ambiguous identity since a transvestite inhabits a liminal gender space. As ghulamiyat, girls were viewed and appreciated as boy sex objects while performing but were otherwise identified as biological females. The mughanniyat cut their hair short and donned boy's clothing, but they were not the only cross-dressing performers in 'Abbasid times. Male and female transvestites were common forms of entertainment in the medieval courts of Baghdad, though they also performed in private households.[30] Unlike the ghulamiyat, the male transvestites (*mukhannathun;* sing., *mukhannath*) were generally freemen. They willingly performed alongside the ghulamiyat as singers, musicians, dancers, and comedians. The gender transformation of the mukhannathun involved shaving their beards, wearing women's adornments, playing musical instruments traditionally reserved for women, and donning women's clothes. Both the male and female transvestite performers of the 'Abbasid court were associated with dishonor and profligacy, as were all entertainers in the Islamicate world. Those who lacked social status, namely slaves and gender benders, were suited for such undignified and public positions as court entertainers. Both the ghulamiyat and the mukhannathun belonged to the "world of professional pleasure-givers."[31] The only acceptable forum in which a respectable Muslim could enjoy the entertainment of cross-dressers and slaves was one that highlighted their abjectness.

## BEARING A CHILD

The various social, moral, and gender ambiguities the qiyan submitted to were not entirely insurmountable. One way to transcend these ambiguous realities was through motherhood. The legal benefits conferred on ummahat awlad have already been discussed here, and in the case of the palace qiyan, the benefits could be even greater than the bare facts of acquiring certain legal protections for themselves and their children. A slave girl could have a son who became a caliph. Several 'Abbasid caliphs did indeed have slave mothers. Caliph al-Ma'mun's mother was a Persian *jariya* (female slave; pl., *jawari*) named Marajil, and al-Mu'tasim's mother was a slave named Marida. Al-Mu'tasim himself went on to marry two *jawari*, both of whom became mothers of caliphs. Qaratis had a son named al-Wathiq, and Shaja' gave birth to Ja'far al-Mutawakkil.

The historian 'Abd al-Karim al-'Allaf has astutely observed that the only 'Abbasid jawari whose names have come down through history are the um- mahat awlad and the most famous singing slaves. The others have mostly languished in obscurity.[32] The tombstone of an umm walad named Umm Muhammad of the 'Abbasid caliph al-Ma'mun's household has survived. According to her epitaph, she had at least twenty children and grandchildren.[33] While the epitaph does not reveal much about her relationship with the elite household, the existence of a tombstone bearing a warm epitaph for a slave woman speaks to her importance for the family. And certainly, other jawari knew full well the importance of bearing a caliph's child (preferably a son) or otherwise winning his sympathy. Competition among them for the caliph's attention and favor would necessarily have been intense. 'Arib herself was the concubine of eight caliphs and linked to several court no- tables but never bore them any children. She was, however, married briefly to a Khurasani officer named Muhammad ibn Hamid and had a daughter by him. Her fame and reputation alone may have given her a privileged standing with the caliphs, thereby lessening the need to bear them children as a tool for greater autonomy.[34] Al-Jahiz felt that the qiyan "set up snares and traps for the victims [of their seduction]. . . . She corresponds with him, . . . swearing to him . . . that she desires no other than him, prefers nobody else to her infatuation for him, never intends to abandon him, and does not want him for his money but for himself."[35] The qiyan could be ardently competitive about winning an admirer's affection. Leslie Peirce, in referring to a similar phenomenon among women in the seventeenth-century Otto- man royal harem, terms this competition to bear a ruler's child the "politics of reproduction."[36] In Peirce's estimation each sexual encounter between a harem woman, be she slave or free, and the sultan held the potential for pregnancy, which the wives and concubines intensely desired. In addition to the political and legal advantages of having a caliph's child, there were also important psychological benefits. Having a child would provide a slave with another consciousness through which to mediate her own and also start a familial community of her own.

David Brion Davis has called on historians of American slavery to start "challenging the boundaries of slavery," in his book of the same name. In the Muslim world such a call to reexamine the relationships between the enslavers and the enslaved has the potential to showcase the intimacies that can complicate the power differential in these associations. Sexuality and motherhood are useful lenses through which to examine the uses of power in slave systems. As shown in this chapter, the politics of motherhood could prove intricate for medieval slave women in the Muslim world, particularly for women disadvantaged not only by their status as slaves, but also by their reputation for sexual availability. However, in the case of the qiyan, motherhood offered more life security and social validation than the liminal existence that was the lot of most singing female slaves.

## NOTES

1. Shaun Marmon, introduction to *Slavery in the Islamic Middle East*, ed. Marmon (Princeton: Markus Wiener, 1999), x.

2. For an explanation of the term Islamicate, which was coined by Marshall G. S. Hodgson, see his *The Venture of Islam: Conscience and History in a World Civilization*, 3 vols. (Chicago: University of Chicago Press, 1974), 1:58–59.

3. Orlando Patterson, *Slavery and Social Death: A Comparative Study* (Cambridge, MA: Harvard University Press, 1982), 97–99.

4. Sussan Babaie, Kathryn Babayan, Ina Baghdiantz-McCabe, and Massumeh Farhad, *Slaves of the Shah: New Elites of Safavid Iran* (London: I. B. Tauris, 2004), 21.

5. Leslie Peirce, *The Imperial Harem: Women and Sovereignty in the Ottoman Empire* (New York: Oxford University Press, 1993), 252.

6. Abu al-Faraj al-Isbahani, *Book of Strangers: Medieval Arabic Graffiti on the Theme of Nostalgia*, trans. Patricia Crone and Shmuel Moreh (Princeton: Markus Wiener, 2000).

7. Some notable treatments of female slavery in Islam include Nadia Abbott, *Two Queens of Baghdad: Mother and Wife of Harun al-Rashid* (Chicago: University of Chicago Press, 1946); Peirce, *Imperial Harem*; Nicola Lauré al-Samarai, *Die Macht der Darstellung: Gender, sozialer Status, historiographische Re-Präsentation: Zwei Frauenbiographien aus der frühen Abbasidenzeit* (Wiesbaden: Reichert, 2001).

8. Muslim ibn al-Hajjaj al-Qushayri, *Sahih Muslim*, trans. Abdul Hamid Siddiqi (Lahore: Sh. Muhammad Ashraf, 1971), 735.

9. Ibid., 734.

10. The Arabic language has various names for the singing slave girls. The term *qayna* (pl., *qiyan*) refers specifically to a female slave who has been trained as a singer, poet, or musician (or all three). *Qayna* is the feminine form of *qayn*, skilled worker. Other terms in use do not embody the meaning of female singing slave. *Jariya* (pl., *jawari*) means simply female slave, and *mughanniya* (pl., *mughanniyat*) designates a female singer. These

two words are often used independently in medieval Arabic literature to signify singing slave girl. But if an author wants to avoid any ambiguity, he couples the terms, and the resulting phrase *jariya mughanniya* (pl., *jawari mughanniyat*) is synonymous with qayna.

11. Charles Pellat, "Kayna," Encyclopedia of Islam, 2nd ed. (Leiden: E. J. Brill, 1954-), 4:821-22. The qiyan in modern Tunisia are described at length in Hasan Husni 'Abd al-Wahhab, "Taqaddum al-musiqa fi-sharq wa-l-andalus wa-tunis," *Waraqat*, 3 vols. (Tunis: Maktabat al-Manar, 1965-72), 2:202. Tovia Ashkenazi describes twentieth-century Palestinian male slave poets in *Tribus semi-nomades de la Palestine du Nord* (Paris: Geuthner, 1938), 98-99.

12. Alfred Kremer, *Kulturgeschichte des Orients unter den Chalifen*, 2 vols. (Aalen: Scientia, 1966), 2:108-9.

13. Franz Rosenthal, *Ahmad b. at-Tayyib as-Sarahsi* (New Haven: American Oriental Society, 1943), 95-96.

14. Ibn al-Nadim, *The Fihrist of al-Nadim: A Tenth-Century Survey of Muslim Culture*, ed. and trans. Bayard Dodge, 2 vols. (New York: Columbia University Press, 1970), 1:309, 317, 324.

15. Female slave poets (*ima' shawa'ir*; sing., *ama sha'ira*) also entertained 'Abbasid aristocrats and rulers and occupied similar social roles as the qiyan. This category of slave performers will not be examined in this study, although its inclusion could only enrich the discussion. For more information on these poets, see Abu al-Faraj al-Isbahani, *Al-Ima' al-Shawa'ir* (Beirut: Dar al-Nidal, 1984), a biographical dictionary that details the backgrounds and literary accomplishments of thirty-three 'Abbasid-era female slave poets.

16. Sami A. Hanna, "Al-Jawari al-Mughanniyat: The Singing Arab Maids," *Southern Folklore Quarterly* 34, no. 4 (1970): 327.

17. Richard Burton, ed. and trans., *The Book of the Thousand Nights and a Night: A Plain and Literal Translation of the Arabian Nights Entertainments*, 10 vols. (s.l.: privately printed by the Burton Club, 1900), 5:193-94.

18. Al-Jahiz, *The Epistles of Singing-Girls of Jahiz*, trans. A. F. L. Beeston (Warminster, UK: Aris and Phillips, 1980), 27.

19. All translations of this poem come from Akiko Motoyoshi, "Sensibility and Synaesthesia: Ibn al-Rumi's Singing Slave-Girl," *Journal of Arabic Literature* 32, no. 1 (2001): 5-8.

20. 'Abbas ibn al-Ahnaf, *Diwan Abi al-Fadl al-'Abbas ibn al-Ahnaf* (Constantinople: Matba'at al-Jawa'ib, 1881), 148-50.

21. Cited in B. F. Musallam, *Sex and Society in Islam: Birth Control before the Nineteenth Century* (Cambridge: Cambridge University Press, 1983), 94, from Ibn Qutaybah, 'Abd Allah ibn Muslim, *'Uyun al-Akhbar*, 4 vols. (Cairo: Al-Mu'assasah al-Misriyah al-'Ammah li-l-Ta'lif wa-al-Tarjamah wa-al-Taba'ah wa-al-Nashr, 1964), 3:286.

22. Al-Jahiz, *Epistles*, 34.

23. Denise A. Spellberg, "Political Action and Public Example: 'A'isha and the Battle of the Camel," in *Women in Middle Eastern History: Shifting Boundaries in Sex and Gender*, ed. Nikkie R. Keddie and Beth Baron (New Haven: Yale University Press, 1991), 50-51.

24. Khaled Abou El Fadl, *Speaking in God's Name: Islamic Law, Authority and Women* (Oxford: OneWorld, 2001), 232-41.

25. Al-Jahiz, *Epistles*, 26.

26. Rosenthal, *Ahmad b. at-Tayyib*, 98. The name of 'Abbasid caliph Harun al-Rashid is here rendered as ar-Rashid, reflecting in print the convention of dropping the 'l' sound before the 'r' in spoken Arabic.

27. Abu al-Faraj al-Isbahani (d. 897), himself a poet and musician, compiled five centuries' worth of artists' biographies and historical anecdotes about music in a ten-thousand-page work known as *Kitab al-aghani*, or *The Book of Songs*. He devoted considerable space to Caliph Harun al-Rashid, a famed admirer of the qiyan and patron of the arts.

28. For this last activity, see Matthew S. Gordon, "The Place of Competition: The Careers of 'Arib al-Ma'muniya and 'Ulayya bint al-Mahdi, Sisters in Song," in *'Abbasid Studies: Occasional Papers of the School of 'Abbasid Studies, Cambridge, 5–10 July 2002*, ed. James E. Montgomery (Dudley, MA: Peeters, 2004), 61–82.

29. Abu al-Faraj al-Isbahani, *Kitab al-aghani*, 24 vols. (Cairo: Matba'at Dar al-Kutub al-Misriyah, 1927), 21:54.

30. Everett Rowson, "Gender Irregularity as Entertainment: Institutionalized Transvestism at the Caliphal Courts in Medieval Baghdad," in *Gender and Difference in the Middle Ages*, ed. Sharon Farmer and Carol Braun Pasternack (Minneapolis: University of Minnesota Press, 2003), 50.

31. Ibid., 65.

32. 'Abd al-Karim al-'Allaf, *Qiyan Baghdad fi al-'asr al-Abbasi wa-al-'Uthmani wa-al-akhir* (Baghdad: Matba'at Dar al-Tadamun, 1969), 37.

33. A. Elad, "An Epitaph of the Slave Girl of the Grandson of the 'Abbassid [sic] Caliph al-Ma'mun," *Le Muséon* 111, no. 1 (1998): 227–44.

34. J. E. Bencheikh, "Les musiciens et la poésie," *Arabica* 22, no. 2 (1975): 144.

35. Al-Jahiz, *Epistles*, 32.

36. Peirce, 13.

# 7

## BECOMING A *DEVŞIRME*

*The Training of Conscripted Children in the Ottoman Empire*

GULAY YILMAZ

For centuries the military-administrative positions of the Ottoman state were manned by slaves who were carefully recruited and painstakingly educated. Different variations of this institution have existed in Islamic societies since the 'Abbasid caliphate—the traditional source of the enslaved military-administrative stratum had always been war captives. The Ottomans, however, enslaved young Christians within their empire through a method called the *devşirme* system.[1]

According to the prevailing paradigm, the devşirme were privileged vis-à-vis the masses and completely loyal to authority, enabling the autocratic regime of the sultan to be effective in all spheres of life. The unquestioned loyalty of the slave-based military-administrative strata, which contrasted starkly with the position of the freeman in the West, was the most crucial strand of the orientalist argument, which asserts that Eastern societies lacked autonomous institutions. This argument is the basis of the Oriental despot model in the literature. The orientalist paradigm depicted Ottoman society as having a sharp dichotomy—the ruling elite bolstered by the devşirme system versus the ruled, that is, the tax-paying *re'aya*. It was the unquestioned loyalty of the devşirme that underlay the despotic powers of the sultan over Ottoman society, in which the re'aya were tranquil and obedient. This essentially obedient and loyal nature of both groups is given as the core reason why Ottoman society was unable to create the freedom that was considered the most significant feature of the urban culture of the West.

Scholarly criticism of this view of the devşirme emerged when closer examination of the military-administrative strata revealed the more intricate links of this class to the sultanate and society. Delineating the various types of loyalties a devşirme developed in Ottoman society, and considering the change in the recruitment methods that transformed the military-administrative strata during the late sixteenth and early seventeenth centuries, refuted the orientalist depiction of Ottoman society as being divided into neat opposing groups.

## THE DEVŞIRME SYSTEM

The practice of allotting one-fifth of war captives as booty to the sultan for use as soldiers was followed in the Ottoman Empire from the beginning. It derived from earlier usage in Islamic societies, and had been determined by Islamic law.[2] In the Ottoman Empire, this tradition was formalized in the Pençik Law—*pençik*, a Persian word, means one-fifth.[3] However, rapid Ottoman expansion during the fifteenth century increased the demand for more soldiers, and Ottoman officials were forced to search for new sources for conscription. After the Battle of Ankara in 1402, state officials decided to conscript the non-Muslim youth of the empire to form a new military force, called the janissary army (the New Corps). The system was institutionalized under the Kavanin-i Yeniçeriyan,[4] or Janissary Law, which is the main primary source for this study.

Of all the institutions of the Ottoman state, the devşirme has perhaps been the most debated by scholars, with the main issue being its legality. According to the shari'a, non-Muslims living under the authority and supremacy of the Islamic state received *zımmi* (protected) status and were treated differently than *harbis*, or non-Muslims living outside the empire, that is—in the *dar-ül harb* (domain of war). The non-Muslim societies of the empire were thus protected.[5] Some scholars have therefore interpreted the devşirme system as an infringement on zımmi status,[6] while others have stressed the fact that devşirme boys were conscripted from among those who had never been granted genuine zımmi status; thus, this practice did not contradict Islamic law.[7] The devşirmes were conscripted from among the zımmis of the empire, as opposed to the practice of taking one-fifth of the non-Muslim youth of newly conquered areas. Plus, the situation is complicated by the fact that the Ottoman state solidified the idea of conscription among the zımmis of the empire as allowable by law, claiming that it was a form of tribute in kind. This has led many to conclude that, even though the devşirmes were conscripted among the zımmis, this was not against Islamic law.

On the other hand, the legality of the pençik system, which continued to be practiced alongside the devşirme system, was clear. According to
Islamic law, the sultan had the right to kill war captives, to enslave them, to
make an agreement with them whereby they became zımmis, or to release
them upon the payment of *bedel* (redemption money). During negotiations
with captives, immunity from the Pençik Law was often used as a bargaining tool by the Ottomans. One noted example was Mehmed II's grant of
exemption from child tribute to the Genoese colony at Galata after the
Genoese offered him the keys to the town during the siege of Constantinople in 1453.[8]

The enslavement of war captives (*pençik oğlanı*) and recruitment of the
children of Christian subjects (devşirme) differed not only in legality and
methods of conscription but also in the way they were trained. War captives
were not given the education offered to devşirmes or subjected to conversion to Islam and the adoption of Ottoman culture. Hence, most of the
time they preserved their Christian identity.

How then did the recruitment process for this military-administrative
stratum work? Who were selected as devşirmes? What were the stages a boy
passed through in becoming a devşirme? What were the attributes that the
boys were expected to learn? And what kind of loyalties did they form in
the process? There were specific rules on the selection of recruits, and the
whole process was under the control of the janissary officers. The *Kavanin-i
yeniçeriyan* is a fertile source as it provides a detailed description of the recruitment procedure. The candidates had to be between the ages of ten and
eighteen or thereabouts, able bodied, good looking, clever, unmarried, and
uncircumcised.[9] It was forbidden to take the only son of a family or more
than one boy from the same family, because the family would need at least
one son to continue cultivating the land. Moreover, only one boy could
be taken from every forty households.[10] Predominantly Serbs, Greeks, and
Albanians were recruited. Jews, Gypsies, Kurds, Persians, and Turks could
not be devşirmes.[11] This division can partly be explained by the strict shari'a
prohibition against enslaving Muslims, but the exclusion of certain groups
of non-Muslims from the devşirme is puzzling. These constraints on the
ethnic background of the boys are perhaps indicative of whom the state
defined as "us"—the Ottomans—and whom it rejected as the other. Here
the concept of the other is being fueled by ethnic stereotyping—for example,
considering Jews as unsuitable for warfare, or Gypsies as unreliable.

The conscription process began upon the request for a new levy by the *yeniçeri
ağası* (chief of the janissaries). Such a decree was issued every three to four years
indicating the number of boys needed and the places of recruitment.[12] Once

this was done, specially appointed janissary officers[13] were sent to Christian villages where they asked village priests for a list of baptized boys.[14] Those who tried to hide children from the officers were strictly punished. Villagers sometimes attempted to prevent the village boys from being conscripted by falsifying baptism registers, circumcising them, or declaring them married.[15] However, in some cases parents asked the sultan to consider their children eligible for recruitment, in order to be exempted from certain taxes. For example, during the reign of Sultan Mehmed II, Bosnians asked to be conscripted.[16] However, it has generally been considered that these recruitments were resented, as shown in a song from Epirus:

> Be damned, Emperor, thrice be damned
> For the evil you have done and the evil you do.
> You catch and shackle the old and the archpriests,
> In order to take the children as janissaries.
> Their parents weep, their sisters and brothers, too
> And I cry until it pains me;
> As long as I live I shall cry,
> For last year it was my son and this year my brother.[17]

Despite the resentment of parents, the boys were scrupulously selected in the village center. Orphans were not accepted because they were believed to lack a proper upbringing and to be greedy.[18] By scrutinizing the lists that the village priest provided, well-brought-up boys of good birth were initially selected. Then they were examined for bodily and facial perfection. When the desired number of boys had been chosen, they were organized into groups of one hundred, one hundred and fifty, or two hundred for transport to the capital; such a group was called a *sürü* (crowd). They were dressed in *kızıl aba* (red clothing) and *külah* (a hat) in order to discourage any escapes or kidnapping during the transfer.[19] These precautions attest to the generally involuntary nature of the procedure as well as the concern on the part of the authorities to prevent any abuse of the boys during the journey.

When the sürü was brought to the capital, the children were allowed to rest for two to three days. Then they were stripped in the presence of the chief of janissaries and examined for bodily defects. All were then converted to Islam, circumcised, and given Muslim names.[20] We do not know how much the boys were informed in advance about the process by their kin or by officers after being selected, yet it was perhaps at this moment that they sensed their enslavement. This was also the point at which the most talented and handsome were selected and sent to the palaces. The rest were registered as *acemi oğlans* (novices). Those who were selected for palace service were placed in one of four palaces: Iskender Celebi, Galatasaray, Edirne, or Ibrahim Pasha. In those palaces the children were taught Turkish and Arabic languages and literature, the Koran, Muslim jurisprudence, theology, or law, and were given military training.[21] Every three to seven years the most talented were selected to continue their education in the Enderun, the Palace School, and the rest were sent to the *kapıkulu* corps to become soldiers.[22]

The transition of the talented to the highly coded palace culture began as soon as they arrived. They were subjected to clearly defined rules of behavior. Immediately after registration, they were introduced to officials and older pages. They were taught to be humble and polite, to show reverence by holding their heads bowed with their hands crossed before them, and to kiss the hands of their superiors as a sign of respect. Their daily schedule was meticulously organized; each hour had its appointed task. The times for waking up, praying, eating, sleeping, exercising, and studying were all specified. They had to walk sedately, eat slowly, bathe weekly, shave regularly, wear well-pressed clothes, and perform the five daily prayers.[23]

There were five preparatory and four occupational schools in the palaces. On average full training lasted fourteen years, of which the preparatory period lasted for seven or eight years. The novices received an allowance of seven or eight *akçes* per day, whereas those in the higher ranks received ten to twelve.[24] Not all the students who graduated from preparatory school continued to the occupational schools. The great majority were appointed to lower posts in the kapıkulu corps and government according to their grades and chosen for different ranks in the ruling class. The curriculum of the schools was carefully designed not only to prepare candidates for further specialization but also to supply trained personnel for appointments to military and administrative posts. N. M. Penzer argues that the palace schools functioned like regiments. They fostered a strong solidarity among the students.[25]

The four occupational schools specialized in different subjects. The expeditionary force chamber provided mainly musical training but also taught sewing, embroidery, leatherwork, arrow making, and gun repair.[26] The commissariat chamber taught students to prepare royal beverages, whereas Treasury chamber trained pages in financial responsibilities. The royal bedchamber trained those who would be responsible for the protection of the Holy Relics.[27] After their graduation, pages would petition for the posts they wanted, and their promotions were mostly to the higher posts of the military or state administration.

The rest of the conscripted boys, on the other hand, became acemi oğlans and passed through a two-stage training. First, they were hired out by the army to a Turkish family in Anatolia or Rumelia—in return for payment—for approximately five years.[28] If a boy was conscripted from Rumelia he would be sent to Anatolia, and vice versa. Placing the boys in locations far from their villages helped prevent them from fleeing, indicating that their participation was often not voluntary.[29] The object was to acquaint the boys with the Turkish language and customs and Islamic practices while they worked for their host families. The children were thus transplanted into a Turkish-Islamic environment different from their ethnic, cultural, and religious background.

The second stage of training occurred in the barracks. The boys who had been hired out to Anatolian and Rumelian villagers would be recalled to the barracks when the existing acemi oğlans were promoted to the kapıkulu corps. The new boys were taught literacy, the principles of governance, and the precepts of the Qur'an.[30] They were assigned general tasks such as sweeping, carrying, or cooking for themselves and for the city, as well as continuing their training as professional warriors. They were also used on the ships carrying wood and ice to Istanbul.[31] They replaced the janissaries when they went on campaigns and also served as night watchmen, firemen, and police within the city.[32] When new soldiers were needed, selected acemi oğlans were enlisted in the kapıkulu corps.

Among the kapıkulu corps, janissaries are the most prolific in Ottoman historiography. Janissaries were divided into regiments (ocaks) and instructed under the same tutor (hoca). Sharing similar experiences in the early phase of their lives in Ottoman society, the boys developed special attachments to each other. This attachment was referred to as ocakdaş or hocadaş—being in the same regiment or trained under the same tutor.[33] Every regiment had its own symbol, etched as a tattoo on every janissary's body. These tattoos were also symbols of loyalty.

Besides their loyalty toward the regiment, religion had an important impact on janissary identity. The janissaries were also referred to as Zümre-i Bektaşiyan (a group of Bektaşi followers) or Bektaşi Oğulları (sons of the Bektaşi). Each ocak of the janissary corps had its own leader (çorbacı), and they were all supervised by an ortacı. The ortacı was regarded as the official representative of Hajji Bektash Veli, the founder of the Bektaşi sect.[34]

While the existence of a close relationship between Bektaşis and janissaries is commonly accepted by scholars, no work has specifically considered this relationship, although there are sporadic references in the literature. Suraiya Faroqhi mentions, for example, that janissary novices and janissaries were the participants and the protectors of the biggest annual Bektaşi ceremonies in Seyit Ghazi lodge toward the end of the sixteenth century.[35] She also provides a document from 1730 indicating that the members of the Ramazan Baba lodge in Bursa were *emekderan-ı ocak-ı Hacı Bektaş* (retired janissaries).[36] Louis Massignon shows once again that the janissaries were the followers of the Bektaşi order, and they were very much influenced by the chivalric character that persists in the teaching of Hallaj, the famous martyr-mystic of Islam who became not only a symbol for those who seek God but also for those who have been imprisoned or tortured by unjust governments.[37] He also cites that the "gibbet of Mansur" was part of the initiation rite of the Bektaşis; moreover, to give reference to the gibbet of Mansur was very common among Bektaşi poets, especially the ones affiliated with the janissary army.[38] Another source that indicates a connection between this sect and the janissaries is Esad Efendi's *Üss-i Zafer*, written to support the annihilation of the janissaries in 1826. There he mentions that at the same time as the annihilation of the janissiaries, the Bektaşi lodges were also shut down due to the close ties established with the army. In fact, Faroqhi uses the *'ayniyyat defters*, registers of properties confiscated from the Bektaşi lodges during the annihilation of the janissary army by the Ottoman state, in her research on Bektashism in Anatolia.

The solidarity among the janissaries also had an economic dimension. Strong economic ties were established among janissaries through *oda sandığı* (regiment *waqfs*, pious endowments). No research has yet been done on the function and role of these waqfs but as far as we can learn from *Kavanin-i yeniçeriyan*, every member of the regiment had to give a certain percentage of his salary. The money was used to support those in need, such as the families of dead janissaries. These waqfs were also used as sources for lending money that would be paid back with interest. Tahsin Özcan regards the regiment waqfs as a form of cash waqf,[39] which were important endowments that provided money to people and injected capital into the economy.[40]

How these loans were used is still an unanswered question, but an educated guess can be made. It is known that the janissaries opened small businesses and entered guilds from the mid-sixteenth century.[41] Cemal Kafadar notes that the ruling elite and the janissaries were involved in production and exchange even before the sixteenth century. Kafadar gives examples of various pashas involved in commercial enterprises and mentions that contrary to what *Kavanin-i yeniçeriyan* law requires, the janissaries were shopkeepers in cities. He even gives an example of janissaries who leased shops from the Ayasofya foundation under Bayezid II, which indicates that janissary entrepreneurialism was permitted at the higher state ranks.[42] Halil Inalcık,

examining the economic transformation of Ottoman society in the seventeenth century, also stresses the rapid increase of commercial activities of
janissaries in big cities as urbanization developed.[43] Eunjeong Yi's research
on Istanbul court records reveals that the commercialization of janissaries
gained momentum at the beginning of the seventeenth century and that
by the mid-seventeenth century janissaries were actively present in guilds.[44]
Examining the account registers of the regiment waqfs may provide us with
more information in answering whether these waqfs functioned as an institution for giving investment loans in the urban market and whether there
was an economic policy in choosing investors.

Recognizing the economic importance of the janissaries in the urban
market prompts us to question other dimensions of orientalist and declin-
ist narrative concerning Ottoman society that conceived janissaries as
troublemakers, who rebelled for their own benefit, attacked city dwellers,
and disturbed daily life. While recognizing the oppressive acts of the soldiers
against city dwellers, the outcome of their economic intertwining with the
city should also be taken into consideration, since economic alignments
would lead to common interests. This commonality made janissaries the
mediators and sometimes even the representatives of the cities vis-à-vis
the sultan's power.[45]

Christoph Neumann argues that the janissaries were the most influen-
tial group to voice the opposition of the urban population against the state.
Neumann notes that, in *Tarih-i Cevdet*, Ahmet Cevdet defined the abandonment of the janissary army in 1826 as "the weakening of the power,
fraternity, and solidarity *asabiye* in Islam."[46] The term *'asabiye* is used very
specifically to denote a community tie, a bond of brotherhood within the regiments, which has always been more powerful than their bond to the sultan.
As Cevdet put it, the reason for the janissary rebellions was not the lack of
discipline (*nizam*) but the existence of a solidarity that could work against
the sultan (*karşı nizam*).

Once this solidarity is recognized, the janissary uprisings have to be seen
not as mob revolts but as popular rebellions.[47] Şerif Mardin argues that
there were certain elements in the social construction of a rebellion in
Ottoman society. Before rebellions, disapproving gossip was spread, mainly
about the behavior or decisions of the sultan or his officials; the gossip
then gained more formal structure when it was expressed during sermons
in mosques. The janissaries then joined the rebellion, which was supported
by religious students and merchants in the city bazaars.[48] However, as Cengiz Kırlı emphasizes, janissaries' mingling with the bazaar population, and
their active presence at the coffeehouses, where the gossip was generated,

made them the figures that initiated the oppositional urban movements against the state.

## THE STATUS OF A DEVŞIRME

An attempt to understand janissaries within their complex social network reveals that rather than being loyal slaves who ensured the despotic rule of the Ottoman sultan, the janissaries became the intermediaries between the state and society, mostly voicing and negotiating the demands of society with the state. In the light of these considerations, the status of a devşirme in Ottoman society should also be examined carefully. In legal terms the devşirmes were the kuls of the sultan. *Kul*, though generally translated into English as slave, is a multifaceted word. The fundamental problem is to describe the different usages of *kul* so as to produce a more accurate interpretation of Ottoman social structure, that is, one that would presumably defy such neat oppositional classes. In a general sense, *kul* was used for all the subjects of the Sultan: every person living under the rule of the Ottoman state. In a narrow sense, kuls were the servant-officers and soldiers of the sultan, whether they were genuine slaves or not.[49] More specifically, as a third layer, this group was used for the servants of the sultan coming from slave origins, that is, Christian boys reduced to slavery, converted to Islam and involved in patronage networks and socialized into various levels of society.

Yet, *kul*, even when used to refer to the devşirmes with slave origins, had a different sense from the term *'abd*, which designated purchased slaves. Purchased slaves can clearly be seen as being in a master-slave relationship. However, the relationships of the devşirmes involved more dynamic power relations, negotiations, and reconciliations. The devşirmes, as kuls, enjoyed the privilege of being members of the imperial household.[50] They were paid salaries, exempted from tax and allowed to own property, including all types of slaves of their own.[51] As the "servants of the sultan"—the true Ottomans—they earned privileges that distinguished them from the subjects of the empire.

The servant status was a patron-client relationship rather than one of master and slave, primarily because of its reciprocal nature. Ehud Toledano describes devşirme status as "a continuum of various degrees of bondage rather than a dichotomy between slave and free."[52] A devşirme was absorbed into the owner's social group and engaged in the political, economic, and cultural life of Ottoman society according to the power of that group. Therefore, the concept of social alienation does not shed light on the devşirme's position in Ottoman society, predominantly due to his excessive involvement in his patron's social group.

The negotiating power of the devşirmes in their relationship with their patron, the sultan, gave rise to differing linkages and loyalties within the ruling elite. The devşirmes, having been conscripted between the ages of ten and eighteen, remembered their birthplaces and maintained ties with them. Sokullu Mehmet Pasha gave special patronage to the region of his birth, while Koci Bey, a prominent intellectual at the end of the sixteenth century, was buried in his birthplace of Gümülcine (in the Thrace region of modern Greece) in accordance with his will.[53] More important than ties to birthplaces, devşirmes were able to maintain kinship ties. Traditional arguments claim that slave soldiers were socially alienated, but this was not true in the Ottoman case. Metin Kunt gives examples of devşirmes who spoke their native languages or dressed in the traditional clothing of their region such as Mere Huseyin Pasha and Ibshir Mustafa Pasha.[54] These cultural attachments also led to stronger links among devşirmes with the same family background. Kunt explains that in accordance with the family solidarity of the newly appointed grand vizier, there was a great chance that the new administration would be formed along kinship lines.[55] This solidarity, as well as other loyalties, such as belonging to the same regiment, are important for our understanding of how the devşirmes were involved in the power dynamics of Ottoman society.

Conscripted boys were filtered through to various positions, from military to administrative, and the social power and prestige of these positions varied. There were devşirmes who ended up performing no more than general labor and who were marginalized within the system. Others reached high-ranking administrative and military positions. The solidarities that stemmed simply from being introduced into Ottoman society through enslavement might have cut across the loyalties that were tied to social positions, generating an improved social network among the various ranks and an upward mobility. Kunt, for example, tells of a pasha who helped a janissary because they had both been taught by the same tutor in the same regiment.[56]

The theme of overlapping loyalties needs to be investigated further. Yet another important issue in relation to this is the transformation of the recruitment process itself during the seventeenth century and the introduction of Muslim subjects into the military-administrative stratum alongside non-Muslims, a phenomenon that generated more conflicting loyalties.

## OPENING THE DOORS TO COMMONERS

The recruitment process for the military-administrative stratum gradually evolved in the direction of conscripting re'aya (tax-paying Muslim commoners) toward the end of the sixteenth century, and it transformed both the nature of the servant body and the role of devşirmes in Ottoman society. The reasons for this transformation were numerous and closely related to the demographic, economic, and military crisis on the European and Asian continents.[57] The effects of a vast population increase, the influx of silver from the New World, the price revolution, and most crucial for our case, military developments in Europe, all hit the Ottoman Empire. One action the state took to adapt to these conditions was to recruit soldiers from the Muslim population.

European armies were composed of musketeers by the seventeenth century. The number of soldiers in European armies increased due to this use of firearms, since it was easier to teach commoners how to shoot than to train them as professional warriors.[58] In response, the Ottoman state enlisted commoners in the regiments of the janissary army, as well as recruiting the offspring and brothers of the existing janissaries in order to acquire more firearm-bearing soldiers. Scrutinizing the contemporary accounts of şemandanizade, Virigina Aksan asserts that almost "the entire population of both Rumelia and Anatolia was passing itself off as janissaries. Anyone who claimed to be a janissary was accepted as such."[59] Hence, the peasants, who had been kept in their low status as a tax resource, and barred from the military-administrative stratum, gained access to these ranks for the first time. The figures Rhoads Murphey provides for the three successive reigns of Murad III (r. 1574-95), Mehmet III (r. 1595-1603), and Ahmed I (r. 1603-17) show that there was a 140 percent increase in the numbers of those recruited for military and administrative staff.[60]

As already mentioned, the administrative apparatus was also transformed from a devşirme body to a hybrid group consisting of converted slaves, freeborn officers, and sons or relatives of those groups.[61] Kunt defines the holders of military-administrative posts as those who had attained ümera status, professionals in the state ranks who themselves enjoyed different social standings.[62]

This new state policy, which blurred the boundaries between the ruler and the ruled, was perhaps one of the most debated issues among Ottoman intellectuals of the time. Many of them, in nasihatnames (advisory epistles to the sultan), mentioned the negative effects of these innovations and interpreted them as responsible for the decline of Ottoman society. Thus, Lutfi Pasha, the grand vizier of Suleyman the Magnificent, notes the deteriorating conditions within the empire and suggests "returning to the good old days" in his Asafname (1542). However, it was the Risale of Koci Bey, completed in 1630, that developed the idea of a Golden Age of Ottoman power and that diagnosed the empire as being in decline. Here, the most important issue was the corruption of the janissary army by the enlistment of commoners, and the provincial administrative positions and grants likewise given to the latter.[63] In 1631, Aziz Efendi reiterated the same concerns in his *Kanun-name* and urged the sultan to act against the infiltration of the janissary army by members of the taxpaying classes.[64]

The intellectuals who contributed to this genre of advice literature, however, were devşirmes themselves, and their main issue was with the infiltration of the Muslim-born into their class. Yet state policies did not change in response to these warnings; instead other precautions were taken. Inalcık argues that the devşirme system could not provide sufficient soldiers for the expanding infantry, therefore, the central administration opened up the janissary ranks to outsiders from the Muslim urban and rural population.[65] He stresses the reasons that pushed the state to develop these strategies. Karen Barkey depicts the change in state policies toward recruitment methods as a reflex reaction. Consequently, it can be concluded that the recruitment of commoners to the ruling class was a conscious policy, but to what extent it was a reflex reaction or a new political strategy is hard to say. It might be that the political agenda shifted toward commoners in consequence of a growing mistrust of the devşirmes in the seventeenth century. Janissary rebellions broke out during the two military triumphs of Selim I's reign (1512–20)—the defeat of the Savafids in 1514 and the conquest of Egypt in 1517—and this led to suspicion of devşirme loyalties.[66] Selim I's frustration with the janissaries drove him to reduce the devşirme element in both the military and the administrative ranks. He, for the first time, conscripted devşirmes from among Turks in Anatolia and selected his grand vizier, Piri Mehmed Pasha, from among the Turkish population.[67] We do not know how strong a consensus there was for supporting the elevation of commoners to state rank, yet the population increase and economic crisis of the era seem to have triggered the mobility of commoners, and the sultans who considered devşirmes a threat to their power might have been responding more willingly to the demands of commoners.

The so-called opening of the doors to commoners started a new era in the Ottoman Empire, though it was perceived by the devşirme intellectuals as a deterioration of society that would inevitably lead to the decline of the state. Hence, in the face of such opposition, it could only have been a conscious policy on the part of the sultans not only to adapt to new circumstances but also to manage power relations within the ruling elite. This fact defies the orientalist argument in support of the supposed absolute loyalty of the enslaved military-administrative stratum to the sultans. It was the network of linkages and loyalties generated by the devşirmes in Ottoman society that might well have led the sultans to welcome new elements into the ruling elite.

## NOTES

1. V. L. Menage gives one of the best descriptions of the system as "the forcible removal of the children of the Christian subjects from their ethnic, religious, and cultural environment and their transplantation into Turkish-Islamic environment with the aim of employing them in the service of the Palace, the army, and the state, whereby they were to serve the Sultan as slaves or freemen and to form a part of the ruling class of the State." Menage, "Some Notes on Devşirme," *Bulletin of the School of Oriental African Studies* 29, no. 1 (1966): 64.

2. J. A. B. Palmer, "The Origins of the Janissaries," *John Rylands Library Bulletin* 35, 462.

3. For facsimile, transliteration, and concise interpretation of *Kanunname-i Pençik*, see Ahmet Akgündüz, *Osmanlı Kanunnâmeleri ve Hukukî Tahlilleri*, vol. 2, *Beyazid devri kanunnâmeleri* (Istanbul: Fey Vakfı Yayınları, 1990), 128-34.

4. For facsimile, transliteration, and concise interpretation of *Kavanin-i yeniçeriyan*, see Ahmet Akgündüz, *Osmanlı Kanunnâmeleri ve Hukukî Tahlilleri*, vol. 9, *Ahmet Devri Kanunnameleri* (Istanbul: Fey Vakfı Yayınları, 1990), 127-367.

5. Hakan Erdem, *Slavery in the Ottoman Empire and Its Demise, 1800-1909* (London: Macmillan, 1996), 19-20.

6. Palmer, "Origins of the Janissaries," 464.

7. P. Wittek, "Devshirme and Sharia," *Bulletin of the School of Oriental and African Studies* 17, no. 2 (1955): 276-77.

8. Vryonis gives the translation of the related part of the Capitulations of Galata: "Since the archontes of Galata have sent to the Porte of my domains their honored archontes . . . who did obeisance to my imperial power and became my slaves [he translates *kuls* as slaves], let them (the Genoese) retain their possessions . . . their wives, children, and prisoners at their own disposal. . . . They shall pay neither *commercium* nor *kharaj*. . . . They shall be permitted to retain their churches . . . and *never will I on any account carry of their children or any young man for the Janissary corps*." Speros Vryonis, "Isidore Clabas and the Turkish Devsirme," *Speculum* 3, no. 3 (1956): 440-41 (emphasis in original).

9. Akgündüz, *Osmanlı Kanunnâmeleri:*, 139.

10. Ibid., 138.

11. Ibid., 143.

12. İsmail H. Uzunçarşılı, *Osmanlı devleti teşkilatında kapıkulu ocakları* (Ankara: Türk Tarih Kurumu Basımevi, 1943), 14-15.

13. Ibid., 15.

14. Albert Howe Lybyer, *The Government of the Ottoman Empire in the Time of Suleiman the Magnificent* (Cambridge, MA: Harvard University Press, 1913), 53.

15. *Kavanin-i yeniçeriyan*, 141.

16. Ibid., 141.

17. Apostolos E. Vakalopoulos, *The Greek Nation: 1453-1669: The Cultural and Economic Background of Modern Greek Society*, trans. Ian and Phania Moles (New Brunswick, NJ: Rutgers University Press, 1976), 36-37.

18. Ibid., 138.

19. Uzunçarşılı, Osmanlı devleti, 21.

20. Ibid., 23.

21. İbrahim Emiroğlu, Tarihi dekor içinde özel dersler ve evreleri: Saray eğitimi, padişahların hoca ve lalan (İzmir: Cumhuriyet Matbaası, 1992), 33.

22. Uzunçarşılı, Osmanlı devleti, 2–4. Kapıkulu corps were composed of acemis, yeniceris, cebecis, topçus, and top arabacıs as foot soldiers, and sipah, silahdar, sağ ulufeciler, sağ garipler, and sol garipler as cavalry. To soldiers lağımcıs and humbaracıs were added during the seventeenth century. Devşirmes were posted to any of these regiments.

23. Ülker Akkutay, Enderun mektebi (Ankara: Gazi Üniversitesi Gazi Eğitim Fakültesi, 1984), 127–28.

24. "Fifty agchas had the value of one Venetian gold ducat." Barnette Miller, The Palace School of Muhammad the Conqueror (Cambridge, MA: Harvard University Press, 1982), 102–3, 128–29.

25. N. M. Penzer, The Harem (London: George G. Harrap, 1936).

26. Ibid., 134.

27. Miller, Palace School, 123.

28. Kavanin-i yeniçeriyan, 137.

29. Uzunçarşılı, Osmanlı devleti, 24.

30. Ignatius Mouradgea d'Ohsson, Tableau général de l'empire othoman, vol. 7, L'état actuel de l'empire othoman (Paris: Firmin Didot,1824), 327.

31. Kavanin-i yeniçeriyan, 156.

32. Menage, "Notes on Devşirme," 66–67.

33. Metin Kunt, "Ethnic-Regional (Cins) Solidarity in the Seventeenth-Century Ottoman Establishment," International Journal of Middle East Studies 5, no. 3 (1974): 238.

34. John Kingsley Birge, The Bektashi Order of Dervishes (London: Luzac Oriental, 1994), 75.

35. Suraiya Faroqhi, Anadolu'da bektaşilik (Istanbul: Simurg Kitabevi, 2003), 139.

36. Ibid., 140.

37. Louis Massignon, "La légende de Hallace Mansur en pays turcs," Revue des Études Islamiques (1941–46).

38. Louis Massignon, The Passion of al-Hallaaāj, Mystic and Martyr of Islam, trans. Herbert Mason, 3 vols. (Princeton: Princeton University Press, 1982), 2:254.

39. Tahsin Özcan, Osmanlı para vakıfları: Kanuûnii dönemi Üsküdar örneği (Ankara: Türk Tarih Kurumu, 2003), 85–86.

40. Murat Çizakca, "Cash Waqfs of Bursa, 1555–1823," Journal of the Economic and Social History of the Orient 38, no. 3 (1995): 313–54.

41. Although the economic and social involvement of janissaries in urban life is stressed by modern scholarship, it would not be wrong to assume that the same process was experienced in other regiments as well, as with cebecis in fortress cities.

42. Cemal Kafadar, "On the Purity and Corruption of the Janissaries," Turkish Studies Association Bulletin 15, no. 2 (Spring 1991), 275–76.

43. Halil İnalcık, "Military and Fiscal Transformation in the Ottoman Empire (1600–1700)," Archivum ottomanicum 6 (1980), 283–339.

44. Eunjeon Yi, Guild Dynamics in Seventeenth Century Istanbul (Leiden: Brill, 2004).

45. Şerif Mardin, "Freedom in an Ottoman Perspective," in *State, Democracy, and the Military: Turkey in the 1980s*, ed. Metin Heper and Ahmet Evin (Berlin: W. de Gruyter), 29.

46. *"Ehl-i Islamın kuvve-i asabiyesine zaaf geldi."* Christoph K. Neumann, *Araç tarih amaç Tanzimat: Tarih-i Cevdet'in siyasi anlamı*, trans. Meltem Arun (Istanbul: Tarih Vakfı Yurt Yayınları, 2000), 122.

47. Şerif Mardin, "Freedom."

48. Cengiz Kırlı, "Kahvehaneler ve hafiyeler: 19. yüzyıl ortalarında Osmanlı'da sosyal kontrol," *Toplum ve bilim* 83 (2000): 58-79. Kırlı mentions that by the nineteenth century there were approximately one thousand coffeehouses in the neighborhoods of Eyüp and Hasköy and another thousand on the European side of the Bosporous. According to the registers of the artisan inspectors (*esnaf yoklama defterleri*), one shop in seven was a coffeehouse, and one-third of these coffeehouses belonged to janissaries. Moreover, half the janissaries who dealt with small businesses ran coffeehouses.

49. Erdem, *Slavery*, 6.

50. Menage, "Freedom," 66. Households were an important characteristic shaping the Ottoman elite, which reached its full form after the reign of Sultan Suleyman I (1520-66). A household mainly comprised a household head and those under his patronage, regardless of kinship ties. The most important household in Ottoman society was the imperial household. Those who enjoyed the patronage of the sultan were not only the domestic members from the kitchens, gardens, or women's quarters, but also the military members such as the pages, the students of the training school, and the guards. For more detailed information on households, see Jane Hathaway, *The Politics of Households in Ottoman Egypt: The Rise of the Qazdaglis* (Cambridge: Cambridge University Press, 1997), 18-19.

51. Ehud R. Toledano, "The Concept of Slavery in Ottoman and Other Muslim Societies," in *Slave Elites in the Middle East and Africa: A Comparative Study*, ed. Miura Toru and John Edward Philips (London: Kegan Paul International, 2000), 164; Metin Kunt, " Kulların Kulları," *Boğaziçi üniversitesi dergisi* 3 (1975): 27-42.

52. Toledano, "Concept of Slavery," 167.

53. Koçi Bey, *Koçi bey risalesi*, ed. Zuhuri Danışman (Ankara: Kültür ve Turizm Bakanlığı, 1985), 9; Lewis Thomas, A *Study of Naima*, ed. Norman Itzkowitz (New York: New York University Press, 1972), 9, 20-22.

54. Kunt, "Ethnic-Regional Solidarity," 236.

55. Ibid., 237.

56. Ibid.

57. Karen Barkey, *Bandits and Bureaucrats: The Ottoman Route to State Centralization* (Ithaca: Cornell University Press, 1994), 48.

58. Knud J. V. Jespersen, "Social Change and Military Revolution in Early Modern Europe: Some Danish Evidence," *Historical Journal* 26, no. 1 (1983): 2; Clifford J. Rogers, ed., *The Military Revolution Debate: Readings on the Military Transformation of Early Modern Europe* (Boulder: Westview, 1995).

59. Virginia Aksan, "Mutiny and the Eighteenth Century Ottoman Army," *Turkish Studies Association Bulletin* 22, no. 1 (1998): 117.

60. Rhoads Murphey, "Kanun-name-i sultani li Aziz Efendi (Aziz Efendi's Book of Sultanic Laws and Regulations: An Agenda for Reform by a Seventeenth-Century Ottoman

Statesman)," *Sources of Oriental Languages and Literatures* 9 (1985): 45. The number of janissaries rose from 21,094 in 1574 to 45,000 in 1597 and 47,033 in 1609 (a 123 percent increase). The number of soldiers in six cavalry regiments shifted from 5,957 in 1574, to 17,100 in 1597 and 20,869 in 1609 (a 250 percent increase). The auxiliary troops recruited 2,124 soldiers in 1574 and 7,966 in 1609 (a 275 percent increase). The 6,978 palace staff in 1574 jumped to 10,964 in 1609. The grand total for the military-administrative stratum shifted from 36,153 in 1574 to 86,832 in 1609. The figures are taken for 1574 at the reign of Murad III from Koçi Bey, those for 1597 from Mustafa Ali in his *Künh al-ahbar*, and those for 1609 from Ayn-i Ali in his *Risale*.

61. Metin Kunt, *The Sultan's Servants: The Transformation of Ottoman Provincial Government, 1559–1650* (New York: Columbia University Press, 1983), 35.

62. Ibid., 44.

63. Koçi Bey, *Koçi bey risalesi.*

64. "The reason for their [janissaries] becoming so numerous and for their corruption has been the adoption of the two new recruitment categories of *ibtidadan boluk* and *veledesh* which has allowed entry into the ranks of the cavalrymen of nondescripts, disgraceful Djelali rebels, Turks, men of low character, and city boys." Murphey, *Kanunname-i Sultani*, 7.

65. İnalcık, "Military and Fiscal Transformation," 288.

66. Uzunçarşılı, *Osmanlı devleti*, 144, 167.

67. Kavanin-i yeniçeriyan, 141-43.

# 8

## THE THIRD GENDER

*Palace Eunuchs*

BOK-RAE KIM

Societies using eunuchs have two common characteristics: first, they possess a despotic monarchy and a strong state autocracy, second, they practice polygamy or concubinage. In premodern China concubinage is officially recognized by Confucian ideology. The Forbidden City, home to the Imperial Palace of the Ming and Qing dynasties, was divided into two sections: the inner court, or living quarters, and the outer court, or working area. Only the emperor and his sons lived in the inner court, where three hundred court ladies, including the empress, perfumed the air with their cosmetics. Owing to this temptation (and in order to run a palace household on such a grand scale), it was necessary to employ eunuchs to guard the inner court because they were not "real" men. Their responsibilities were mostly related to the emperor's sexual life. A eunuch was allowed to carry naked concubines into the emperor's bedroom on his back or to give a lady who had won the emperor's favor an imperial gift.[1]

One would expect that no man would be more melancholy than a sexually impotent one; yet people without physical defects or disabilities emasculated themselves. It was the avenue to power, as was shown when eunuchs ruined the Qin dynasty (221–206 BC), dethroning three emperors and killing four. They also enthroned a total of seven rulers during the three hundred years of the Tang dynasty (618–907). In Korea a eunuch named Man-saeng Choe assassinated King Kongmin (r. 1351–74) of the Koryo dynasty (918–1392).[2] The mystery is how such a strange group came into being and harnessed such power. If the eunuch system was a necessary practice of so-called Oriental despotism, why did it not exist in Japan? What alternate system existed there? In order to answer these questions, the origins and practice of the system must be examined. We must compare the recruitment and functions of Korean eunuchs with those of their Chinese counterparts.

## THE FIRST EUNUCHS

Chinese scholars presumed that eunuchs existed before the Zhou dynasty (1046–221 BC) on the basis of the Zhouli (Rites of the Zhou), which contain the first historical record of the eunuch system. According to the Zhouli, the emperor had "one queen, three madams, nine concubines, twenty-seven varied ranks of consorts, and eighty-one court ladies." These women all had to be guarded by eunuchs.[3] In this book, Zhou Gong describes castration as a form of severe punishment ranking somewhere between amputation and decapitation. Castrated prisoners were kept as palace servants. Oracle bone ( jiagu) inscriptions found among the relics of Wu Ding (Martial IV, China's first historic ruler) are the oldest known documentation of a eunuch system, dating to around the thirteenth century BC, during the Shang dynasty (1600–1046 BC). According to the hieroglyphs, King Wu Ding was interested in knowing whether he could make captive Western Barbarians, called qiangren, into eunuchs.[4] Even though the castration of prisoners has existed since prehistoric days, it is difficult to say for certain whether or not the eunuch system was firmly established as an institution during the Shang period.

In Korea eunuchs were variously referred to as nae-si (Chinese, nei-shi), hwan-kwan (huan-guan), or hwa-ja (huo-zhe). During the later Koryo period, the Chinese eunuch system was introduced into Korea under the influence of the Yuan dynasty (1271–1368), which ruled the Korean peninsula for close to one hundred years. In the beginning the nae-sis were government officers charged with secretarial tasks and serving as a royal guard for the king; they had no relation to castrated males. A maximum of twenty good-looking men suited for the civil service were selected. Gradually, the number increased, augmented by the children of powerful families and successful candidates for the civil service examination.[5] The Korean nae-si system was limited in the beginning, but became grotesque during the Yuan dynasty, when castrated eunuchs were offered as tribute. A Mongol princess married to the Koryo king Chungyol (r. 1274–1308) dedicated the Korean eunuch Su-myong to the first Mongol emperor of China, Shizu (Qubilai Qan, r. 1260–94).[6] Thereafter, the demands of the Yuan dynasty (1206/79–1368) for Korean eunuchs as tribute became excessive. With this heightened demand for Korean eunuchs, a surgical method of castration was introduced.

(Before that, castration had been accomplished by dog bite.) In general, Korean eunuchs succeeded in winning the Yuan royal family's favor. They were then redispatched as special envoys to Koryo. The government was often obliged to grant them the title of prince. Their families, and even their remote relatives, also enjoyed greater influence. As a result a father would castrate his son, or an elder brother his younger brother, as becoming a eunuch at the Yuan court was considered to be a golden opportunity for success.

In Korea the office of eunuchs was first established in the fifth year of King Kongmin's reign (1355). Before that, a minority of eunuchs were engaged in miscellaneous services without belonging to a government office. With this "institutionalization," eunuchs were now given important posts in the royal court. They gained power through proximity to the king and began to intervene in politics and seize sizable estates. Under the last king, Kongyang (r. 1389-92), the number of eunuchs reached one hundred. After the collapse of the Koryo dynasty, the office of eunuchs was inherited almost intact by the Chosun dynasty (1392-1910). Their numbers increased to 240, with fifty-nine receiving an official rank.[7] Although most of the evil practices seen during the Koryo period vanished, eunuchs continued to make their fortunes by attending the king and queens.

## THE RECRUITMENT OF EUNUCHS

It is not known for certain when castration began in China, but it was one of the five punishments during the Han period (206 BC–AD 220), along with decapitation, cutting off the nose, cutting off the heel, and tattooing the crime on the face. In two particular periods, the Qin (221-206 BC) and Han dynasties, castrated prisoners acted as the main source for new eunuchs. It was only under the Sui dynasty (581-618) that castration was completely abolished. In the Sui or Tang (618-907) periods, only volunteers could be selected. Nevertheless, a few eunuchs were still recruited from among the ranks of condemned criminals, neighboring barbarians (as tribute), prisoners of war, foreigners, and so on.[8]

Most so-called self-castrated eunuchs—those deliberately castrated for their political or social advancement—were castrated in early childhood through the will of their parents rather than their own. Parents might tightly bind the genitals of their newborn son with a silk thread. The part below the knot would then die and eventually fall off.[9]

In front of the western gate to the Forbidden City there was a building where several "knifers," recognized by the government as qualified to perform castrations, ran their businesses. The existence of these professionals proved there was a significant demand for eunuchs. A male candidate was tied to an operating table and was asked one last time if he would ever regret being castrated. If the candidate had no doubts, both penis and testicles were swiftly cut off as close as possible to the body with a small curved knife.[10]

The main supply center of eunuchs was located in the southern part of China. At the end of the Ming dynasty (1568–1644) there were one hundred thousand eunuchs and nine thousand court ladies. Some scholars estimate the total number of eunuchs during the Shang and Qing dynasties to have been around 10 million.[11]

In Korea not many sexually impotent or castrated males were available, unlike China, where the palace eunuch system was fully developed. Additionally, there is no literature that explains exactly how palace eunuchs were recruited in Korea. According to the vague testimonies of descendants of eunuchs, their ancestors had become eunuchs by accident. For example, being bitten by a dog during childhood. U-chol Yi divides eunuchs into four categories: involuntary eunuchs, accidental eunuchs, congenital eunuchs, and self-castrated eunuchs.[12] He pays particular attention to the latter category (which includes what he calls semi-self-castrated eunuchs). In the *Koryo-sa* (History of Koryo, 1452) self-castration is mentioned but the method of the castration is not; probably castration was considered taboo.[13] Voluntary castration was primarily limited to the lower classes. This included *nobis* (slaves), who underwent self-castration to escape poverty, the extortion of local officers, the domination of owners of nobi, or military service. Unlike in China, castration was never instituted as a form of punishment in Korea. This complicated the recruitment of eunuchs. Jae-ryun Cheong records that when he was young, he heard the following statements from several old eunuchs. "There was a noble [yangban] boy with underdeveloped genital organs. A eunuch adopted him as his child."

The adoptive system was also used to recruit eunuchs, especially during the Chosun dynasty (1392–1910). According to Chosun adoptive law, it was customary to adopt a child with the same family name. However, the Chosun government permitted eunuchs to adopt a child with a different family name, to prevent the extinction of their lineage. The *Kyongguk taejon* (Complete Code of National Law, 1470) prescribed that a child adopted by the eunuch class should be under three years old, but that rule was not strictly enforced.[14] There are many cases of eunuchs adopting intrinsically impotent or postnatally castrated boys (or occasionally normal boys) as their heirs. For instance, under the reign of King Sejong (1418–50) the eunuch Yong-gi Kim raised a child from infancy and made him a palace eunuch. Under the reign of King Myongjong (1545–67), the number of baby eunuchs dramatically increased, causing political tension. At times there were as many as four or five adopted baby eunuchs per person, doubling the expenditure of the royal warehouse.[15] A shortage of eunuchs could also create political tension. Under the reign of King Songjong (1469–94), an ordinance was promulgated prohibiting the raising of baby eunuchs within the residence of high- or middle-ranking government officials. The ordinance prevented private individuals from keeping baby eunuchs as domestic nobis in order to meet the royal court's demand for eunuchs. This form of prohibition was then repeated. According to the *Daejonheotong* (Final Code of National Law), in 1865 there were ninety baby eunuchs in the royal court.[16] It is thus probable that eunuchs were recruited by simply bringing up adopted baby eunuchs in the court. Rich and powerful eunuchs often enjoyed the benefits of their high positions. For example, they could adopt several children. In addition, some had wives and even concubines. Their colleagues who had neither children nor spouses looked upon them with envy.

Unlike their Chinese counterparts, Korean eunuchs were said to have sexual relations. In many cases of self-castration, only the testicles were cut off, leaving the penis intact. Thus, although a man's generative power quickly died away, sexual intercourse was said to be possible for some time. According to the *Diary of Prince Yonsan* in 1507, there were love affairs between eunuchs and court ladies. In such cases, the guilty parties were expelled from the royal palace.[17] It is not known exactly whether the men whose sexual power remained intact were false or authentic eunuchs. In the event, eunuchs were occasionally obliged to take their pants off in public to provide physical proof. In this respect, the Korean eunuch system was nonsystematic and somewhat vague in comparison to the Chinese system.

## THE FUNCTIONS OF EUNUCHS

In the beginning, Korean eunuchs usually engaged in various petty works at court. However, as they took the place of the nae-sis (precursor form of eunuchs), they progressively took over their former duties. Those duties can be divided into six categories: administration of the royal harem and concubines, public works, transmission of royal orders, inspection of the loss of crops or the condition of people (as a special envoy dispatched to the provinces by royal order), protection of the crown prince, and administration of the office for hunting with hawks or breeding them.

In both Korea and China the supreme ruler tended to have as many wives and concubines as possible, though their number was often subject to certain restrictions, primarily due to financial problems. According to the encyclopedia *Tongdian* (Comprehensive Manual), written by a minister of the Tang dynasty, Du You (735–812), the emperor had four wives, four being a sacred number that symbolized the four cardinal directions. During the Shang dynasty, the number of wives and concubines increased to thirty-nine. Under the Zhou dynasty their number increased to 121, which was proportionate to the extension of royal authority during that time.[18] Assuming that a single concubine would have twenty-five lady attendants on average, the total number of court ladies could exceed three thousand. This number seemed too much for one man, even though it may have included many older women whose beauty may have faded. It also cost a great deal. The emperor, called the Son of Heaven, under the pretext of having as many heirs as possible, had many wives and concubines. The practice of polygamy, however, often led to quite contrary results. There are many examples in which those emperors who overindulged in carnal pleasures ended up injuring their health and dying at a young age without leaving any successors, and this led to political disorder.

Moreover, the history of the imperial harem was far from romantic and quite devoid of common sense. Each concubine had a green nameplate. After the emperor finished dinner, the chief eunuch would offer him a score of nameplates on a silver tray. If the emperor put a nameplate upside down, the concubine could serve him that night. However, without the consent of the empress, whose seal was needed on the document in which the name of the concubine was recorded, even the emperor could not have his way. The exercise of this veto depended not only on the empress's mood or health but also on the power of her clan, that is, the status of her family. Even with the approval of the empress, the emperor could spend only a limited time with his chosen concubine. The duration of the visit varied according to periods and dynasties but, generally speaking, it ranged from two to four hours. When the fixed time came to an end, the chief eunuch would announce loudly, "Time is up!" If the concubine failed to come out, or if she or the emperor were unduly stubborn, the eunuch would remove her from the emperor's bedroom by force.[19] According to this example, it seems that eunuchs were quite powerful. In accordance with the emperor's special order, the eunuch would document the visitation as a form of proof. If not, he took measures to prevent conception. Thus, the emperor's ex post facto indication in the form of a gift bestowed as a pledge of affection if the concubine greatly pleased him was for concubines a matter of primary concern, as the status of a concubine depended on whether she could give birth to a son or not. Using this process, some eunuchs once more exhibited their trickery. They modulated the length of the visitation, which could vary to some degree, according to their whim.

Taking advantage of their proximity to the supreme ruler both day and night, eunuchs ingeniously manipulated him. If the emperor was not clever, he would be like a marionette in their hands. If he was clever they were convenient instruments that operated according to his direction. However, with time the system gradually expanded. In proportion to their octopuslike expansion, the eunuchs' institutional and politico-economical power increased. Even though they suffered through massacres and harsh retrenchments of their organization, their inscrutable power as an eccentric castrated group permitted them several times to win key positions in government.

In Korea the first precise documents on royal concubines appeared during the Koryo dynasty. The Korean royal concubine system was a miniature of the Chinese one, but the rank of Korean concubines was nonetheless equal to that of their Chinese counterparts during the Koryo period. The founder of the Koryo dynasty, Wang Kon (r. 918–943), had no less than six queens and more than twenty madams. Through politically expedient marital arrangements and settlements he won over powerful family clans and meritorious subjects.[20] In the Chosun period, under the ideology of *sadae*, or serving the Great (toadyism)—which was instrumental in shaping both Korea's foreign policy and cultural identity—the title given to the king's legitimate spouse deteriorated to that of queen consort. Royal concubines were granted the official rank of court ladies. According to the *Kyongguk taejon* (Complete Code of National Law), the office of court ladies (*naemyongbu*) comprised not only the court ladies charged with miscellaneous services and administration but all royal concubines.

Court ladies were chosen from among the four-to-five-year-old daughters of *yangban* (noble) families to receive training in court manners and etiquette. Court ladies were highly disciplined. They could not marry any male except the king, and their dress, ornamentation, and salary differed according to their position or class. Their average salary is estimated to be around 240 (old) Korean won during the middle of the Chosun dynasty (approximately 1.5 million won today). Even a lady's maid-of-all-work was granted either the ninth rank of government office (which was nominal) or funeral expenses for her parents and herself. It is not surprising that eunuchs or court ladies serving the king and his royal concubines received such preferential treatment. According to an old Korean proverb, "If you wear your skirt wrong-side-out, you will come into unexpected fortune."[21] This proverb originated from the tradition of the royal harem. If a court lady who managed to attract the king's attention by chance succeeded in sleeping with him, she received the fourth rank of naemyongbu. For the following few days, she should wear her skirt wrong side out. This odd behavior was to publicly show that she had taken off her skirt. In other words, nobody but the king could now take off her skirt. This was viewed by the outside world as a token of royal favor. Most court ladies, those who could not receive the king's favor, were expected to live and die as virgins. Court eunuchs were best suited to protect the purity of all court ladies, and to enforce the strict court laws placed upon them. Since the private life of kings was nothing but a history of the royal harems, that made placing eunuchs in charge of the royal harem a necessity.

By royal order eunuchs also engaged in construction work. The eunuch Sa-haeng Kim (d. 1398), for example, took a very active part in palace construction. In 1357, under the reign of King Kongmin (r. 1351–74), Kim began construction of the royal palace. This led to an exhaustion of Korea's resources and widespread economic distress. As soon as King U (r. 1374–88) procured the throne, Kim's fortune was confiscated as he was charged with starting the large-scale public work by deceiving the assassinated King Kongmin with flattery. This was followed by his exile as a public nobi (slave). He was released and rehabilitated in 1391, under the reign of King Kongyang (1389–92). After the foundation of the Chosun dynasty, he succeeded in winning the favor of the first king, King Taejo (r. 1392–98). The king ordered him to survey land in order to construct an ancestral shrine for the royal family, an altar to the state deities, a royal palace, market, towns, and so on. During the first rebellion of princes, Kim was charged with conspiracy and decapitated. His head was displayed as a warning to the people.[22] Thereafter, the responsibility for public work was assumed by civil officials, though they were still accompanied by eunuchs. During the reign of King Taejong (1400–1418), the eunuch Yu-chi Kyom supervised construction of the main building of the palace by royal order. During the reign of Prince Yonsan (1494–1506), the eunuch Ja-won Kim constructed the residence of a princess and won the king's favor.[23] It is clear that Korean eunuchs were actively engaged in the construction of royal palaces, temples, and various other public works embodying the authority and prestige of the king.

Aside from such duties as guarding the royal gate, cleaning, and cooking, the eunuch's most important responsibility was the transmission of royal orders. Officially, this was the responsibility of the royal secretariat (sung-jongwon), but in reality it was through the office of the nae-sis (eunuchs) that documents were transmitted to and from the king. When a censor-general advised the king verbally, for example, the chief secretary would dictate this to the eunuch again, and then the latter would report it to his majesty. Through the use of two- to threefold reports, a biased interpretation could be obtained by the eunuchs. During the reign of King Sejong, on account of problems during the transmission of royal orders, the king separated the duties of the royal secretariat from those of the office of the censor-general (the Saganwon). Charging the censor-general with the transmission of royal orders, he ordered that all reports be in written form and that all officials' opinions be announced through the royal secretariat without transmitting them directly to eunuchs. However, most officials preferred giving an oral report to a eunuch rather than giving it in written form by way of a secretary.[24] King Munjong (r. 1450-52) thus made it a rule to report all opinions through the royal lecture sessions held between king and subjects.[25] In theory there were six secretaries reporting directly to him, but these rules were not observed in practice. Gradually, the eunuchs assumed responsibility for the transmission of royal orders. Under this system of informal politics, personal relationships and informal networks played an important role behind the scenes, while often also providing the basis for factional politics. The shadow power of eunuchs who secured information grew and contributed in part to King Sejo's coup d'état in 1455. As in China, the main reason eunuchs in Korea could hold power was that they were able to play a part in deciding the succession to the throne.

Beyond these functions, the eunuchs also acted as the king's special envoys. This role involved the inspection of crop loss, flood damage control, and monitoring the condition of starving people within the provinces. The eunuchs investigated not only natural disasters but also the diligence of local governors. However, documents indicating this are found only from the early Chosun period. If the Chinese demanded virgins as a tribute, or if the Korean royal family was selecting a spouse for a prince, eunuchs were also dispatched to look for suitable candidates. During the reign of King Taejong, for example, the virgins selected by the eunuch Um Hwang were criticized as "too plain."[26] Thus, the king redispatched the inspectors of the provinces to be accompanied by a different eunuch. During the early Chosun period, the eunuchs took part in the selection of the crown princesses, but under the reign of King Songjong this role passed to civil officers. Also, the protection of a crown prince by eunuchs was a target of criticism among officials, including ministers. During the reign of Taejong, the bureaucrats of the Saganwon admonished the king to separate the prince from his eunuchs: "A group of eunuchs was bent on currying favor with the young prince. Thus, it is necessary to keep the flattering eunuchs at a distance." The king reportedly replied, "Your demands are entirely right. But the eunuchs undertake the cleaning of the royal court, so I could not abolish them."[27] Several eunuchs brought up young princes or princesses within their own homes. For instance, under the reign of Yejong (1468-69) the eunuch Kyun Chon raised the crown prince in his house. And because he had assisted the young prince, the eunuch Jung-kyong An was able to secure a high government position for his brother. The famous eunuch Han-jong Park also reared a crown prince and received many bribes as a result.[28]

The administration of hunting with hawks and breeding them was one of the main tasks of the eunuchs. These activities became especially important as the Yuan dynasty increasingly demanded hawks as tribute. The hawk was necessary not only for the tribute, but also for the king's hunt. Under the reign of King Sejong, the eunuch Duk-bu Yun, a trainer of hawks, practiced extortion in the province of Hamkil under the pretext of investigating the conditions for hawk-hunting. The eunuch Jon Chong became a high-ranking officer due to his great hawk-training skill.[29] Eunuchs also engaged in memorial services for ancestors and the maintenance of the royal family shrines. After the death of the king some eunuchs became guardians of the royal tomb. From the cradle to the tomb, the eunuchs took charge of their king's public and private life.

## JAPAN'S LACK OF A EUNUCH SYSTEM

Several hypotheses attempt to answer why the eunuch system did not exist in Japan. First, unlike other European and Asian countries, Japan was not subject to foreign rule. In fact, the Japanese had little contact with the outer (soto) world before the open-door policy created by the Meiji reform of 1868. Thus, on the Japanese archipelago there were no foreign prisoners, presumed to be the first object of castration in other societies. Second, Japanese society depended essentially on the growing of cereal crops. Therefore, the culture of animal castration was unfamiliar to them. Third, a system of absolute (or despotic) monarchy was not established in Japan. Finally, the Japanese have seldom engaged in wars with foreign countries. Although they fought fiercely among themselves, the nation's ethnic homogeneity was so strong that all members were administrated under the dominance of inner (uchi) logic, in spite of a rigid social hierarchy based on the norms of domination-obedience.[30]

The eunuch system never existed on the Japanese archipelago, but did a similar system exist in its place? The Japanese king is called tenno (emperor); however, the position of the tenno lost much of its political power with the advent of the samurai shogunates. After the Meiji reform the offspring of a concubine could no longer become a member of the royal family.[31] In the Heian period (794–1192), the civil officers guarded the entrance to the emperor's royal harem, but any man with a royal permit was allowed free access to it; this was quite different from the case in China, Korea, or even

Japan in the later period of the Tokugawa shogunate. According to *Nihon shoki* (Chronicle of Japan), the office of *nai-ju* (eunuchs) existed as early as the middle of the Nara period (710–94). In the memorial to Chinese empress Wu Zetian (r. 690–705), during the Tang period, it was recorded that the nai-ju worked at the royal harem.[32] However, it appears that the Japanese nai-ju were not castrated. For example, among nai-jus the renowned litterateur Oumi no Mifune (722–85) and the brave warrior Takakura Fukunobu were not only married but sired many children. Thus, the *nai* (inside) *ju* (boy) was merely a boy with disheveled hair rather than a eunuch. Probably due to Japanese social repugnance regarding castration, the nai-ju class was not composed of castrated eunuchs but of (still sexually immature) errand boys engaged in miscellaneous services around the royal harem.

As the emperor's authority was merely symbolic during the twelfth century, true national power rested with the leading vassal of the emperor, the shogun. If we consider the Japanese royal harem, it is much better to examine the *ooku*, the shogun's exclusive harem. It was not until the establishment of the Tokugawa shogunate that the Japanese royal harem was institutionalized by Kasuga no Tsubone, who was the nurse of Iemitsu Tokugawa (r. 1623–51), the third shogun during the Edo (or Tokugawa) period (1603–1868). The women of the ooku were charged with guarding the royal court at all times, without relying on eunuchs. These women were divided into twenty-seven different ranks, each with a different salary. Women of ranks one to twenty were called *ome mie*.[33] They were allowed the honor of meeting the shogun and his legal wife. In theory, they had to work twenty-four hours a day, seven days a week, 365 days a year. But the maids in the ranks below twenty could not only take holidays once a year but could also quit their jobs with permission. These low-ranking maids were mostly commoners.

Serving in the ooku was not only a great family honor but a guarantee for good marriage. To enter the ooku required three qualifications: personal connections, wealth, and pleasant physical appearance. Special agents designated by the ooku were responsible for recommending ooku candidates from within the country. There was serious competition among these agents to discover beautiful and talented women of good pedigree because the promotion and power of the ladies they recommended was directly linked to the agents' wealth and power. However, these women, with the exception of the shogun's favorites, were partnerless—although on occasion a select few were lucky enough to wear their skirts wrong side out, as in Korea. That said, almost all women except the general maids were forbidden to have contact with men. With the exception of a rare group viewing of Kabuki, they remained in an entirely women's world. This extreme sexual repression led to two distorted outlets. One was autoeroticism or lesbianism. The other was the smuggling of a man inside a crate bound for the ooku. Later, such practices became open secrets. Even the shogun deliberately overlooked them, fearing a strong reaction from the ooku. The seventh shogun, Ie Tsugu, who died as a child, was too young to take an interest in the ooku. Seizing this opportunity, a court lady (Eshima) fell in love with an actor. With momentum from this scandal, the splendor, extravagance, decadence, and political power of the ooku was soundly attacked by the tight-money policy launched under the initiative of Arai Hakuseki (1657–1725), chief counselor to the sixth shogun. At that time, around fifteen hundred persons of the ooku were executed, condemned to exile, or ousted from their position by the system of guilt by association. In a sense, Eshima was a scapegoat for the ooku purge-through-retrenchment policy. After the great purge, the Kansei (1787–93) and Tembo reforms (1841–43) were carried out by regent-minister Matsudaira Sadanobu (1758–1829), and later by Mizuno Tadakuni (1794–1851), to reverse the decline of Tokugawa through restructuring finance, enacting a sumptuary law, and controlling public morals.[34] The stronger the retrenchment policy became, the greater the reaction from the ooku. The reforms failed due to pressure from the ooku, and Mizuno was removed from office. Even the rulers of the shogunate were unable to reform. There seemed to be a common thread between the eunuchs and the women at the ooku, the latter having substituted for the former.

Korean eunuchs would not have appeared on the historical stage if the yoke of Mongolian rule had not been imposed on the Korean peninsula for over a hundred years. During the intervention period of the Yuan dynasty, Korean-Japanese diplomatic relations nearly reached a standstill. Thus, there was (fortunately) no political background with which the Chinese custom could be transplanted onto the isolated Nihon archipelago.

So, if the eunuch system is supposed to be a byproduct of so-called Oriental despotism, let us consider it within this context. In China it is rumored that the eunuchs stemmed from the jealousy of the Chinese people, but the eunuch system was more closely linked to power than to psychology. It is said that appetite comes from eating. Anyone coming into power aspires to have absolute power and to maintain it permanently, if possible. By avoiding presenting himself openly, a leader begins to be deified, making his body sacred and inviolable. However, a king ruling over an entire country could not be completely separated from the everyday world. An unchallenging, asexual mediator was needed. The mediator could not be a real man, hence the neutral eunuch. For example, entering the Buddhist priesthood requires becoming newly born, transforming oneself into a being different from other worldly men. Thus, the monk has his head shaved as a token of otherness or transcendence. In premodern Japan the physician attending the emperor in royal court had to have his hair shaved, in order to examine the sacred and inviolable body of a royal family member without violating such a sanctuary. In a sense, this shaven physician was not a human being, but an outer being.[35] In any period, the power holder is in need of close associates devoted to him and in whom he can put his confidence. In the early stages of the Ming dynasty (1368-1644) people called the eunuch *huozhe,* from the Hindu *khoja* (castrated man), implying that many eunuchs were imported from India. Indeed, the Yongle (Everlasting Joy) emperor (r. 1402-24) was surrounded by a variety of foreign eunuchs (Koreans, Mongols, Annamese, Arabians, etc.).[36] In Islamic countries neither black nor white eunuchs were uncommon. Foreign eunuchs were in fact quite welcome. They seemed more appropriate to keep the despotic monarch's secrecy, dignity, and sacredness. There were, of course, many Chinese eunuchs, like Sima Qian (145-86 BC), involved in composing the *Shiji* (Records of the Grand Scribe). Most of these eunuchs were prisoners whose punishment was castration. There was a gradual increase, though, in the number of self-castrated eunuchs, so as to be exempt from corvée or to attain greater wealth and power.

Surgical castration was extremely dangerous. Somewhere between one-fifth and one-half of all candidates died during or shortly after surgery. Nevertheless, the voluntary castrati who overcame the dangers and difficulties stubbornly clung to wealth and power. During the recruitment of palace eunuchs in 1621, the second year of the Ming emperor Tianqi (r. 1621-28), about twenty thousand candidates flooded the gates of the Forbidden City.[37] In a sense, there was a connection between the emperor, who was a solitary being despite his limitless power, and the eunuchs, who were also alienated from society.

Since the reign of the Yongle emperor, eunuchs were responsible for the network of espionage under the emperor's direct control and for secretly administering the firearms belonging to the military. The large-scale appointment of (inner) eunuchs during the Ming period was partly due to the emperor's distrust of (outer) bureaucratic officials. Shih-shan Henry Tsai writes, "The Ming eunuchs were not just household servants hewing wood and drawing water. They actually made up a 'third administrative hierarchy,' participating in all of the most essential matters of the dynasty."[38] In China the eunuch system was used by the distrustful leaders to hold the bureaucrats in check.

For the eunuchs who served the king as tools, acquiring royal confidence was imperative if they were to gain a high position. Thus, some cunning eunuchs paved their career paths by successfully separating the emperor from politics. In the farewell speech of the Tang eunuch Zi-liang Chou, who wielded considerable power while serving six successive emperors, the key to success was in blinding the emperors through a life of debauchery.[39] There was no quota for eunuchs. Their numbers increased or decreased according to their emperor's mandate. The more debauched the emperor's sexual life, the greater the number of eunuchs. The founder of the Song dynasty (r. 960-975) limited the number of eunuchs to fifty by imperial order, but by the end of the dynasty (960-1279) their number had increased to 180. In the early Ming period, the number of eunuchs is estimated to have been less than one hundred, but their number had reached seventy thousand in Beijing. If we add to this figure those eunuchs owned by (feudal) princes in Nanjing and in other provinces, the number would have been over one hundred thousand, a situation the Qing emperor Kangxi (1661-1722) deplored: "in the Ming period the number of court ladies reached ninety thousand, and that of eunuchs, one hundred thousand. Some of them died of starvation." The Qing emperor Shunzhi (r. 1644-61), who died of smallpox, left a will abolishing the eunuch system. However, like a phoenix, the eunuch system soon revived, and the number of eunuchs reached 2,866. However, in 1911, when the last emperor, Xuantong (r. 1909-11), abdicated the throne, they numbered only eight hundred.[40]

At the end of the Koryo period, the eunuch system was institutionalized in Korea under Chinese influence before and after the fourteenth century. Unlike China, Korea did not have "shadow cabinets" like the Dong Chang and Xi-Chang, which were composed of eunuchs and exercised virtually unlimited power. As a result, Korean eunuchs seem to have been far less destructive than their Chinese counterparts. Nonetheless, their rank was disproportionately high, even in the case of inferior eunuchs engaged in what we now consider menial tasks. Laundrymen, for example, eunuchs of the ninth rank, were equal to the high-ranking inspectors of the Office of the Inspector-General. And even a eunuch in charge of lighting lamps enjoyed an equal rank with accounting inspectors or the chief teachers of Confucianism.

In the premodern political system of both China and Korea, where nepotism and favoritism prevailed, those in closest proximity to the supreme leader possessed the most power. The eunuchs not only kept a vigilant eye on the emperor's bedroom but were the only ones to whom the emperor could lay bare his heart. In compensation for their absolute loyalty, the ruler ranked

TABLE 8.1

## Rank and functions of Korean eunuchs

| Rank | Functions | Number | Notes |
|------|-----------|--------|-------|
| 1 | Preparation of royal meals, banquets, king's ancestor-memorial services, etc. | 2 | Eunuchs from first to fourth rank were charged with the preliminary royal meal testing to guard against poisoning. |
| 2 | Responsible for wine and liquor | 1 | |
| 3 | Responsible for charge of tea | 1 | |
| 4 | Chinese medicine | 1 | |
| 5 | Transmission of royal orders, acting as intermediaries between king and subjects | 2 | |
| 6 | Custody of royal seal and sealing, records on royal-family history (birth, marriage, death, royal harem, concubines, etc.), all kinds of ceremonies. Also responsible for list of books for royal family's reading and its administration | 3 | |
| 7 | Choice and administration of royal clothing, ornaments, other articles (folding screens, chairs, flags for national ceremony, cushions, etc.) | 4 | |
| 8 | Court finances, accounting | 4 | |
| 9 | Laundering, handling, storing of royal clothing | 4 | |
| 10 | Custody of court lighting system | 4 | |
| 11 | Administration of fuel, underfloor heating system (hypocaust) | 4 | |
| 12 | Building and repairs at court | 6 | |
| 13 | Cleaning, extermination of vermin (mosquitoes, flies, fleas, etc.) | 6 | |
| 14 | Operation, guarding of royal gate | 5 | |
| 15 | Night watch, protection, fire prevention | 6 | |
| 16 | Gardening | 5 | |
| | | Total: 58 persons | |

them above all other retainers and subjects. The eunuchs, entrenched with the royal family through their unusual fidelity and devotion, were a necessary evil under a despotic monarchy.

But were premodern China, Korea, or Japan really despotic? The label of Oriental despotism results from applying a Western concept of despotism as repressed individualism. Some Western philosophers have supported a view of China as a despotic state by documenting a lack of individual freedom in China, where accomplishments are attributed to parents, ancestors, and ultimately the emperor; where corporal punishment was common; or where subjects were judged guilty by association. Nonetheless, China—truly the mecca of the eunuch system—viewed from the inside is a traditional but not a despotic culture. The relative absence of individualism is not necessarily perceived as repressive by the Chinese. Under the *Gemeinschaft* (community) characterized by traditional practices and a personal sense of belonging, the relationship between master and servant transcends our contemporary thinking. During the reign of the tyrant Yonsan, there was a loyal old eunuch called Cheo-sun Kim (d. 1505) who attended four different kings. He knew well young Yonsan's violent temper, but at the risk of his life remonstrated several times against the lascivious king's misconduct. In a fit of rage, the prince shot an arrow through his eunuch's heart. However, Kim continued to rail tenaciously, grabbing the arrow lodged in his chest. In a fit of anger Yonsan cut off Kim's legs, and finally his tongue, claiming he was tired of listening to his ardent remonstration. The prince gave his dead body to a tiger, then ordered the demolition of the grave of Kim's parents, and the removal of the Chinese character Cheo in all personal and geographical names.

## NOTES

1. Jun-yop Kim [in Korean], *The Sleeping Lion: A History of the World* (Seoul: Hyunamsa, 1971), 9:112–16.

2. Yong-su Kang [in Korean], *Korean, Chinese, and Japanese Cultures* (Seoul: Nanam, 2000), 257–58.

3. Ibid., 259.

4. Ibid., 259–60; Hee-hung Chang [in Korean], "Research on the Eunuchs during the Chosun Period" (PhD diss., Dongkuk University, 2003), 9.

5. Chang, "Eunuchs," 1.

6. Ibid., 22–23.

7. Ibid., 42–46.

8. Kang, *Korean, Chinese Cultures*, 261–63.

9. Ibid., 264.

10. Mary. M. Anderson, *Hidden Power: The Palace Eunuchs of Imperial China* (Buffalo, NY: Prometheus, 1990), 307–11.

11. Kang, *Korean, Chinese Cultures*, 264.

12. U-chol Yi [in Korean], "The Eunuchs in the Koryo Period," *Historical Research* 1 (1958): 18–23.

13. Chang, "Eunuchs," 3.

14. Ibid., 3–4.

15. Sum Hong et al. [in Chinese], "The Fifty-eighth Year of the Sexagenary Cycle," *Annals of King Myongjong* 33 (1571).

16. Chang, "Eunuchs," 4.

17. Kang, *Korean, Chinese Cultures*, 289.

18. Ibid., 267–68.

19. Ibid., 269–70.

20. Ibid., 293.

21. Ibid., 295.

22. Chang, "Eunuchs," 21-22.

23. Ibid., 23.

24. Bo-in Hwang et al. [in Chinese], "The Twenty-fourth Binary Term of Sexagenary Circle," *Annals of Sejong* 113 (1473).

25. Chang, "Eunuchs," 24.

26. Ibid., 38.

27. Kye-ryang Byon et al., "The Forty-sixth Binary Term of the Sexagenary Cycle," *Annales of Taejong* 7 (1431).

28. Chang, "Eunuchs," 39.

29. Ibid., 40.

30. Ibid., 306-7

31. Ibid., 300.

32. Ibid., 309

33. Ibid., 301

34. Ibid., 303.

35. Ibid., 310.

36. Kim, *Sleeping Lion,* 114-15.

37. Ibid., 115-16.

38. Shih-shan Henry Tsai, *The Eunuchs in the Ming Dynasty* (Albany: State University of New York Press, 1996); Tsai, "Eunuch Power in Imperial China" in *Eunuchs in Antiquity and Beyond,* ed. Shaun Tougher and Raanan Abusch (London: Classical Press of Wales and Duckworth, 2002), 231.

39. Kang, *Korean, Chinese Cultures,* 270.

40. Ibid., 281-84.

# 9

## THE WELL-BEING OF PURCHASED FEMALE DOMESTIC SERVANTS (*MUI TSAI*) IN HONG KONG IN THE EARLY TWENTIETH CENTURY

PAULINE PUI-TING POON

By the early twentieth century, human beings in China had been purchased like a commodity for many centuries. They were wanted for adoption, domestic servitude, marriage, prostitution, and overseas indentured labor. Generally for the Chinese community, the buying and selling of human beings were morally acceptable so long as the transaction was aimed to alleviate the financial difficulty of poverty-stricken families. Filial piety and interest were inherent in the concept of patriarchy—an ingrained social practice of the Chinese. The ideas of individual entity, freedom, and rights were all alien to the Chinese.[1] The purchase of *mui tsai* entailed one such socially justified transaction of human beings.

### THE MUI TSAI SYSTEM

A mui tsai, Cantonese for little sister, was a girl transferred to another family to be a domestic servant. Money was advanced by the prospective master or mistress to the girl's family. A mui tsai seldom received a regular wage, but her master was obliged to provide her with lodging, clothing, and medical care, and to arrange marriage for her when she reached a marriageable age, usually eighteen. If the mui tsai's parents or other family members desired to recover the girl, they had to repay the master the money they received during the transfer.[2] The system, if not abused, saved many surplus daughters

TABLE 9.1

## Major occupations of Chinese in Hong Kong, 1921

| Occupation | Number Engaged |
| --- | --- |
| Coolies (road, cargo, coal) | 30,918 |
| Shop assistants | 16,327 |
| Needlework | 14,392 |
| Cooks | 13,069 |
| Hawkers | 9,142 |
| Mui tsai | 8,653 |
| Carpenters | 8,600 |

TABLE 9.2

## Major occupations of Chinese women in Hong Kong, 1921

| Occupation | Number Engaged |
| --- | --- |
| Needlework | 14,326 |
| Domestic servants | 10,284 |
| Mui tsai | 8,653 |
| Cooks | 4,362 |

whose poverty-stricken parents could not support them from being left to die. It was therefore considered a charitable practice.

The age-old mui tsai system was still prevalent in Hong Kong, as it was in China itself and in Chinese communities abroad, in the late nineteenth and early twentieth centuries. Since mui tsai were seldom paid wages, their masters could come from either wealthy or relatively poor classes. Some of them were wealthy and sold precious Chinese medicines like ginseng and pilose antlers, or owned rice shops, groceries, or charcoal shops; others were shoemakers, blacksmiths, shop assistants, or hairdressers.[3] This implies that the cost of procuring and raising a mui tsai was not high, and by extension, that families who sold their daughters were usually in dire poverty.

According to the census for 1921, the only census containing statistical information about mui tsai in the colony, there were 8,653 mui tsai in Hong Kong, of whom 5,959 were under fourteen years old. Being a mui tsai was one of the most common occupations of the day, both in the Chinese community as a whole and among Chinese females.[4]

Notwithstanding the theoretical moral obligation of masters to look after the girls, some mui tsai were maltreated. In Hong Kong in the early twentieth century, the Po Leung Kuk (Society for the Protection of the Innocents, founded in 1878), the Society for the Prevention of Cruelty to Mui Tsai (1921), and the Anti–Mui Tsai Society (1921) were the main Chinese organizations concentrating on the rescue of maltreated mui tsai. Since the registration of mui tsai was loosely enforced, it is difficult to know how extensive this mistreatment was. But documents in the Po Leung Kuk archives clearly show abuse within the mui tsai system (see table 9.3).[5]

TABLE 9.3

## Types of abuse handled by Po Leung Kuk, early twentieth century

| Nature of abuse | Year | No. of cases |
|---|---|---|
| Masters inflicting gross cruelty on mui tsai | 1901 | 10 |
| | 1923 | 22 |
| | 1929 | 56 |
| | 1930 | 34 |
| Masters reselling or intending to resell mui tsai as prostitutes | 1901 | 3 |
| | 1923 | 2 |
| | 1929 | 3 |
| | 1930 | 2 |
| Girls abducted or decoyed to be sold to other masters as mui tsai or prostitutes | 1901 | 19 |
| | 1923 | 21 |
| | 1929 | 11 |
| | 1930 | 5 |
| Mui tsai sexually harassed by masters or males at workplace | 1923 | 3 |
| | 1929 | 1 |

### THE PO LEUNG KUK

By 1940 a number of ordinances had been enacted that legitimized the work of the Po Leung Kuk against the abuse of the mui tsai system. They included the Offences Against the Person Ordinances of 1865 and 1929, which prohibited kidnapping; the Female Domestic Services Ordinance of 1923, which forbade overwork and gross cruelty to and further employment of mui tsai (as well as its amendment, in 1929, which set up regulations for the registration of mui tsai and their remuneration); and the Ordinance for the Protection of Women and Girls of 1897 and its amendment of 1929, which forbade the kidnapping of females for immoral purposes.

The daily running of the PLK was generally regulated by the Rules for the Society for the Protection of Women and Children (hereafter, the Rules), adopted in 1882, and the Incorporation Ordinance for the Po Leung Kuk (1893).[6] These detailed regulations governed everything from the election of committee members, to the procedures of offering assistance to the destitute, reporting to and seeking advice from the Secretary for Chinese Affairs (SCA; before 1913, the Registrar General), and the appointment of investigative staff. The Incorporation Ordinance also made the SCA the ex-officio president of the board of directors, who monitored the work of the PLK.

From 1880 the Po Leung Kuk employed two special Chinese detectives.[7] Whenever a PLK detective found a suspect, he would first inform the SCA of the case and take the person to the SCA's office. Very often, the SCA sent the victims to the PLK, where they were interviewed by the board of directors.[8] Maltreated mui tsai discovered by the police or the harbormaster's office would also be taken to the SCA's office, which would keep a record of them. Then, they would be referred to the PLK for further investigation.[9] Ordinary people, as revealed by the documents in the PLK archives for 1901, 1923, 1923, and 1940 and the Anti-Mui Tsai Society's annual report for 1930, would also report on abuses (see below).

A mui tsai would be questioned by at least two directors at the PLK about such personal particulars as her family, her living situation, and whether she was willing to reunite with her family.[10] The girls' testimonies were compiled as *Testimonies of the Destitute Staying in the Po Leung Kuk*. In fact, not only the girls, but all persons involved in a case would be questioned by the directors, to ensure that the information obtained was reliable. This was compiled as *Testimonies of Outsiders*, "outsiders" being persons not maintained by the PLK. The directors discussed each case based on the testimonies. If they believed that certain persons had cruelly treated their own mui tsai or were kidnappers, they would suggest that the police or the SCA prosecute them.

To prevent further abuse of the girls, a number of complicated procedures had to be carried out—usually family reunion, adoption, marriage, or restoration to their masters.

If a girl agreed to a family reunion, the PLK might request individuals and institutions in the colony—charitable organizations, shops and firms, chambers of commerce, same-native-place societies—to look for her family members. If the family members resided outside the colony, usually in their hometowns on the mainland, the PLK would turn to the institutions nearest the hometowns for help. Among many such institutions were the Guangren Shantang (Society of Benevolence) in Guangzhou and Wuzhou,

Guangshan Tang (Society of Philanthropy) in Leizhou, the chamber of commerce of Zengcheng, and Kiang Wu Hospital in Macau.

In the nineteenth century, if a mui tsai failed to state clearly her home address, a collaborating institution would post outside the institution and in public places a piece of red paper that contained all important particulars about her.[11] In the twentieth century, the information was published in the vernacular newspapers of the girl's native place.[12] It was hoped that anyone who knew her would contact the institution concerned.

Next, the collaborating institutions or individuals would investigate to verify the parents' identities and whether the girl's interests would be safeguarded if she was restored to her family.[13] The PLK and the investigating parties updated each other on the development of the investigation. Correspondence between them was compiled as *Inbound Correspondence* and *Outbound Correspondence*.[14] Follow-up meetings would be held based on the information at hand. The minutes were compiled as *Records of Events*.[15]

Collecting parties (for example, the girl's parents or relative), once they were determined to be reliable, would be questioned at the PLK about themselves and the mui tsai concerned to preempt any impersonation and to have their identities verified. Finally, the directors would propose to the SCA a family reunion. The girl would be restored to her family upon obtaining the SCA's consent to the recommendation. Collecting parties arriving in the colony from the neighboring regions had to undergo the same procedures.[16]

As a rule, the collecting party had to obtain a surety. In most cases, the guarantor was a shop owner in Hong Kong. Occasionally, land was also accepted.[17] Once both the collecting party and the guarantor were proved trustworthy, they would draw up a guarantee slip at the PLK and the SCA's office respectively, promising that the girl would be properly treated, such as that she would not be retransferred or be subjected to cruel treatment.

Since collecting parties living outside the colony, usually in China, had difficulty getting sureties in Hong Kong, each could find a guarantor in his or her own district, while the girl would be maintained by a charitable organization there. Meanwhile, the institutions and individuals nearest to the collector's and guarantor's district of residence would investigate such details as the background and occupation of the collector and comments on his personality by his neighbors or other acquaintances. Finding both parties honest, the collecting party could pick up the girl at the charitable organization. Both the collecting party and the guarantor would sign a guarantee slip, which eventually would be kept by the PLK.[18]

If the collecting party was found not absolutely trustworthy, he would be required to produce the collected girl before the directors to ensure that he conformed to the pledges he had made in his guarantee.[19] If it was believed that the interests of the girl could barely be safeguarded by family reunion, then adoption or marriage would be recommended.

Some young girls, ranging from four to fourteen years old, were homeless because their parents or close relatives were dead, untraceable, or unreliable. In most of these cases the directors would propose adoption. In general, the adoptive individuals were middle-aged married women who were childless or had given birth to sons only. Their husbands' occupations and financial statuses varied. The men might be shop assistants, seamen, or workers. They were not wealthy but neither were they impoverished. A number owned real estate in their native place. As for widows, they might have a regular source of income derived from the rents of their husband's landed property, or their children had grown up.[20]

If the homeless girls had resided at the PLK for more than three months or even half a year without appropriate adoptive parents coming forth, they would be adopted with prior consent of the SCA by charitable organizations like the Victoria Home and Orphanage of the Church Missionary Society or the Italian Convent run by the Canossian Sisters of the Catholic Church.[21]

Some older girls (fifteen or older) preferred marriage arranged by the PLK.[22] The girls were married only as first wives, not concubines.[23] The *Registers of Marriage and Adoption* reveal that the men wishing to marry the PLK's inmates were generally twenty-five to thirty years old, by Chinese reckoning.[24] Like the other collecting parties, the men were required to provide a surety, obtain approval of the SCA, and eventually sign a guarantee slip, known as a wedding slip, at the PLK and the SCA's office respectively.[25]

Naturally, mui tsai abused by their owners would refuse to return to their workplace. But those who were kidnapped or had lost their way on the street might ask to be restored to their masters. The investigative and collecting procedures were the same as those for the other circumstances.[26]

## POWER RELATIONS BETWEEN
## THE SOCIAL ELITE AND THE GOVERNMENT

Insights into the Po Leung Kuk, from its establishment to its daily operation, and the legislative protection for mui tsai will show the political maneuverings and carrot-and-stick policy of the government toward the social elite of the Chinese community. On the one hand, the PLK was directly responsible to the SCA, who reviewed all the recommendations for the settlement of the abused mui tsai. On the other hand, the necessity for securing the support of the wealthy and prestigious leaders of the Chinese community for social and political stability and economic prosperity shaped the government's attitude toward the custom of mui tsai.

To combat the abuse of the mui tsai system, the government had to rely on Chinese charitable organizations like the PLK, which had a wide social network. But the government also feared that the PLK would become independent of it. For one thing, the PLK was run by notable leaders of the Chinese community in the colony, who were often the retired or concurrent members of three other prominent Chinese economic and charitable organizations, the Chinese General Chamber of Commerce, the District Watch Force, and the Tung Wah Hospital.[27]

The wide social network and prestige that the social elite could secure both inside and outside the colony was regarded with suspicion by the British community in the late nineteenth century. Hence the Po Leung Kuk Incorporation Ordinance 1893 restrained the PLK's autonomy.

The board of directors of the PLK believed that the mui tsai system was benevolent in itself. They also thought that the merits of the system outweighed its evils. What they were appalled at was the abuse of the custom.[28] It is not surprising, therefore, that many of the PLK's board also served on the Society for the Prevention of Cruelty to Mui Tsai, established by the defenders of the system in 1921.[29]

The government's attitude toward the mui tsai custom was pragmatic—to tolerate and accommodate, rather than to interfere with and confront, an ingrained Chinese tradition for Hong Kong's stability and prosperity. Members of the elite institutions were respected as "the representatives of the Chinese" and their opinions were interpreted as "the opinions of the Chinese community." The views of other Chinese social groups were largely ignored.[30]

The government's contempt for the Anti–Mui Tsai Society completely reaffirmed its prejudice in favor of the defenders of the system. Governor Cecil Clementi (governor 1925–30) described the Anti–Mui Tsai Society as an incompetent and disgraceful organization.[31] However, the records of the Anti–Mui Tsai Society for the years 1921 to 1933 and those of the Po Leung Kuk show the Society's devotion to the rescue of maltreated *mui tsai*.[32]

From this political maneuvering, one can see that the government was unwilling to implement any fundamental change. The Female Domestic Service Ordinance of 1923, which forbade further employment of mui tsai and the taking of girls under ten as domestic servants, was not strictly enforced.[33] Nor was the provision that girls under eighteen or their parents were free to apply to the SCA for terminating the domestic servitude without the need to repay their masters the money advanced during the purchase observed.[34] Moreover, the registration, inspection, and remuneration of mui tsai, agitated for by the opponents of the mui tsai system since the early 1920s, was not made statutory until the enactment of the Female Domestic Service Ordinance of 1929. Nonetheless, the new ordinance was loosely enforced.[35] The concern for masters' economic interest and conditional benevolence partly served to perpetuate the mui tsai system.

## THE SOCIAL ATMOSPHERE OF EARLY-TWENTIETH-CENTURY HONG KONG

From the late nineteenth through the early twentieth centuries, one of the most common justifications of the government for not taking fundamental reforms on the mui tsai issue was the necessity to carry out gradual reforms that would have the support of the Chinese community.[36] The authorities also believed that the predominance of Chinese patriarchy would hamper the abolition of the mui tsai system. Gradual reforms by means of educating the public should, therefore, be adopted.[37] With such a strong emphasis on the role the public could play in the abolition of the practice, it is important to analyze the survival of the mui tsai custom from both top-down and bottom-up approaches; in other words, to analyze the general social atmosphere of the day.

As we have seen, a number of ordinances had been enacted by 1940 to combat the abuse of the mui tsai system. In addition, a proclamation declaring the right of oppressed mui tsai to express their grievances before the SCA was issued and published in the local Chinese press on 14 April 1922. However, on the one hand, the provisions were loosely enforced; on the other hand, a mere publication of the provisions could not be an effective means of propaganda in a place with a high illiteracy rate. For instance, in 1931 just around 50 percent of the population could read and write Chinese.[38] The 1921 census showed that mui tsai who were able to read and write formed only 9 percent of the total.[39] The extensive social networks and social influence of the community leaders within and outside the colony were not used to carry out verbal propaganda. As a result the public and the mui tsai were generally ignorant of the girls' rights.

Reports of cruelty could be made at the SCA's office and at police stations. But a famous Chinese proverb reads, "Don't go to the authorities while living and don't go to hell after death." Traditionally, the average Chinese feared the authorities as much as hell. As a result, they were hesitant to report to government officers.[40] Some reported to the Anti-Mui Tsai Society and the Po Leung Kuk instead. Yet they often did not have the courage to testify openly in court. Not surprisingly, mui tsai also had the same mentality. Moreover, they were afraid of the consequences of reporting their resentment to the authorities. They worried that if discovered, they would suffer further or heavier cruelty.[41]

Despite the general ignorance of the Chinese public and the mui tsai about personal rights and fear of the authorities, public sympathy to the girls' misfortune was growing in the early 1920s. For instance, the formation of the Anti-Mui Tsai Society in 1921 signifies that a number of Chinese in the colony, for the first time, were organizing themselves to bring about the abolition of the mui tsai system. Once it started recruiting members, the Anti-Mui Tsai Society secured a membership of four hundred—a number more or less the same as that of its rival society, the Society for the Prevention of Cruelty to Mui Tsai.[42] The pillars of the Anti-Mui Tsai Society were Chinese Christians[43] who, contrary to patriarchal values, agitated for personal freedom. The "opinions of the Chinese" of the custom were in fact not homogeneous, as the government claimed.

Besides, there were articles in the colony's Chinese newspapers and Chinese operas showing sympathy for mui tsai or contempt for the practice, but these were few.[44] Self-reporting of abuse by victims and reports by witnesses also accelerated, from at least ten in 1923 to no less than twenty-six in 1930.[45] The records of the PLK for 1940 show that of the cases involving maltreatment of mui tsai or adopted daughters, at least fifty were reported by the victims themselves or witnesses.[46]

Of course, the cases reported by victims or a third party constituted only a very small share of all the cases handled by the Po Leung Kuk. Nor can we exaggerate the consciousness or the courage it took for the Chinese to give up deep-rooted attitudes and report abuses. However, the sense of self-help and the desire to help, as well as sympathy for the oppressed mui tsai, had been stirred up since the early 1920s. Tribute should be paid to both the critics and defenders of the system. The former—such as the Anti-Mui Tsai Society, the YMCA, the YWCA and the churches—published circulars and organized speeches at schools, trade unions, churches, and voluntary associations, educating the public with ideas of individual freedom, humanitarianism, and equality of man, and even held an essay competition about the mui tsai system.[47] As for the defenders, though they did not organize the same activities as their opponents, their work in protecting the girls from abuse served to make the public aware of the problem.[48]

Oppressed mui tsai might be helpless victims or arbiters of their own fate. By the early twentieth century, there were Chinese charitable organizations like the Po Leung Kuk and the Society for the Prevention of Cruelty to Mui Tsai and ordinances that suppressed the malpractice of the system and public sympathy for the plight of the girls was growing. If the oppressed mui tsai, being themselves ignorant and helpless, could win the sympathy of the masses, it was more likely that the witnesses of oppression would report the abuse to the colonial authorities or voluntary associations. The girls themselves, however, were often too young or too intimidated to seek help and their plight could be revealed only by a system of inspection.

Registration of mui tsai was not required until 1929. Nonetheless, Sir William Peel (Hong Kong's governor from 1930 to 1935), objected to the appointment of inspectors on financial grounds. Consequently, inspection was carried out by a female Chinese inspector of the Hong Kong Society for the Protection of Children established in January 1930, and a European police inspector attached to the SCA for work related to the Ordinances for the Protection of Women and Girls of 1897 and 1929.[49] From December 1930 to May 1931, only two special tours of inspection of registered mui tsai were taken.[50]

The inspectors were dedicated to their work, but their achievement was constrained by the severe disproportion of their number to that of registered mui tsai, which was 3 to 2,000 between December 1934 and June 1935, for instance.[51] It was not until 1937 that the girls could be visited twice a year as each year, a number of the registered mui tsai were written off from the register.[52] By 1939 the frequency of inspection was reportedly more or less the same.[53]

The economic interests of the girls' masters, and eventually the social and political stability of the colony, were decisive factors in establishing how far the interests of the girls should be protected. The so-called welfare of mui tsai was not merely a matter of the well-being and happiness of the girls. Although Chinese community held different opinions about the mui tsai system, the colonial government never needed to achieve any conciliation because it largely sided with the defenders of the system. The inertia of the government and Chinese community leaders like the board of directors of the Po Leung Kuk to carry out more effective measures to combat the evils or abolish the system—together with the general social mentality of the day, such as patriarchy and the fear of reporting to the authorities—served to perpetuate the mui tsai system and hence its abuses.

## NOTES

### Abbreviations

CFPLK    Correspondence from the Secretary for Chinese Affairs (Huamin Zhengwusi lai xinbu)

CIPLK    Correspondence Inbound for the Po Leung Kuk (Gefu lai xinbu)

CO        Colonial Office records
COPLK   Correspondence Outbound for the Po Leung Kuk (Jie gefu xinbu)
CSCA    Correspondence From/To the Secretary for Chinese Affairs (Huamin
          Zhengwusi wanglai xinbu)
CRG     Huamin Zhengwusi wanglai xinbu (Correspondence From/To the Registrar
          General (Huamin Zhengwusi wanglai xinbu)
HKAR    Administrative Reports (Hong Kong Government)
HKGG    Hong Kong Government Gazette
HKSP    Hong Kong Sessional Papers
PLK     Po Leung Kuk
RDLPLK  Records of the Destitute Leaving the Po Leung Kuk (Nanfuyu chuju dengji)
RE      Records of Events (Zhishilu)
RMA     Registers of Marriage and Adoption (Linghun dengji: fu lingyu)
TDSPLK  Testimonies of the Destitute Staying in the Po Leung Kuk (Nannu nanmin
          kougongbu/Liuju kougongbu)
TO      Testimonies of Outsiders (Wailai kougongbu)

This chapter is taken from my dissertation, "The Mui Tsai Question in Hong Kong (1901–1940), with Special Emphasis on the Role of the Po Leung Kuk" (University of Hong Kong, 2000). I thank Dr. Elizabeth Sinn for reading this chapter and for her valuable comments.

The names of places and social organizations in Hong Kong have been romanized according to the Cantonese system (and as they appear in the *Hong Kong Government Gazette, Civil Service Lists, Anglo-Chinese Directory, Hong Kong,* and all other local sources), as are local colloquial terms, such as *mui tsai*. All other Chinese terms are romanized in pinyin. To respect the privacy of the individuals mentioned in the documents of the Po Leung Kuk archives, their names are not reproduced in full.

1. Risley, 18 May 1918, CO129/448: ref. no. 23769, 241.

2. Wilfrid Woods, *Mui Tsai in Hong Kong and Malaya: Report of the Commission* (London: HMSO, 1937), 22.

3. Ginseng and pilose antlers: PLK, Testimonies of Outsiders, 28th day of 11th moon, case of Peng Juan; rice shops: PLK, *TO,* 4th day of 4th moon, 1901, case of Chen Xian, Wang Mei, Hong Gui; groceries: PLK, *TO,* 2nd day of 4th moon, 1901, case of HanYou; charcoal shops: PLK, *TDSPLK,* 28 May 1923, case of Mai Di; shoemakers: PLK, *TO,* 22nd day of 4th moon, 1923, case of Tan Huan; blacksmiths: PLK, *TDSPLK,* 3 April 1923, case of Tan Hao; shop assistants: PLK, *TO,* 11th day of 4th moon 1901, case of Huang Mei, 29th day of 3rd moon, case of Hong Xiang; hairdressers: PLK, *TDSPLK,* 25 April 1929, case of Ling Xin.

4. Hong Kong, Census Department, "Occupations of the Chinese Population of the Colony, Census Report for the Year 1921," in *Hong Kong Census Reports, 1841–1941* (Hong Kong, 1986).

5. The work of identifying and obtaining a full picture of the cases concerning mui tsai was impeded by a lack of indexing and the sometimes piecemeal nature of the documents. I came across a number of common names of the day, like *damei, chunxi,* and *wangxi,* to name but a few. Usually, the identity of the girl in question, whether a mui tsai or in any other status, was recorded in testimonies. But if an investigation

was required, only words like "girl damei" would be written on the record at such a preliminary stage of investigation. Cases spanning more than a year would create further difficulty, as the status of a girl might have been mentioned in the records of the preceding year (e.g., 1928); and therefore became unclear in the records for the year 1929. I encountered the same problem while keeping track of the proceedings of cases and final settlement of the girls. Tremendous verification efforts are required. Therefore, the figures that this paper presents on the number of abuse tackled by the Po Leung Kuk can only reflect part of the story.

6. Rules: PLK 1978, Chinese section, 137, 138, 212; Incorporation: PLK 1978, English section, 74-78.

7. PLK 1978, Chinese section, 211-12; HKGG 1882, notification no. 318, 5 August 1882.

8. PLK 1978, Chinese section, 317.

9. CTRG, 1 April 1901, no. 63; COPLK, 27th day of 2nd moon, case of Tang Kuan, alias Li E; CSCA, 22 January, no. 18; TDSPLK, 22 January 1923, case of Liu Qian.

10. PLK 1978, Chinese section, 317.

11. Sun Guoquan and Chao Zongpo, eds., *Juhua–bei fanmai haiwai di funu*, trans. Kani H. (Tokyo, 1979); Sun and Chao, *Kindai Chugoku no kuri to choka* (The Coolies and Slave Girls of Modern China) (Chengzhou: Henan Remin, 1990), 322 of the translated edition.

12. PLK, *CIPLK*, 11 December 1929, case of Liang Mei.

13. PLK 1978, Chinese section, 317.

14. See, for example, PLK, *CIPLK*, 18 November 1929, case of Huang Xing, alias Guo Xing.

15. See, for example, PLK, *RE*, 29, 30 October 1929, case of Huang Xing, alias Guo Xing.

16. PLK, *RE*, 13 May 1929, case of Yang Feng.

17. PLK, *TDSPLK*, 9, 22 April 1923, cases of Chen Jin and Mai Ying.

18. PLK, *COPLK*, 14th, 16th, 22nd, 25th, 27th, 30th days of 2nd moon; 2nd, 3rd, 5th, 6th days of 3rd moon, 1901, case of Tang Kuan.

19. PLK, *CFSCA*, 25 May 1929, no. 120, case of Liang Lan; Sun and Chao, *Juhua*, 320.

20. PLK, *RMA, 1922-28*.

21. Victoria Home Extension and Rural Home, Taipo, Report (Hong Kong and the Home), 1; Fr. Sergio Ticozzi, "The Social Concern of the Catholic Church for Hong Kong People, 1841-1945," in *Church History of Hong Kong*, ed. Centre of Asian Studies, University of Hong Kong (Hong Kong: University of Hong Kong, 1993), 6-7.

22. PLK, *TDSPLK*, 20 April 1923, case of Tan Hao.

23. Stubbs to Churchill, 4 October 1921, no. 381, CO129/469, ref. no. 57511, 165.

24. The 1921 and 1931 censuses reveal that most Chinese males got married by age thirty-five.

25. PLK, *RE*, 3 June 1923; CFSCA, 4 June 1923, no. 127; RMA, 19th day of 4th moon, 1923, case of Tan Hao.

26. PLK, *RE*, 29 September 1901; RE, 7 January, 23 March 1902, case of Huang Hua, alias Wang Hua; *TDSPLK*, 20 February 1929; TO, 21 February 1929; CFSCA, 20, 22 February 1929, nos. 36, 38; RDLPLK 1929, 88, case of Wu Jin.

27. Henry James Lethbridge, "The District Watch Committee: The Chinese Executive Council of Hong Kong?" in *Hong Kong: Stability and Change: A Collection of Essays*, (Hong Kong: Oxford University Press, 1978), 104-29; HKAR 1913, 1915; Tung Wah Board of Directors, *Development of the Tung Wah Hospital, 1870-1970* (bilingual) (Hong Kong, 1961); Tung Wah Board, *One Hundred Years of the Tung Wah Hospital, 1870-1970*, 2 vols. (bilingual) (Hong Kong, 1970).

28. PLK 1978, English section, 30-39. The defense for the system was also mentioned in a report by the registrar general and protector of the Chinese, James Russell, "Report on Child Adoption and Domestic Service among Chinese." See "Extracts from Correspondence respecting Child Adoption and Domestic Service among Chinese (Including Mr. Russell's Report)," reprinted in F. H. Loseby, "*Mui Tsai* in Hong Kong: Report of the Committee Appointed by His Excellency the Governor Sir William Peel, KCMG, KBE," in HKSP 1935, no. 8, 238.

29. Mai Meisheng, ed., *Fan tui hsu pei shih lueh* (A History of the Anti-Mui Tsai Campaign) (Chinese), (Hong Kong: Fu xing zhong xi yin wu ju, 1933), 3-5.

30. CO129.

31. Climenti to Amery, 22 February 1929, HKSP 11/1929, 234.

32. Mai, *Fan tui hsu*, 315-88; RE, 25 December 1929; CSCA, 22 January 1930, no. 19, case of Auyang Xi; TDSPLK, 7 January 1929; and CSCA, 5 June 1940, no. 121, case of Zhao Xian.

33. Woods, *Mui Tsai*, 39, 51.

34. CSCA, 17 March 1923, no. 62; RE, 18 March 1923, case of Tan Ping; RE, 30 September 1929, case of Huang Mei.

35. Pui Ting Poon, "The Mui Tsai Question in Hong Kong (1901-1940), with Special Emphasis on the Role of the Po Leung Kuk" (PhD thesis, University of Hong Kong, 2000), chaps. 5-7.

36. Viscount Milner to Stubbs, 28 September 1920, CO129/461, ref. no. 43493, 438.

37. Risley, 18 May 1918, CO129/448, ref. no. 23769, 241; A. E. Collins, 31 May 1921, CO129/473, ref. no. 29711, 137, 139; Stubbs to Winston Churchill, 28 October 1921, no. 397, CO129/469, ref. no. 61734, 237.

38. Hong Kong, Census Department, "Education, Census Report for the Year 1931," in *Hong Kong Census Reports, 1841-1941* (Hong Kong, 1986).

39. "Extract from Report on the Census of the Colony for 1921," in CO129/478, ref. no. 8660, 304-5.

40. Mai, *Fan tui hsu*, 206.

41. J. D. Bush, Secretary of Anti-Mui Tsai Society, to R. A. C. North, Secretary for Chinese Affairs, 20 March 1929, CO129/516/7, ref. no. 62838, 59.

42. Mai, *Fan tui hsu*, 45, 138; Poon, "Mui Tsai Question," 5-21, 51-114.

43. Mai, *Fan tui hsu*, 43; Carl T. Smith, "The Chinese Church, Labour, Elites and the Mui Tsai Question in the 1920s," in *A Sense of History: Studies in the Social and Urban History of Hong Kong*, ed. Smith (Hong Kong: Educational Publishing, 1995), 240-65, esp. 253, 255.

44. *Chinese Mail*, 2 June, 20 June, 20 July, and 26 July 1921.

45. PLK documents; Mai, *Fan tui hsu*, 1933.

46. The Domestic Service Ordinance of 1929 required the registration of mui tsai. Some masters evaded registration by calling their maidservants adopted daughters

instead. Although the author is unable to identify all the camouflage, the figure fifty serves to illustrate the growing public sympathy to the destitute, and the sense of self-help and courage that it took for victims to report to authorities. See *TDSPLK 1940; CSCA 1940; RE 1940.*

47. Mai, *Fan tui hsu,* 90–134.

48. The Chinese might have been influenced by a number of feminist campaigns as well as the May Fourth movement, advocating the emancipation of women from their social bondage. Susanna Hoe, "Mrs. Little and Big Feet," in *The Private Life of Old Hong Kong: Western Women in the British Colony, 1841–1941* (Hong Kong: Oxford University Press, 1991), 225–31; Hoe, *Chinese Footprints: Exploring Women's History in China* (Hong Kong: Roundhouse, 1996), 96, 101, 118, 127, 252; Sha dongxun, *Wusiyundong zai Guangdong* (The May Fourth Movement in Guangdong) (Chinese) (Beijing: Zhongguo jing zhi chu ban she, 1989), 39–43, 168–72; *Huazi ribao* (Chinese Mail), 13 January 1922.

49. The ordinance generally combated the traffic of women and girls for immoral purposes. CO129/532/4, ref. no. 82759, pt. 1, 33.

50. Peel to Passfield, 23 June 1931, no. 293, CO129/532/3, ref. no. 82758, 125.

51. Woods 1937, 61, 62, 218; W. T. Southorn to Malcolm MacDonald, 3 July 1935, no. 404, CO129/551/2, ref. no. 53502, 76.

52. The girls were reported by their masters as having died, returned to their parents or relatives, run away or disappeared, left the colony permanently, married, left their masters to earn their own living other than as mui tsai, or been handed over to the custody of the SCA or charitable organizations. Poon, "Mui Tsai Question," 158.

53. HKAR 1939, C1.

# Part B
*Children in Commercial Slaveries*

# 10

## SLAVE AND OTHER NONWHITE CHILDREN IN LATE-EIGHTEENTH-CENTURY FRANCE

PIERRE H. BOULLE

It was fashionable in early-modern aristocratic circles to own an African male child as a domestic servant. So prevalent was the fashion for "little blacks" dressed in exotic costumes in France, notably in the late eighteenth century, that a governor of Senegal, the chevalier de Boufflers, on a short visit home, brought a number of them, along with parrots and other exotic presents, to various ladies of the court as a means of advancing his career.[1] Louis-Sébastien Mercier mocked the practice:

> The monkey, which used to be a favorite of ladies . . . has been relegated to their antechambers . . . and women have taken little blacks instead. . . . The little black . . . burned by the sun . . . only appears the more beautiful for it. He climbs onto the knees of a charming lady . . . presses her breast with his languid head, applies his lips to her rosy mouth; his ebony hands set off the whiteness of her dazzling neck. With his white teeth, his thick lips, his silky skin, a little black caresses better than a spaniel or an angora.[2]

History has retained the memory of at least one of these turbaned pets, Zamor, the young black (in fact, a Bengali) of Madame du Barry, who remained in her service after he had become adult and was involved in his mistress's trial during the Revolution. After her execution he lived in poverty in Paris until his death, in 1820, having earned a reputation as "the black who betrayed the Du Barry."[3]

How exceptional were these so-called little blacks who fill the pages of literary works and nearly monopolize contemporary artistic depictions of nonwhites? A census taken in 1777 of nonwhites in France may provide some answers. The term *census* here, of course, does not refer to the type conducted in modern societies but rather to the statistical information collected by the State in the latter part of the eighteenth century on all sorts of subjects—including hygiene, the economy, the state of roads, taxation, and population—on the basis of *états*, or lists established by local agents, notably the intendants, at the request of the central authorities. In the case of nonwhites, the printed forms to be filled by local authorities contained columns where the name of each individual was to be entered, along with his or her age and racial identification, occupation, place of residence, date of arrival in France, status (slave or free), master's or employer's name, along with whatever comment the local official judged significant. These documents, ranging in date from late 1776 to early 1778, plus various allied declarations of blacks and related correspondence, were collected by the ministry but, perhaps owing to the growing involvement of French Marine officials in the American War of Independence, were never amalgamated into a coherent whole. They now reside in three cartons in the French National Archives, where they have been consulted by a few historians who, before the advent of computers, could only sample their contents.[4]

These documents contain a substantial number of lacunae, owing in part to the refusal of local officials, for one reason or another, to comply with the minister's orders, to losses due to various incidents over time, and, most significantly, to the reluctance of certain privileged segments of society to comply with the laws that required them to register their nonwhite employees or slaves. However, some of these lacunae can be filled through the consultation of departmental and municipal archives. Copies of some of the *états* lost in Paris can be found at the local level. Local admiralty records can also provide the information that some officials refused to compile. Finally, additional material can be gathered from such records as parish registers.

In total, I have been able to compile for the year 1777 a list of 2,240 nonwhite French residents (2,053 certain and 187 possible ones), representing between 41.6 percent and 44.8 percent of the approximately five thousand nonwhites estimated to have lived in France at any time during the latter part of the eighteenth century.[5] However, this figure expresses a certain bias in favor of the less privileged, who were more likely to obey laws requiring the registration of nonwhites, and perhaps toward coastal regions and the capital, which were better controlled and where officials were more

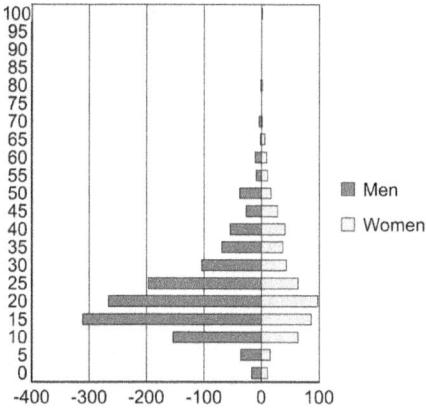

FIG. 10.1. Age pyramid of nonwhite residents in France in 1777[6]

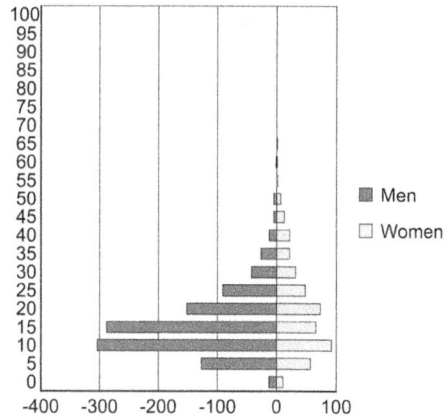

FIG. 10.2. Age pyramid of nonwhite residents in 1777, at the time of their arrival

conscious of color differences. Nonetheless, it forms a sufficiently large sample from which to reach conclusions about the population as a whole.

A first observation concerns gender. My sample includes 1,519 males, but only 663 females. The remaining 58 individuals could not be identified by gender. As for age, they represented a typical immigrant population (fig. 10.1)—relatively young (notably the males), but with few very young children (under thirteen years of age). Half the 1,301 males whose ages are recorded were younger than twenty-one years, and half the 540 females younger than twenty-three. The largest group of males was between the ages of thirteen and seventeen and the largest group of females between eighteen and twenty-two.

The age at which these individuals had arrived in France is even more significant. Of the 1,069 males and 447 females for whom we know both the age in 1777 and the date of arrival (67.7 percent of the sample), half the males had arrived in France before they had reached fifteen years of age and half the females before they had reached eighteen. Children aged eight to twelve form the largest age group for both genders. On average, females tended to have been in France half a year longer than males (7.43 years versus 6.91 years). On the other hand, among those born in France—the one group in which near parity between the sexes would be expected—there are nearly four times as many males as females (161 versus 41). Assuming that males and females were as likely to be declared, this suggests that female children were more likely to be sent back to the colonies.

Between 13.3 percent and 13.5 percent of the corpus were under thirteen years old[7]—close to the period of puberty, at least for boys—which is here taken as the time of transition to adulthood. This has the distinct advantage of avoiding the fifteenth year, which tends to be an approximate age in many declarations. Moreover, many individuals aged thirteen or fourteen already performed adult tasks. Boys predominate slightly more among nonwhite children (70.5 percent boys; 29.5 percent girls) than among all nonwhite residents (69.6 percent males; 30.4 percent females), probably because women tend to live longer than men. However, a much larger proportion of girls than boys is listed as free (40.5 percent, compared to 25.1 percent). In part, this is due to the fact that a significant number of the children (between 14.7 percent and 15.2 percent) were born in France, many of free parents, and that the gender imbalance characteristic of immigrant populations does not apply to them (20–23 boys, 14–17 of them freeborn; 21–22 girls, 16–17 freeborn).

Those born in France were frequently of mixed parenthood, often the product of a marriage between a freed black and a white woman. This was the case of the children of Pierre Almoradin ("the little Moor"?), who in 1735, at the age of two, was brought to France from the Guinea coast and in 1760 married Marie-Anne-Geneviève Fabre, a boilermaker's daughter. In 1762, they settled at the comte d'Eu's estate at Bû, in Normandy, and there raised fourteen children, of whom eight were alive in 1777.[8] Conversely, a Monsieur Barbeaux of Paris declared as nonwhite the three children born to his wife, the demoiselle LeBlanc. The latter came from Pondicherry, suggesting that she was a Tamil and her children half-Indian.[9] Yet others were the illegitimate children of slave women brought to France by planters. Thus, Olive-Rose, the slave of the widow Cottin, made her pregnancy declaration on Christmas Eve 1777, stating that she had been seduced by another black in the Cottin household, and gave birth the next day to a daughter, baptized Hortense-Marguerite.[10] Another case was that of Anne, the daughter of Marie-Françoise, the black slave of a resident of Port-au-Prince named Bouvier, whom she accompanied on a trip to France, where he planned to be treated for an unspecified illness. Bouvier died onboard ship and Marie-Françoise, left on her own, later claimed to have been abused by the ship's captain, a certain De Noües. Having become pregnant, she found her way from Bordeaux to Nantes and obtained asylum in the household of Bouvier's mother-in-law, the widow Royne, where she gave birth to a daughter named Anne. Her pregnancy declaration, which named the ship's captain, noted that she "reserves the right to pursue claims against the sieur Des Noües as she will deem appropriate,"[11] but a subsequent declaration by the mother-in-law indicates that "as soon as she [Marie-Françoise] will have recovered from the delivery, she and the daughter will be returned" to Bouvier's widow in Port-au-Prince.[12]

Cases of abandoned pregnant women are not rare. Indeed, pregnancy declarations were designed specifically to deal with a situation that would otherwise place an "unjustified" burden on the resources of municipal hospitals. However, more heartwarming stories can be found. Particularly revealing is that of Esprit Fauchier and his unnamed brother, planters from the West Indian island of Grenada, who returned to France when it was ceded to the British following the Seven Years' War. They were accompanied by Franchine and Nanette, two black women whom they had freed, and their progeny. Because of "their attachment to these blacks and mulattoes," the intendant of Provence reported, the Fauchiers asked to be allowed to retain them in France; "should they be required to get rid of them," they threatened to settle outside French jurisdiction, in the Comtat Venaissin or in Nice. They (or at least Esprit) finally settled in Brignoles, their native city, with the entire group. Esprit spent his few remaining years establishing the children, having them trained in various crafts, and marrying the older girls to various Brignoles craftsmen. His will left a life annuity to the two older women and three thousand livres to each of the nine children. By 1777 there were in Brignoles, in addition to the two original women who worked as seamstresses, four of their married daughters, three unmarried ones, and one son, also unmarried, plus seven grandchildren, all under the age of thirteen; another son lived in Marseille with his wife.[13] Two other planters, returning from the Grenadines, settled in Roquebrune-sur-Argens with five young children, clearly their own, whom they planned to "educate and raise in the Christian religion until they were fifteen or sixteen, and then send back to America."[14] Finally, one may mention the chevalier de Rouvray, who declared that he had been entrusted with Moÿse, the son of his plantation's manager, and intended "to provide him with all the education possible."[15]

Not surprisingly, the more African the child's ancestry, the more that child was likely to be a slave. Among those of African descent, over 90 percent of boys and girls declared to be black were slaves. The proportion for mulattoes was 57.1 percent for boys and 60 percent for girls, for quadroons (nonwhites with only one black grandparent), 16.7 percent and zero percent respectively. The two octoroons (nonwhites with only one black great-grandparent) included in the sample were free. The terms *noir* (black), *nègre* (negro), or *mulâtre* (mulatto), when used to describe individuals born in India, pose an important problem of interpretation, as it is impossible to know, unless other physical features such as the form of the hair are described, whether they refer to the skin color (the swarthiness of certain East Indian groups) or to descendants of Africans brought to India as slaves.

Nevertheless, there appears as close a correlation between skin color and slave status for East Indian children in France as for African children. Eighty percent of those of both sexes described as full Indians were slaves, as were 63.6 percent of boys and 75 percent of girls labeled as black. By contrast, no East Indian labeled a mulatto had slave status. The declaration of an East Indian mother, married to a white, and of her two children, "equally white," is just as noteworthy, given that it was made to conform to the law requiring the registration of nonwhites in France. That the parents were from Bourbon Island, in the Indian Ocean (present-day Réunion), may explain this oddity, for the terms *white* and *black* did not refer to color there, but to whether the individual was free or not.[16] This case also confirms that the clerks who registered declarations simply recorded what was told them by the declarants concerning origins, status, age, and other details.

According to the legislation dating from the first half of the century, only plantation owners were permitted to bring slaves to France and only for religious education or to learn a craft. They could remain in France for no more than three years and their use as domestic servants was specifically prohibited.[17] The corpus demonstrates that these laws were regularly flouted: the average stay of nonwhites in France was more than double the maximum allowed; even though most children came from the West Indies, notably from Saint-Domingue (see table 10.1), more than one in seven (nearly one in five for boys alone) were brought directly from Africa and all but three declared as slaves—an infraction of the law that permitted such a status only for nonwhites coming from plantation colonies. Eleven out of the eighteen arrivals from India were slaves—although there were no plantations there at that time. Indeed, the proportion of slaves from Africa and India was probably even larger, as only two were declared free and one was hostage to a slave trader, a status tantamount to slavery. The status of the seven or eight remaining is unclear; they too were probably slaves.

The elite proved particularly neglectful, so that few declarations came from the court at Versailles, despite the presence there of little black domestics. Faced with the refusal of the duc de Chartres, the king's cousin and future Philippe-Égalité, to register his black domestics, the minister of Marine was even obliged to ask the Paris lieutenant-general of Police to do so in his stead.[18] The only declared nonwhite son of an aristocrat who came to France as a child was the chevalier de Saint-George. The illegitimate child of M. de Bologne de Saint-George, an aristocratic planter, and his slave, Nanon, and hence a slave at birth according to French law, Saint-George was at the age of eight brought to France by his father and given an aristocratic education; he mixed in elite circles as a renowned violinist, composer,

TABLE IO.I

## Origins for nonwhite children, ages 0–12, residing in France, 1777

| Origin | Boys | | Girls | | Both sexes[a] | |
|---|---|---|---|---|---|---|
| | Number | Percent | Number | Percent | Number | Percent |
| West Indies | 95 (104)[b] | 67.9 (69.3) | 42 (43) | 84.0 (84.3) | 137 (147) | 72.1 (73.1) |
| St-Domingue[c] | 65 (70) | 46.4 (50.0) | 25 (26) | 46.7 (51.0) | 90 (96) | 47.4 (47.8) |
| Mascarenes | 4 (4) | 2.9 (2.7) | 2 (2) | 4.0 (3.9) | 6 (6) | 3.2 (3.0) |
| Africa | 26 (27) | 18.6 (18.0) | 3 (3) | 6.0 (5.9) | 29 (30) | 15.3 (14.9) |
| India | 15 (15) | 10.7 (10.0) | 3 (3) | 6.0 (5.9) | 18 (18) | 9.5 (9.0) |
| Total foreign-born | 140 (150) | 100.0 (100.0) | 50 (51) | 100.0 (100.0) | 190 (201) | 100.0 (100.0) |
| French-born | 27 (27) | | 23 (23) | | 57 (62) | |
| Unknown | 23 (23) | | 9 (9) | | 32 (34) | |
| TOTAL | 190 (200) | | 82 (83) | | 279 (297) | |

a   The numbers in this column include fourteen cases (seven certain, seven conditional) of individuals whose gender is unspecified, mostly infants born in France.
b   Numbers in parentheses include conditional files.
c   The numbers for Saint-Domingue are also included in those for the West Indies.

and swordsman. His declaration under the name Joseph Ritondaine was made by the master-at-arms to whom he had been entrusted, probably as a measure of self-protection at a time when nonwhites were threatened with expulsion from France.[19] An equally famous mulatto, the future revolutionary General Dumas—the son of the marquis de La Pailleterie and the father of the novelist Alexandre Dumas (père)—who came to France in similar circumstances as a fourteen-year-old in 1776, was never declared.[20]

Flouting the law was not the preserve only of the upper aristocracy. Royal officials and naval officers as well as captains and owners of merchant ships took advantage of their visits to the colonies or Africa to obtain cheap and more dependent, hence reliable, servants. Although many of these domestics were adults, some children were also involved. Thus while visiting Madagascar, the explorer Yves-Joseph de Kerguelen de Trémarec, after whom Kerguelen Island in the Indian Ocean is named, bought an eight-year-old who accompanied him to France and, during Kerguelen's imprisonment at Saumur, following his court-martial for insubordination, served as his domestic servant.[21] Among the many other naval officers who availed themselves of such servants, one can cite Charles-Louis de Ternay, chef d'escadre (commodore), who admitted in his declaration that "he currently holds with him in his castle of Ternay in Loudunois a little black named Le Samorin, aged ten to twelve and born in Goa, who came with him [to France] on the frigate

*La Belle Paille,* upon his return from Île de France [now Mauritius], where he served him as his slave."[22] Not all naval officers were as forthcoming. A Marine official complained that he could not enforce the registration law in Brest, where "no sooner do I require a naval officer to conform to His Majesty's wishes than I am accused of an indiscrete zeal and risk being reported to the minister of Marine as a busybody."[23]

Captains and officers on merchant ships had similar opportunities. Slave traders in particular frequently selected from their ship's cargo young blacks to bring to France, as domestic servants for the shipowners, as cabin boys and interpreters on their subsequent trips to Africa, or simply to sell in France. For instance, the shipowner Dumoutier l'aîné made a declaration in La Rochelle to the effect that "his ship, the *Baron-de-Montmorency,* brought [back] a black aged eleven years purchased on the Angola coast . . . to whom he has given the name of Prospert and whom he plans presently to have instructed in the Catholic religion . . . then taught the cooper's trade," and added, "he's already had him baptized."[24] Again, ship captain Jean Michel of Saint-Malo declared Antoine, a twelve-year-old purchased in Mozambique, to be employed as "interpreter on his master's voyages," and Salomon Le Prévôt of Le Havre declared he planned to use Mafonga, an eleven-year-old from the Gold coast, for the same purpose.[25]

Slave ship manifests from Nantes often include as crew members black youths, as cabin boys or cooks. Some were paid normal wages and may be assumed to have been free; the extremely low wages of others suggest that they were slaves of the captain or shipowner. For example, Silvain was brought from India at the age of about seven for the Nantes shipowner Augustin de Luynes. Originally declared in 1777, so as to conform somewhat with regulations, as someone who would be taught "a trade when his age makes it possible, and then sent back to the colonies," he appears the very same year as a ten-year-old *maître d'hôtel* (cabin boy) on De Luynes's ship, the *Comte-de-Maurepas,* sailing for Port-au-Prince. As the slave of the ship's owner, he is indicated as receiving no wage.[26] Jean-Joseph, the twelve-year-old slave of Captain Richer de La Haye, was luckier. He was paid five, then six, livres per month—still a low wage—as maître d'hôtel on three separate trips of the *Guerrier* between 1772 and 1776. Of course, it may be that the captain, as Jean-Joseph's master, collected his wages.[27]

As noted, none of these boys would have been considered legal residents, and it is clear that they were allowed to remain in France only with the connivance of the ports' officials. The *état* sent to the Ministry of Marine by the admiralty of Bordeaux on the basis of the declarations it had received includes numerous cases of slaves specifically indicated as having been purchased in the city from ship officers.[28] Connivance was at times more than passive, as a declaration at the admiralty in La Rochelle makes patently clear.[29] In it, Paul Hardy, the captain of a slave ship, the *Saint-Paul,* explains that, after having purchased 327 captives at Luanga in Angola, he sent Michel Garnier, his lieutenant, to take the ship's leave from the local ruler. During the meeting,

> the said king asked him [Garnier] to deliver to the declarant a young black approximately three feet five inches tall that the king gave him as a free gift to enjoy as he saw fit [*en pur don et aventage*] . . . and as it is in the interest of the sieur Hardy to justify that he belongs to him in full ownership as a result of the gift made to him . . . he makes the present declaration, so that in case the young black escapes, he can reclaim him whenever and wherever he may be found, and also, in case he acts the libertine or is guilty of bad conduct, he can be punished as he [Hardy] will see fit.

Someone must have warned the captain that his declaration was contrary to law, for it is crossed out and replaced by another, which claims that Kikuye, the young black in question, was the younger brother of another youth whom Hardy employed aboard ship as an interpreter, and that, on the occasion of a trip to Luanga, the interpreter's parents expressed their gratitude for the way Hardy had treated the older brother and asked him to educate their younger son in the same manner, before returning both children to their native land. "This is what the declarant has done, at the request of the father and all the relatives of the two little blacks who are indeed in his service." Hardy indicated that he would provide Kikuye with a religious education and "will have him taught whatever craft proves compatible with his disposition." The declaration ends by copying from the disused text the clause concerning potential escape and punishment for bad behavior, but this time applied to both Kikuye and his older brother. As free individuals sent to France for training, these two boys no longer fell under the regulations established by the 1738 royal declaration. On the other hand Hardy, as their guardian, could enjoy rights of control akin to those of a slave master.

A similar story is told by another merchant ship's officer, concerning an African child entrusted to him by an Angolan chief. The boy was being trained as a *perruquier* (wig maker or, more likely, wig dresser), hardly an appropriate craft for someone allegedly meant to be returned to Africa, but a useful one for a cabin boy serving a ship's officer.[30] Charles-Augustin Bridon, a

Nantes ship captain, was more forthright. He openly declared that he possessed Adonis, "a young black from . . . Ouidah whom he obtained at the said place as a hostage for a sum owed to him." Bridon did state that he intended to take Adonis back to his native land "according to the laws," but claimed he could not specify when that might be, as trade had been interrupted by rumors of war. In the meantime, he had Adonis baptized, indicating him on the parish register no longer as a hostage but as his slave.[31]

Such legally suspect practices could at times result in conflicts. Children were usually too young to resist exploitation or learn of potential recourses, but some, when older, attempted to free themselves through flight or by seeking legal recognition of their freedom, notably in Paris, where the admiralty court (*Table de marbre*) was particularly receptive to such appeals and where a support network for escaped slaves appears to have come into existence.[32]

Several such cases are worth citing. A fifteen-year-old East Indian named Juliette was declared in Paris by Louis-Roger de Charlevoix-Villers, a naval engineer. He claimed that she had been

> kidnapped when she was seven by a black at Gorétic[?] in Bengal, sold to a mulatto who resold her to M. de Corbin, at the time an officer of His Majesty in Bengal, who brought her to Lorient in 1773. Since then she has been treated as a slave by the sieur and dame Corbin, but as she was born a free person, she declares that she left [their service] because of ill treatments . . . and proposes incessantly to petition [the courts] to be declared free.[33]

Three days later, the dame Corbin, who lived on her estate at Courtem-pierre, near Montargis, made a parallel declaration in Paris, concerning Juliette, age ten, and another slave—thereby laying claim to the escaped girl. Four days later, Corbin obtained a royal warrant (*ordre du Roi*) for Juliette's arrest and so appears to have claimed her back from the naval engineer.[34] From the declarations, it is clear that Juliette had taken advantage of accompanying her mistress on a trip to Paris to seek her freedom. Villers may have been part of the slave-support network there; in any event, he provided her with a place of refuge. A royal warrant, in withdrawing a slave from the jurisdiction of the courts, was usually the initial act in the reexpedition of a slave to the colonies. In this case, it seems to have resulted only in the return of Juliette to the Corbins. The reasons for the conflict in age in the declarations are not entirely clear, though the Corbins are more likely to have known her age. By claiming her to be older, Villers may have wished to indicate a mature decision on the part of Juliette.

Louis-René-Charles-Camille *dit* Crispin, another "black born in Bengal," appealed for freedom to the Paris admiralty court at the age of fifteen. He had been brought to France from India at a very early age by a naval officer, the sieur de Chateauneuf, who subsequently sold him to a friend, the sieur de Besse. Crispin served Besse for seven years, traveling throughout France and always wearing a silver collar, "like a dog." The collar, which he exhibited to the court, identified him as belonging to Besse. In this case, the petition was successful and Crispin quickly made his own declaration as a free man, noting the court's decree and indicating his new address with M. Pelé, an attorney (*procureur*) at the Paris *parlement*.[35]

Zamor, a native of Ouidah who had been brought to Rochefort by a naval officer and sold there to a *commissaire des guerres* named Thibault de Lange-court, was less successful. He escaped to Paris, where he sought recognition of his freedom and back wages from the admiralty court, but Langecourt, who had attempted on several occasions to recapture him, obtained a royal warrant for his arrest. Zamor's new employer, a captain in the dragoons named Le Sousteleur de Gaudret, attempted to prevent his transportation to the colonies by posting bail for him with the Paris lieutenant-general of Police. To no avail: despite the court's decision to place him under its protection and Gaudret's bail money, Zamor was transferred to the port of Cherbourg in anticipation of his being shipped to the West Indies. The affair came to the attention of the minister of Marine, who received a num-ber of reports suggesting that, if it were ascertained that Zamor had been brought to France directly from Africa, he could not be considered "under any circumstances" as a slave and should be released, or at least retained in France until the facts of the case had been fully investigated. The minister, however, refused to intervene, on the grounds that Thibault de Langecourt had declared him in La Rochelle as a slave and thus had fulfilled the letter of the law.[36]

It is clear from the archival evidence that the principal occupation of a nonwhite in France was that of a domestic servant. This is the case even for children below age thirteen, 38.5 percent of whom were declared as such or appear to have functioned in that capacity. Most such cases elicit little comment in the records, simply being listed as "in the service of" a whole array of masters and mistresses, occupying a broad range of French society, from the nobility to the petite bourgeoisie of towns. In this, they (or at least their adult counterparts) differ only slightly from white domestic servants, except perhaps for the dominance of males among nonwhites.[37] The two next most important categories are those for whom no occupation is listed

(24.6 percent) and those who were too young to be trained or who were simply mentioned as part of their parents' declaration (15.8 percent)—as was the case of the children of Hector, a domestic servant of the duc de la Trémoille. Hector had served as a kettledrummer (*timbalier*) in a cavalry regiment and married the daughter of a noncommissioned officer, by whom he had a nine-year-old daughter and two sons, eight years and eighteen months of age respectively. The children lived with their mother and her father at the regiment, and it is likely that the older boy was enrolled there as an *enfant de troupe*.[38]

Other children (7.7 percent) were placed in apprenticeship to local tradesmen.[39] The youngest was a girl eight to nine years old, apprenticed to a seamstress; all the others were at least ten years old, and indeed the proportion of apprentices within the next age group—young teenagers between thirteen and fifteen—increased dramatically, to 18.6 percent. Apprenticeships usually concerned occupations appropriate for domestic servants, most notably to crafts having to do with women's hairdressing or the grooming of men's hair or wigs. Boys were also being trained as cooks and pastry chefs and girls as seamstresses, linen maids, dressmakers, or milliners. Seldom were young slaves or wards trained in occupations related to production—coopers, carpenters, shipwrights, locksmiths, cabinetmakers—precisely the types of crafts useful to the colonial economy and therefore presumably anticipated in the law. Only three boys and one girl were listed as occupying functions beyond apprenticeship: an eleven-year-old cook, two footmen/wig dressers nine and somewhere between seven and fifteen years of age, and an eight-year-old dressmaker. The range of occupations is naturally more varied among young teenagers; also, some of them had completed their apprenticeship.

Some of the more privileged youths were entrusted by parents (usually a planter father) to agents in France who supervised their education. This was often limited to religious instruction and, later, to training in a craft. In a few cases, however, literacy was specified as the principal objective. Thus, several free mulattoes were entrusted by their fathers to correspondents and placed by them with private tutors to master reading and writing. For example, Jean Laurent, a free mulatto, was sent by his father to a Nantes correspondent for religious instruction and "to have him taught to read and to write," as were Emmanuel Siphorien and Etienne Pezant, also in Nantes, Claude Gaspard in Libourne, and the octoroon Jean Guité in Bayonne.[40]

Some were placed in various institutions in Nantes and Agen (*Écoles chrétiennes*), La Ciotat, and Étampes, although the type of instruction (other than religious) received in these colleges is not certain. The case of

Étampes concerns a whole family "received from the sieur Gilbert Espagnol" of Saint-Domingue. The three boys, eleven, twelve, and seventeen years old respectively, were placed at the College of the Bernatins and the four girls, nine to fifteen years old, at the Convent of the Congregation. The declarant indicated that they would be sent back to Saint-Domingue "once they have received instruction in the different estates to which they have been destined." He also noted that the older boy was at the time in Paris, living at the home of a master cartwright and presumably apprenticed to him.[41] The La Ciotat case is more promising, for the individual in question, a quadroon named Dominique Brun, was studying at the College of the Oratorians. Given the Oratorians' good reputation as educators, it is likely that he received a genuine education there. Interestingly, this is the only case of a child sent by a nonwhite parent—a free mulattress of Saint-Domingue.[42] However, apart from the case of the chevalier de Saint-George cited above, the children who received the most advanced education were probably two teenagers (hence in the age group above the one on which we have focused), one a certain Joseph Coucy, apprenticed to an architect and the other a student of surgery at the Hôtel-Dieu in Nantes. Coucy also made separate declarations for his younger sister and brother, and all signed their names clearly, suggesting a good education—though the sister had been placed with a milliner.[43]

A few of the children even assumed a life of genteel leisure. For example, Catherine and Marie-Thérèse, two mulattresses, twenty and twelve years of age, lived with their aunt in Marmande "off the revenues of plantations" they had inherited from their father, the sieur Lamiré, who had died "in the islands."[44] Alexandre Dumas's father, age fifteen in 1777, also lived the life of a young man of means until he became estranged from his own father and enlisted in the army.[45]

It is among those "in service," notably within aristocratic households, that one would expect to encounter the little blacks mentioned by Mercier at the outset of this article, but aristocrats were precisely those most likely to ignore the law. Even the uncle of the two *rentières* of Marmande, a relatively obscure provincial whose noble status rested on the purchase of the office of king's secretary, initially refused to make a declaration about them.[46] In any case, declaration of those "pets," if they were made, were not likely to refer to them in terms reminiscent of Mercier's description. Nonetheless, a number of cases in our sample suggest the existence of such pets in elite households. Thus Scipion, only four years old, in the service of the duc de Chartres, is unlikely to have been an ordinary domestic servant. Even older boys can be suspected to have served a decorative rather than a functional role, as for instance the eleven-year-old Azor, declared in Paris by the marquise de Marsan, or Aza and Jean (nicknamed César), two East Indians also both eleven years old, living at the homes of the marquise de Bremoy and of Madame de Montignan, respectively.[47]

Looking beyond our corpus of children, and through cases of non-whites for years other than 1777, we get some hints of what happened to these little blacks. Some remained in the service of their initial masters, though not always happily so, as the case of Madame du Barry's Zamor shows. Other slaves, once they became adults, sought their freedom and payment of back wages from the courts, usually claiming some sort of ill-treatment. Another means of obtaining freedom was simply to escape and attempt to disappear within the community of the free, something more easily achieved in a city than in the countryside. This is reflected in the accounts given by some nonwhites in Paris who declared their freedom. For instance, in 1777 a certain François claimed first to have been freed by Gaspard-Louis de Bompar, governor of Saint-Domingue, and later to have been born free, whereas an earlier declaration shows that he came to France in 1761 as Polidor, the slave of François de Beauharnois de Baumont, marquis de Beauharnois, governor of Martinique.[48] For masters, an escaped slave represented a significant financial loss, so that it is not surprising that most sought to recover their property. Nonetheless, the costs associated with recovery could prove too steep or the returns not worth the effort. This proved to be so for the Nantes ship captain Pierre-Ignace-Liévin Van Alstein, who returned from a voyage to Africa with a young black named Aza, whom he had baptized as Jean-Joseph and apprenticed to a wig maker. While master and slave were on a visit to Paris, Aza escaped and Van Alstein paid three hundred livres for a royal warrant to have him arrested and returned to him. Three years later, Van Alstein foolishly visited Paris a second time with Aza, who promptly escaped again. This time, Van Alstein gave up pursuing him.[49] Indeed, while young black boys might be cute and exotic domestic servants, an adult black may well have been perceived as a threat to the mistress who, when he was younger, had appreciated his caresses.[50] While impossible to demonstrate from the records studied, this type of sexual fear may explain in part why a number of male slaves, upon reaching adulthood, were freed and released to fend for themselves in France while female slaves tended to be retained. Such may have been the case of LaPierre, a black in the employ of a West Indian visitor. In his declaration, the latter stated that "La Pierre [is] claiming to be free, having previously belonged to the marquise de Maille who manumitted him." The declaration was made because LaPierre was caught in a sweep for illegal blacks conducted by Nantes police and there is no evidence that his manumission was anything but informal.[51]

## NOTES

All translations are the author's.

### Abbreviations

AD   Archives départementales
AM   Archives municipales
AN   Archives nationales (Paris)
ANC  Archives nationales, Fonds des colonies

1. Gaston Maugras, La Marquise de Boufflers et son fils, le chevalier de Boufflers (Paris: Plon-Nourrit, 1907), 477-78.

2. Mercier, Tableau de Paris, new ed., 12 vols. (Paris: s.n., 1782-88), 6:290-91.

3. Georges Lenôtre, "La Fin de Zamor," in Paris révolutionnaire: Vieilles maisons, vieux papiers, 6 vols. (Paris: Perrin et Cie., 1929-30), 1:217-24; Philip M. Laski, The Trial and Execution of Madame Du Barry (London: Constable, 1969).

4. See "Police des Noirs," ANC, F/1B/1, 3 & 4. Among early historians who have consulted these documents are Lucien Peytraud, L'esclavage aux Antilles françaises avant 1789, d'après des documents inédits des archives coloniales (Paris: Hachette et Cie, 1897); Jules Mathorez, Les étrangers en France sous l'ancien régime: Histoire de la formation de la population française, 2 vols. (Paris: E. Champion, 1919-21); Shelby T. McCloy, The Negro in France (Lexington: University of Kentucky Press, 1961). Since my study of these files, others have consulted them. See especially Erick Noël, Être noir en France au XVIIIe siècle (Paris: Tallandier, 2006). For the legal background to the census, see Sue Peabody, "There Are No Slaves in France": The Political Culture of Race and Slavery in the Ancien Régime (New York: Oxford University Press, 1996); Pierre H. Boulle, "Racial Purity or Legal Clarity? The Status of Black Residents in Eighteenth-Century France," Journal of the History Society 6, no. 1 (March 2006): 19-46.

5. A generally accepted figure based on estimates of slave numbers made by the Comité de législation coloniale. "Avis," 23 February 1782, ANC, F/1B/4, no. 316.

6. In the declarations on which the états are constructed, the ages of individuals are often given in round numbers (10, 20, 30, etc., or to a lesser extent, 5, 15, 25, etc.). In order to offset this trend, the bars in the age pyramids have been set, except for the first, in five-year segments around these numbers (0-2, 3-7, 8-12, etc.).

7. 279 cases out of 2,053 certain residents; 297 out of 2,240 if we include conditional cases.

8. Paris declaration, 28 February 1778, AN, Z/1D/139, reg. 7, fol. 18v; parish registers of Sceaux, 1760-62, AD Hauts-de-Seine; parish registers of Bû, 1762-81, AD Eure-et-Loir.

9. Paris declaration, 10 February 1778, AN, Z/1D/139, reg. 7, fol. 11.

10. Pregnancy declaration, 24 December 1777, AM Nantes, GG757, fol. 14v; parish register of Nantes (Saint-Nicolas), 1777, fol. 333v, AD Loire-Atlantique. Hortense-Marguerite died four months later (ibid., 1778, fol. 78).

11. Pregnancy declaration, 29 January 1777, AM Nantes, GG756, fol. 164v-65; parish register of Nantes (Saint-Saturnin), 1777, fol. 5, ibid., GG324, which states that Anne was born of "an unknown father."

12. Declaration of the widow Royne, 22 March 1777, AD Loire-Atlantique, B4524, fol. 131.

13. [Des Galois] de la Tour [intendant, Provence] to Choiseul [Ministry of Marine], 12 September 1763, AD Bouches-du-Rhône, C2561; Pellerin [subdélégué Brignoles] to intendant Provence, 5 February 1777, & "Etat des Noirs," 1777, ibid., C4622; Extr. reg. Sénéchaussée Brignoles, 4 February 1778, ANC, F/1B/4, no. 229.

14. Declaration of Pierre-Jean Ginette to Adm. Fréjus, 30 October 1777, ANC, F/1B/4, no. 132; declaration of Jean Ginette to Adm. Marseille, 18 December 1777, ANC, F/1B/3, no. 363.

15. Paris declaration, 12 May 1777, AN, Z/1D/139, reg. 6, fol. 7. A later declaration by Rouvray's wife suggests that Moÿse, age six, has to date only received religious instruction. Tours declaration, 1 October 1777, AD Indre-et-Loire, 2B1447.

16. Paris declaration, 21 May 1777, AN, Z/1D/139, reg. 6, fol. 13v. On the meaning of white and black on Bourbon Island, see Claude Wanquet, *Histoire d'une révolution: La réunion, 1789-1793*, 3 vols. (Marseille: J. Laffitte, 1980), 1:215-17.

17. Royal edict, October 1716, modified by royal declaration, 15 December 1738, in *Le Code Noir ou Recueil des Reglemens rendus juqu'à présent Concernant . . . [l]es Negres dans les Colonies Françoises* (Paris: Prault, 1767; redited in facsimile, Basse-Terre and Fort-de-France: Sociétés historiques de la Guadeloupe et de la Martinique, 1980), 169-81, 372-85.

18. Le Noir to Minister, 4 December 1777, ANC, F/1B/4, no. 397.

19. Paris declaration, 12 May, 1762, AN, Z/1D/139, reg. 5, fol. 2. On the life of Saint-George, see Alain Guédé, *Monsieur de Saint-George, le nègre des Lumières: Biographie* ([Arles]: Actes sud, 1999).

20. Robert Landru, *À propos d'Alexandre Dumas : les aïeux, le général, le bailli, premiers amis* (Vincennes: n.p., 1977), 28-106.

21. Saumur declaration, 18 October 1777, ANC, F/1B/4, no. 396. For Kerguelen's career and court-martial, see Etienne Taillemite, *Dictionnaire des marins français*, new ed. (Paris: Tallandier, 2002), 274; for his visit to Madagascar, see Kerguelen, *Relations de deux voyages dans les terres australes et des Indes, faits en 1771, 1772, 1773, et 1774* (Paris: Knapen et fils, 1782), 83, 87, 154-69, which makes no reference to the purchase of Corentin-Gustave.

22. Loudun declaration, 2 October 1777, AN, F/1B/4, no. 49.

23. Cited in Annick Le Douget, *Juges, esclaves et négriers en Basse-Bretagne, 1750-1850: l'émergence de la conscience abolitionniste* (n.p.: n.p., 2000), 24.

24. AD Charente-Maritime, B258, fol. 4v (16 September 1777).

25. AD Ille-et-Vilaine, C1438; ANC, F/1B/3, no. 369.

26. AD Loire-Atlantique, Marine 120-JJ-444, no. 77.

27. Ibid., 120-JJ-436, no. 25, 440, no. 11, and 442, no. 113.

28. "État des noirs [etc.] . . . déclarés . . . [à l']Amirauté de Bordeaux," ANC, F/1B/4, no. 211.

29. La Rochelle declaration, 23 July 1773, AD Charente-Maritime, B231, fol. 35v.

30. La Rochelle declaration, 9 October 1777, ibid., B258, fol. 18.

31. Nantes declaration, 7 March 1777, AD Loire-Atlantique, B4558, fol. 111v; parish register of Nantes (Saint-Nicolas), AM Nantes, GG279, fol. 129 (26 May 1777).

32. See Peabody, *No Slaves in France.*

33. Paris declaration, 24 September 1777, AN, Z/1D/139, reg. 6, fol. 36v.

34. Paris declaration, 27 September 1777, ibid., fol. 40; "Table alphabétique des Nègres," ibid., letters I/J, [1778], indicating that Mme Corbin "asked for her return from M. de Villiers"; "Ordre du Roi," 1 November 1777, Archives de la Préfecture de Police (Paris), AB370, 288, with the unusual marginal comment: "The warrant was not proposed by the Magistrate [the lieutenant-general of Police]."

35. Petition and Sentence of the Admiralty of France, 6 August 1777, AN, Z/1D/27 & 134; Paris declaration, 8 August 1777, AN, Z/1D/139, reg. 6, fol. 20v.

36. Petition to the Table de marbre (Paris), 27 July 1781, AN, Z/1D/135; report of the Bureau des Colonies, 3 November 1781, and undated comments by the minister, AN, F/1B/1, nos. 35, 40; La Rochelle declaration, 25 September 1777, AD Charente-Maritime, B258, fol. 14; ANC, F/1B/4, no. 388.

37. On white domestic servants, see Jean-Pierre Gutton, *Domestiques et serviteurs dans la France d'ancien régime* (Paris: Aubier Montaigne, 1981); Sarah Maza, *Servants and Masters in Eighteenth Century France: The Use of Loyalty* (Princeton: Princeton University Press, 1983); Cissie C. Fairchilds, *Domestic Enemies: Servants and Masters in Old Regime France* (Baltimore: Johns Hopkins University Press, 1984).

38. Paris declaration, 27 September 1777, AN, Z/1D/139, reg. 6, fol. 39v-40.

39. The royal declaration of 15 December 1738 required that the declaration of a slave include the name of the master craftsman to whom he or she was apprenticed. I have considered as effectively apprenticed only those for whom such a name is given, leaving aside the many others declarations which simply state an intention.

40. Nantes declarations, 22, 24, 29 March 1777, AD Loire-Atlantique, B4558, fol. 124, B4524, fol. 132; AD Gironde, C4557, nos. 23, 23 [bis]; ANC, F/1B/4, no. 148.

41. Paris declaration, 24 October 1777, AN, Z/1D/139, reg. 7, fol. 4.

42. Dominique Brun signs his own declaration, dated 26 January 1778, ANC, F/1B/4, no. 232.

43. Paris declaration of Joseph Coucy, quadroon, 24 September 1777, AN, Z/1D/139, reg. no. 6, fol. 35; Nantes declaration, 24 March 1777, AD Loire-Atlantique, B4524, fol. 133.

44. États, généralité Bordeaux and subdélégation Marmande, 1777, AD Gironde, C3669, C4457.

45. Landru, *Alexandre Dumas,* 68-77.

46. The initial report lists them as male slaves, noting that they belonged to the sieur Dian, who "refused to provide the information requested of him." "État des Noirs esclaves . . . Bordeaux," AD Gironde, C3669.

47. Lenoir to Minister, 4 December 1777, ANC, F/1B/4, no. 397; Paris declarations, 1 August, 10 October 1777, two on 14 February 1778, AN, Z/1D/139, reg. 6, fol. 19; reg. 7, fols. 1v, 8, 14v.

48. Paris declarations, 9 December 1761, 7 May 1762, 10 May, 18 September 1777, AN, Z/1D/139, reg. 4, fols. 4, 12v-13 and reg. 6, fols. 4v, 30.

49. The first part of the story is based on the following documents: Nantes declarations, 20 March 1777, 12 March 1778; baptismal record, Saint-Nicolas parish, Nantes, 29 March 1777; Aza's petition at the Table de marbre (Paris), 24 July 1778; Paris declaration by Van Alstein, 25 September 1778; "Ordre du Roi" for Aza's arrest, 3 August 1778, released 10 September 1778 (AD Loire Atlantique, B4524, fol. 126; par. reg. Nantes [Saint-Nicolas], 1777, fol. 93v; AN, Z/1D/135, 139, reg. 7, fol. 22, loose leaf attached to fol. 6 Arch. Préf. Police [Paris], AB370, 374). The second escape and Van Alstein's abandon is described in Père Dieudonné Rinchon, *Pierre-Ignace-Liévin van Alstein, capitaine négrier, Gand 1733–Nantes 1793* (Dakar: IFAN, 1964), 381.

50. On the development of racial prejudice against blacks in the eighteenth century, and its relationship to sexual phobias, see Pierre H. Boulle, *Race et esclavage dans la France de l'ancien régime* (Paris: Perrin, 2007), sect. 1, "Le concept de race en France."

51. Nantes declaration, 22 March 1777, AD Loire-Atlantique, B4524, fol. 130.

# 11

## THE STRUGGLE FOR SURVIVAL

*Slave Infant Mortality in the British Caribbean
in the Late Eighteenth and Nineteenth Centuries*

KENNETH MORGAN

The enslaved population of the British Caribbean failed to reproduce. This abnormality of human demographic behavior resulted from the low fertility and reproductive difficulties suffered by female slaves subjected to the tough working regime of cultivating sugar, poor nutritional and living conditions, the physical punishments characteristic of slavery, and inadequate treatment of many contagious or fatal diseases.[1] Mortality was also an obstacle to the growth of the British Caribbean infant slave population. Not enough children born to slaves survived into adulthood to reproduce. In 1790 the attorney general for Grenada and its dependencies noted that nearly half the slave children born in the West Indies died before the age of two, most within the first nine days.[2] In 1818 a doctor claimed that 38 out of 141 slave deaths (27 percent) in Clarendon Parish, Jamaica, were infants.[3] In 1817-18 in Grenada 24 percent of slave deaths occurred before the age of five.[4] Details from some slave estates reflect these findings. On the Codrington plantations, Barbados, at least one in every two slave youngsters died before reaching the age of five.[5] Half the slave children born in Trinidad between 1813 and 1816 failed to survive to their fifth birthday.[6] And between 1817 and 1834 approximately 56 percent of slave children born on the Lascelles estates in Barbados and Jamaica died before the age of five.[7] The burden of these estimates is that between a quarter and a half of slave children in the British Caribbean died before they were five. This demographic fact was important for slave work in the Caribbean because children aged six years or above were usually employed in the sugarcane fields alongside adults. They assisted female slaves in the third gang, which carried out less demanding physical work than that allocated to the fittest adult slaves of both sexes. Slave children gained knowledge and experience of the seasonal rhythms and routines of sugar cultivation that they carried into adulthood. High infant mortality was therefore a blow to a productive human resource for planters.

Newborn slave children were the most vulnerable to mortality. During the eighteenth century roughly 80 percent of infant mortality occurred within the first fortnight after birth. By the early nineteenth century, the figure was 50 percent.[8] Evidence from individual islands supports the case for heavy slave infant mortality. Dr. John Castles, who practiced medicine in Grenada in the twenty years after 1766, asserted that fully one-third of slave children died within a month after birth.[9] From 1817 to 1820, birth-deaths (before the seventh day of life) accounted for 40 percent of slave children born on three plantations in St. Vincent and for 41 percent on two estates in St. Kitts. The same records generate mortality of 50 percent in the first month of life for Saint Kitts and 61 percent for St. Vincent.[10]

Calculating infant mortality rates is difficult because the data used for such an exercise are distorted by the underregistration of births. Estate accounts usually recorded only live births, so it is not easy to estimate the number of babies aborted or stillborn. In order to estimate slave infant mortality (children under five), Barry Higman has adopted a methodology widely used by historical demographers to compile model life tables for 1817 through 1832, the period of comprehensive slave registration in the British West Indies. Such tables have the advantage of being specific to each British colony in the islands. For male infants, death rates in individual colonies ranged between 240 and 580 per thousand births, and for females from 200 to 480 per thousand. Four out of every ten children in most of the eastern Caribbean colonies did not live to the age of five.[11] Because model life tables are least accurate for the youngest age group (0–5) owing to the underrecording of infant deaths, these estimates indicate the minimum level of slave infant mortality.[12] These mortality rates were much higher than for infants in Britain during the same period. Despite secular swings, the infant mortality rate in England never rose above two hundred per thousand births in any quarter century between 1580 and 1837. Overall infant mortality in England between 1790 and 1837—covering the slave registration period in the British Caribbean—averaged 141 per thousand births.[13]

Although the subject has attracted scholarly attention, including some helpful synthetic studies, the causes of mortality among slave infants remains the least understood component of the demographic regime in the British Caribbean.[14] Even if some aspects of child mortality remain difficult to interpret, it is useful to examine the major contributory factors, which include the cultural attitudes of slave mothers; dietary and environmental factors; disease and medical treatment. This chapter draws on contemporary explanations and modern medical and demographic studies in order to evaluate the reasons for high mortality among slave infants ages one to five. I argue that slave mothers may have played an unwitting, though in most cases not deliberate, role in the failure of infants to survive; but that greater emphasis should be placed on a combination of nutritional, environmental, health, and disease factors that made infant life a struggle for survival.

Any discussion of infant mortality needs to consider the potential for slave women to refuse to nurture their newborn children in order to prevent their offspring from entering the condition of slavery. Some scholars have identified this ideology as a "gynecological revolt."[15] It has also been claimed that the same ideology of resistance accounted for infanticide and slave mothers' neglect of their infants. Thus one historian has argued that slave women deliberately allowed children they could not prevent being born to die, in order to frustrate the planters' desire to breed slave children.[16] Another has claimed that slave motherhood was restricted by "the potential impulse women may have felt to interrupt . . . obscene calculations made by planters in treating slave mothers as commodities."[17]

The evidence to support such claims is mixed. Certainly high infant mortality was a central factor in the lives of slave women; on Worthy Park plantation, Jamaica, for instance, 70 out of 89 slave women in 1794 had lost children—sometimes many.[18] In these and other locations it is possible that slave cultural practices raised the rate of infant mortality. African mothers had a notion of "ghost children," newborn infants who were seen as the possible embodiments of evil spirits and were in consequence neglected for eight days following their birth. For example, slave women first changed a newborn baby's clothes fully three days after its birth—a practice that encouraged the development of gastroenteritis.[19] Indeed, such was the belief that during this period babies were not yet human, that any child dying within that period was denied a funeral.[20] Thus a midwife told absentee proprietor Matthew Gregory "Monk" Lewis when he visited his Jamaican plantation, "Oh, massa, till nine days over, we no hope of them."[21] If the child survived it was then nurtured, took the family and ancestral names, and was registered in the plantation books.[22] This tradition, common in West Africa, survived the Middle Passage and was widespread in the Caribbean.[23] It may well have contributed to infant mortality while also enabling slave mothers to remain emotionally detached from their offspring during the first, highly uncertain days of their lives.

In addition, slave women indirectly contributed to infant mortality by following the widespread practice of allowing wet nurses to feed their newborns. This was certainly the belief of John Quier, a doctor who practiced at Worthy Park for fifty-five years, who noted the "injudicious Custom of Suckling a new born child for the first week after its Birth, or longer, with the Milk of a Woman who often has a child at her breast a year old or perhaps older."[24] The milk of such a mother would have sufficiently declined in calcium content virtually to guarantee neonatal tetany in a low-birth-weight infant.[25] A doctor with experience of West Indian sociomedical practice recommended that slave children should be at least six weeks old before they received any food other than their own mother's milk.[26] Newborn babies would benefit from the colostrum that their mothers, but not wet nurses, could supply. More crucial to their survival, however, was the degree of cleanliness with which infants were handled.

Planters were also often of the opinion that slave mothers neglected their children. Thus in 1793 the absentee Lord Penrhyn noted to his attorney in Jamaica, "I wish the Mothers could be induced to take more care of their children."[27] Again, in 1810 the manager of La Taste estate, Grenada, who stated that "it is almost universally interest & not affection that makes the Negroe Mother attend to her infant,"[28] proposed giving colored cotton handkerchiefs as rewards to those slave mothers whose children remained alive and healthy a few months after birth. Some observers alleged that neglect of children by mothers intent on amorous adventures contributed to infant mortality. Such women, it is suggested, found children an incumbrance to their "nocturnal meetings and dances."[29] Monk Lewis recorded an instance on his Jamaican plantation where a slave mother took care of her baby until the tenth day after its birth, then claimed her "child" allowance of clothes and provisions before leaving her child to go dancing on a neighboring plantation; the abandoned child was left so long without food that it was taken to the hospital, where it died within a day.[30] Dr. Quier accused slave women of being uncaring to their children, especially when they had changed mates: "many children are lost through neglect, and the want of maternal affection, which these mothers seldom retain for their offspring, by a former husband."[31] However, it is extremely difficult to evaluate from these scattered observations whether slave mothers truly denied their infants care and affection, and so contributed to high slave infant mortality.

It is difficult to accept that the neglect of infants by slave mothers was the rule rather than the exception. The reason lies in the personal beliefs and cultural practices of African slave women in the Caribbean. Such women generally attached great importance to children. This helped to validate their personal worth as women in the face of the trauma and misery of slavery. To give birth to a child was the main way in which a female slave could demonstrate self-respect as a woman. Moreover, African-born slaves, who dominated the British Caribbean black population until the early nineteenth century, had been born in societies where fertility was regarded as women's greatest gift. Motherhood grew out of the ancestral veneration that formed part of West African belief systems. Children were regarded as the life force through which men and women achieved integration into the universe. For these reasons, the impulse to care for a child was very strong among West Indian slave women. Therefore it is difficult to see how allegations of maternal neglect could have wide application.[32]

Barbara Bush has argued that the practice of infanticide, and its links with high neonatal mortality, cannot be discounted in British Caribbean slave societies.[33] However, the evidence summoned to support this suggestion is problematic. It was extremely difficult for planters or officials to determine whether a dead baby had been stillborn or whether the mother had killed it. Indeed, charges of infanticide were harder to prove than any other offense brought before the Jamaican courts.[34] Nevertheless, infanticide sometimes occurred. In one well-publicized case Sabrina Park, tried in Jamaica for the murder of her three-month-old child, stated that "she would not be plagued to raise the child . . . to work for white people."[35] But one cannot extrapolate from this and a handful of similar remarks by other slave mothers who had killed their babies to argue that infanticide was widespread in the British Caribbean during the slavery era, especially as little systematic evidence has been marshaled there for child smothering, though the practice is well documented for slave societies in North America.[36] One intriguing possibility is that slave mothers regarded the killing of a sickly baby as abortion rather than infanticide, owing to the widespread belief, already mentioned, that infants were not regarded as survivors until they reached their ninth day.[37] Although there is scant evidence, such a belief might have reduced the moral burden of allowing the debilities of birth under the harsh conditions of West Indian slavery to take their natural course.

The scant records of slave child mortality during the final phase of British Caribbean slavery provide little evidence of infanticide. For example, the causes of death registered for Tobago between 1819 and 1821 contain some references suggestive of child murder, such as "a fall; supposed by a fall from its mother" and "suffocation; overlaid by mother."[38] Yet not only is interpretation of such references difficult, but they were remarkably few, given that the registration material was full and accurate on causes of slave death. Thus the records for the islands of Grenada and Carriacou for 1820 indicate that only two of the eighty-four registered deaths of children aged under one resulted from suffocation; and one of these stated the cause as accidental.[39] When one considers that planters and their representatives carefully oversaw the health of their slave charges, it seems fair to conclude that had infanticide been widespread it would have left a clearer trail in the historical record.

On the whole slave mothers cared for their children and set great store by nurturing them despite the hostile environment and their own poor nutrition and physical condition which critically affected the neonatal health and survival chances of slave infants. In modern times, high mortality rates for under-fives are important indicators of the severity of malnutrition in a given population.[40] Severe maternal malnutrition is the leading cause of stillbirths in third world countries today,[41] and the same situation obtained for Caribbean slave women. Female physiology requires specific nutrients; for example, women need three times more iron than men. Protein and calcium requirements for pregnant and lactating women are also higher than for adult males: 30 to 50 percent more thiamine (vitamin $B_1$) is required.[42] Slave women deficient in thiamine would have been unable to utilize properly riboflavin and niacin, which in turn would have upset metabolization of all the B vitamins. Yet evidence suggests that the all-important protein rations given to slave families were consumed mostly by men. Traditionally in West Africa it was the men who took priority in helpings from the cooking pot. Similarly, in the Caribbean during the slavery era, men consumed most of the available animal protein.[43]

Similarly, the calorific intake of slave mothers was inadequate. Robert Dirks's data suggest that the average plantation food allowance in the British West Indies amounted to 1,500 to 2,000 calories per individual and approximately forty-five grams of protein each day.[44] Under average conditions men require roughly 3,200 calories a day and women 2,300—women's metabolic rate being slower than men's. Under conditions of exceptionally heavy labor, both male and female workers need an additional 450 calories.[45] These caloric estimates indicate that Caribbean slaves on sugar estates, women at least as much as men, received considerably less food than needed for the heavy work in the cane fields and around the boiling house. In fact, women outnumbered men in the field gangs that carried out the most strenuous cane holing, planting, and harvesting.[46] In 1800 a Barbadian planter noted that it was the usual practice with planters "to work all the negroes together, indiscriminately, as the women with men, and the weak with the strong."[47]

The high incidence of stillbirths among the slaves was directly connected to the nutritional deficiencies of pregnant women—and to the lagged effect of physical exertion. Private ameliorative arrangements sometimes reduced the strain. For example, in the 1780s in Barbados it was recommended that breast-feeding women should not appear in the fields until 7 a.m., an hour after work for others began.[48] But such restraint was not widely observed, with the result that many slave infants, deprived of proper maternal nutrition, failed to survive the first few days of life.

Slave women and their infant children existed on a diet high in carbohydrates and low in protein; the children's food consisted of cornmeal and flour soups with little or no milk. On the Lascelles plantations in Barbados in the 1830s children received smaller food allowances than adult workers.[49] Further evidence suggests that children between one and five years old received only one third of the provisions allocated to adult slaves. Even though children did not require as many calories for their daily food intake as adults, they were usually undernourished; the full food allowance was not given to them until they were twelve, thirteen, or fourteen.[50] Healthy children would have been able to cope with these dietary deficiencies, but infants subject to the diseases and complaints referred to below would have struggled to survive. It is unsurprising that the second largest number of complaints to the Protector of Slaves in Berbice (now part of Guyana) in the 1820s—after allegations of brutal punishment—concerned inadequate supplies of food and especially shortages of food for children.[51]

Environmental conditions compounded the difficulties for slave infants. The slaves' overcrowded, smoky huts spread respiratory infections. Many children died of pneumonia, a virus prevalent in the overcrowded slave quarters, though it is most likely to have occurred in young children after their skin had been chilled by dampness or cool winds. The rooms in slave huts were often hot but cold air circulated through them. This contributed to colds picked up by children; sometimes perspiration stopped and death followed quickly.[52] Changes in temperature can also be extremely dangerous, notably for low-birth weight babies left in the open air for long periods and exposed to heat and rain.[53] In Africa babies were carried on their mothers' backs, wrapped with a cloth, which stabilized the child's temperature. The intense work regime of Caribbean slavery denied such protection to children born there and was disadvantageous to their well-being. In 1784 the Reverend James Ramsay, an antislavery advocate who lived in St. Kitts, described a mother with a three- or four-week-old child whom "she then takes to the field with her. The infant is placed naked, or almost naked, open to the sun and rain, on a kid skin, or such rags as she can procure."[54]

Such lack of clothing added to the battle for survival of many thousands of slave children.

Childhood illnesses were further exacerbated by poor hygiene, inadequate housing, impure water supplies, and lack of facilities for sanitary disposal of excreta and rubbish.[55] Slave children often walked on soil and through water infested with feces, mosquitoes, and flies. Poor water supply can result in dysentery, and children who cannot be properly washed may develop skin diseases. The absence of sanitation on most sugar estates meant that the ground was thoroughly soiled with infested stools, which leads, among other hazards, to the spread of intestinal worms. Poor disposal of rubbish results in increased breeding of flies and other vectors, as well as an increased likelihood of diarrheal diseases.

Inflammation of various bodily organs, malformation of the body, and fevers were common among infant slaves. The most common causes of death recorded for slave children under five were tetanus, lockjaw, yaws, worms, beriberi, "teething," and whooping cough—infections and infestations directly related to poor maternal and infant nutrition and lack of medical knowledge—which rarely seriously affected well-nourished children.[56] Most diseases occurred regularly from year to year, but there were also epidemic outbreaks of infectious diseases such as whooping cough that was widespread in Barbados in 1753, Jamaica in 1770, and Grenada in 1798. In Grenada in 1830 whooping cough was the leading cause of infant slave death.[57]

At each stage of infant life—among neonatals, among those breast-feeding, among those between breast-feeding and weaning—there was an unremitting cycle of infection, which could lead to early death. Tetanus, or lockjaw, was the major killer of newborn slave children. In the 1770s a manager on Hope Plantation, Jamaica, noted that "children don't thrive much here. The reason is a mystery to me . . . they generally die of the jaw-fall or some other disorder when about a week or fortnight old."[58] In 1788 the planter-historian Edward Long estimated that tetanus destroyed around one-third of the children born on his Jamaican sugar plantation.[59] And as late as 1831, John Hancock, who practiced medicine in British Guiana for over twenty years, wrote that tetanus killed half the infants born in Demerara-Essequibo.[60] Modern research suggests that tetanus could have accounted for up to 20 percent of total slave mortality, which would have made it as much of a killer as old age or debility.[61]

There were various causes of tetanus. Excrement, refuse from livestock, and richly manured cane fields created an environment "probably without equal, for generating one of the deadliest poisons known to man."[62] The main cause of neonatal tetanus was "improper treatment of the navel string."[63] When nurses, midwives, or ordinary slaves cut a newborn's umbilical cord with unclean instruments and then dressed the umbilicus with mud, tobacco ash, burnt rag, bark, or arrowroot, as invariably happened, the risk of tetanus infection was high.[64]

Doctors at the time realized the connection between infant deaths and introducing dirt into the body when cutting the navel string but misunderstood the etiology of tetanus, which they confused with lockjaw.[65] Thus one contemporary explanation attributed lockjaw to slaves applying very hot linen to the navel string, causing it to be very sore; any touching of the navel then caused irritation, which in turn brought on the fall of the jaw (lockjaw).[66] Eighteenth-century doctors thought fatalities from lockjaw resulted from babies not being properly freed from the afterbirth discharge—an idea that lingered on in the British Caribbean until the end of slavery.[67] Thus Long wrote of infants "perishing within nine or ten days of their birth by what is called here jaw falling; which is caused by a retention of the meconium," that is, the newborn's initial greenish-black stool.[68] The meconium stool needs to be passed, but it is not a cause of tetanus. James Thomson, who practiced medicine in Jamaica and wrote a book on slave diseases, realized that "improper treatment of the naval cord" resulted in tetanus but still advised "purging"—an aggressive procedure that involved cauterizing, cleansing, and tying the umbilical cord. When carried out with unclean implements, it could prove fatal to an already depleted infant, as often was the common practice of feeding a newborn infant castor oil, a purgative, and rum, a stimulant, until he or she was nine days old.[69]

Many doctors also mistook tetany, or hypocalcemia, for tetanus, which produced similar convulsions in an infant. Thus Thomson noted of the symptoms of what he took to be lockjaw, but which was almost certainly acute tetany—characterized by rhythmic jerks sometimes followed by generalized fits:[70] "[The] jaw is not always fixed: I have seen a child suck till within a few hours of its death; the spasms seize every part of the body indiscriminately, in the most partial manner, and we are often astonished to see death ensue after they have commenced but a few hours, without any degree of violence."[71]

Tetany, which results in a 30 percent death rate and was a major but unrecognized cause of early death, is due to a deficiency of metabolized calcium in low-birth weight babies whose mothers are badly nourished or low in calcium and vitamin D.[72] Infants who escaped tetanus or tetany were often afflicted with beriberi, which was frequently the result of thiamine deficiency among female slaves. In such circumstances babies were born with reduced bodily stores of thiamine and the mother's milk, lacking in vitamin $B_1$, could not compensate for this imbalance. The result was often acute beriberi, characterized by restlessness and screaming, leading to vomiting, breathlessness, convulsions, and sometimes cardiac failure. This deficiency disease damages the heart and the nervous system and between two and four months is rapidly fatal. A distinctive characteristic of widespread beriberi among a population is an unusually high number of mothers who have histories of losing one child after another before infants reach their first birthdays.[73] Monk Lewis described such an example: "This woman was a tender mother, had borne ten children, and yet has now but one alive . . . and [I know other] instances of those who have had four, five, six children, without succeeding in bringing up one."[74]

Prolonged breast-feeding was vital to the survival of infants before cow's milk became widely available, as maternal milk would have provided the only available source of protein for slave babies.[75] However, after six months the infant required additional sources of iron and protein or became "breast starved." Beriberi, which normally declines at about six months and is rare after the age of one, can continue to afflict breast-starved infants chiefly in the form of protein energy malnutrition (PEM), a deficiency disease that causes kwashiorkor, or protein deficiency disorder.[76] During the slavery era the symptoms of kwashiorkor and advanced beriberi were often mistaken for what was called teething, which was registered as the cause of death of a relatively large proportion of infant fatalities in Barbados and Jamaica.[77] The erroneous attribution resulted from the practice of weaning slave children to a high-carbohydrate, low-protein diet at about the time of teething, the consequence of which was PEM. Investigations of the teeth of children excavated from a slave cemetery in Barbados have revealed growth-arrest lines shortly after weaning:[78] Hans Sloane witnessed in Jamaica a one-year-old child that had six or seven convulsions when it was teething.[79] Although the nutritional requirements of the under-fives are proportionally higher for body weight than those of older children or adults,[80] slave children were usually given a less nutritious diet than adults.

The high incidence of hookworm further increased the likelihood of PEM. The larvae of one species (*Ancylostoma duodenale*) penetrated the skin of bare feet, caused itching between the toes, and traveled through the bloodstream to the lymph glands or lungs; if ingested through the mouth, they nestled in the intestines. Colonies of over five hundred larvae cause hookworm disease, which produces dropsy (fluid retention in the limbs), convulsions, or a craving to eat dirt (*mal d'estomac*).[81] There is a correlation between dirt eating (pica), which appears to have been as common in infants as it was in their mothers, and anemia. Iron-deficient mothers tend to give birth to babies with iron deficiency, a condition aggravated by hookworm. Indeed, Long wrote that "worms are extremely fatal to children in this climate and destroy more than any other disease."[82] Worms proliferated among slave children suffering from a low intake of vitamin A. In such cases parasites spread quickly to precipitate kwashiorkor.[83] In tropical regions today where kwashiorkor is prevalent—and it is still a common disease—deaths are often attributed to diarrhea or worms.[84] Contemporary writers on the West Indies described the physical manifestations of kwashiorkor without knowledge of its symptomology. Thus Thomas Roughley's widely circulated planter's manual wrote of the "swelling of youngsters [sic] stomachs to a prenatural size . . . known under the vulgar name of pot belly."[85] Higman finds that deaths attributed to swellings or bloated bodies mainly affected younger slaves.[86]

Protein-deprived children have a markedly lower capacity to produce specific antibodies to diseases such as measles, chickenpox, influenza, and even the common cold.[87] Those suffering from these diseases, and others such as yaws, worms, and whooping cough, were likely to develop kwashiorkor.[88] James Maxwell cited the example of young children "whose constitutions are much impaired by chronic yaws, then contract a habit of eating dirt."[89] In this case, the resort to geophagy probably stemmed from the nutritional debilities that children suffered which could help produce yaws, a bacterial skin infection. Though not usually fatal, yaws was a nonvenereal form of syphilis characterized by ugly skin lumps and lesions on the lips, body, and soles of the feet, often accompanied by permanent bone damage and disfigurement. Because of its contagious and widespread occurrence in the Caribbean, some plantations built "yaws houses" for sufferers by the early nineteenth century. The lack of specific nutrients that produced yaws and geophagy could also result in dysentery, Maxwell noting that "when dysentery follows in the rear of protracted yaws it generally proves fatal."[90]

The connections between geophagy and anemia, hookworms and kwashiorkor, dysentery and yaws, are a reminder, possibly underappreciated by historians, that infant slave children could die from a combination of complaints. Thus Richard B. Sheridan's explanation of the causes of death of slave children in Grenada in 1820 and 1830, the fullest and most accurate for any Caribbean island, omitted combined causes,[91] which constituted the leading cause of death (totaling 12 percent) among slaves up to five years old in Grenada and the Grenadines between 1817 and 1834. In Grenada the five leading causes of death recorded for slaves five and under in that period were: combined causes, 309; fever, 304; worms, 263; lockjaw, 243; marasmus (chronic malnourishment), 193.[92] Combined causes of death included worms and debility, itch and marasmus, dysentery and fever, teething and bowel complaint, cachexia (physical wasting) and diarrhea, lung inflammation and diseased navel, bowel complaint and dropsy, anasarca (edema) and debility, and thrush and chest infection. Thus respiratory complaints were frequently combined with gastroenterital disorders, fevers with malnutrition, and starvation with dietary deficiencies.[93]

What medical remedies were available to counteract these debilitating, potentially fatal, complaints? There is evidence to suggest that there was an African tradition of inoculating children against yaws and smallpox. John Stewart, a planter-author in Jamaica, wrote that "there was no doubt that negro mothers wilfully infected their children with yaws."[94] Although this practice was frowned upon by planters and doctors, it must have been correctly understood by slave women that infectious diseases, such as yaws, tended to be less severe in childhood and gave some immunity later in life. When babies were already severely disadvantaged, however, deliberate infection can only have further endangered their health. Slaves similarly practiced smallpox inoculation, to some good effect, although smallpox remained virulent until European-style vaccination was introduced after 1800. In 1813 a vaccine center was established in Jamaica, and in Trinidad in 1819, when a general vaccination of the population was ordered. In the smaller British West Indian islands, however, many people remained unvaccinated up to emancipation.[95]

Overall, the indications are that possibly 50 percent of slave infants died before they reached their fifth year and that slave infant mortality did not decline sharply until after emancipation, particularly in areas dominated by sugar estates.[96] Yet by the early nineteenth century there were signs that appreciation of the benefits of basic hygiene and decent feeding was ameliorating conditions for some infants. European doctors ended to be more restrained in their use of the harsher aspects of medical orthodoxy; the purging and bleeding so disastrous to a small, weak frame was gradually abandoned. Also by the early 1800s the use of mercury, traditionally given freely to little children as a prophylactic against worms had decreased, as had the incidence of infant tetanus, while smallpox had been virtually eradicated.[97]

High infant and early-childhood mortality among slaves in the British Caribbean resulted from a great variety of factors including the reluctance of some slave women to bring children into a world of slavery, poor health, inadequate diet, and harsh working conditions. It is here argued that female slave agency was not the main cause of slave infant mortality, which was due rather to their own and their infants' malnourishment, and to disease. After the traumas of the first few days of life, when tetanus and tetany killed many infants, the survivors often fell victim to a vicious circle of deficient nutrition, poor hygiene, and diseases, notably kwashiorkor and P.E.M. High slave infant mortality was rarely monocausal in the British Caribbean, where slave children faced an environment so replete with factors now known to be lethal that it is a miracle that any survived to adulthood.

## NOTES

1. Kenneth F. Kiple, *The Caribbean Slave: A Biological History* (Cambridge: Cambridge University Press, 1984), 104-19; Richard B. Sheridan, *Doctors and Slaves: A Medical and Demographic History of Slavery in the British West Indies, 1680-1834* (Cambridge: Cambridge University Press, 1985), 222-48.

2. Evidence of Sir Ashton Warner Byam, cited in *House of Commons Sessional Papers of the Eighteenth Century*, ed. Sheila Lambert (Wilmington, DE: Scholarly Resources, 1975), 71:110.

3. William Sells, *Remarks on the Condition of the Slaves in the Island of Jamaica* (London: J. M. Richardson, Cornhill, and Ridgways, 1823), 19-20.

4. Jeffrey P. Koplan, "Slave Mortality in Nineteenth Century Grenada," *Social Science History* 7, no. 3 (1983): 312-13.

5. J. Harry Bennett, *Bondsmen and Bishops: Slavery and Apprenticeship on the Codrington Plantations of Barbados, 1710-1838* (Berkeley: University of California Press, 1958), 56-57.

6. A. Meredith John, *The Plantation Slaves of Trinidad, 1783-1816: A Mathematical and Demographic Enquiry* (New York: Cambridge University Press, 1988), 156.

7. S. D. Smith, *Slavery, Family and Gentry Capitalism in the British Atlantic: The World of the Lascelles, 1648-1834* (Cambridge: Cambridge University Press, 2006), 286.

8. J. R. Ward, *British West Indian Slavery: The Process of Amelioration, 1750-1834* (New York: Oxford University Press, 1988), 130.

9. Lambert, *House of Commons*, 71:210.

10. B. W. Higman, *Slave Populations of the British Caribbean, 1807-1834* (Baltimore: Johns Hopkins University Press, 1984), 29. However, much lower rates of infant mortality for Grenada (4.7 percent of slave births in 1820 and 5.7 percent in 1830) are reported in Sheridan, *Doctors and Slaves*, 237.

11. Higman, *Slave Populations*, 317-19.

12. S. D. Smith, "Life and Labor on a Jamaican Sugar Plantation: Prospect Estate, 1784-1832," *Wadabagei: A Journal of the Caribbean and Its Diaspora* 9, no. 3 (2006): 86.

13. E. A. Wrigley, R. S. Davies, J. E. Oeppen and R. S. Schofield, *English Population History from Family Reconstitution, 1580-1837* (Cambridge: Cambridge University Press, 1997), 218-19.

14. The main previous studies are Kiple, *Caribbean Slave*, 120-34; Sheridan, *Doctors and Slaves*, 200-219, 234-39; Higman, *Slave Populations*, 26-33, 317-19.

15. For example, Orlando Patterson, *Slavery and Social Death: A Comparative Study* (Cambridge, Mass: Harvard University Press, 1982), 133 (quotation); Stella Dadzie,

"Searching for the Invisible Woman: Slavery and Resistance in Jamaica," *Race and Class* 32, no. 2 (1990): 27.

16. Barbara Bush, *Slave Women in Caribbean Society, 1650–1838* (London: James Currey, 1990), 137-42, 147-49; Bush, "Hard Labor: Women, Childbirth, and Resistance in British Caribbean Slave Societies," in *More than Chattel: Black Women and Slavery in the Americas*, ed. David Barry Gaspar and Darlene Clark Hine (Bloomington: Indiana University Press, 1996), 205-6, 209-10.

17. Jennifer L. Morgan, *Laboring Women: Reproduction and Gender in New World Slavery* (Philadelphia: University of Pennsylvania Press, 2004), 200.

18. Michael Craton and James Walvin, *A Jamaican Plantation: The History of Worthy Park, 1670–1970* (London: W. H. Allen, 1970), 134.

19. Michael Craton, *Searching for the Invisible Man: Slaves and Plantation Life in Jamaica* (Cambridge, Mass: Harvard University Press, 1978), 395.

20. Higman, *Slave Populations*, 27.

21. Quoted in Matthew Gregory Lewis, *Journal of a West India Proprietor 1815–1817*, ed. Mona Wilson (London: George Routledge and Sons, 1929), 96.

22. Thomas Samson to Henry Goulburn, 23 November 1810, Goulburn Collection, 304/J/1/17(9), Surrey History Centre, Woking.

23. Pierre Erny, *Childhood and Cosmos: The Social Psychology of the Black African Child* (New York: New Perspectives, 1973), 120; Maria R. Cutrufelli, *Women of Africa: Roots of Oppression* (London: Zed, 1983), 133.

24. Quoted in Craton, *Invisible Man*, 395.

25. Kiple, *Caribbean Slave*, 124.

26. A Physician in the West-Indies [James Grainger], *An Essay on the More Common West-India Diseases; and the Remedies which that country itself produces* (London: T. Becket and P. A. De Hondt, 1764), 16.

27. Lord Penrhyn to Mr. Falconer, 17 April 1793, Penrhyn Manuscripts, Bangor University, Wales.

28. Quoted in Susanne Seymour, Stephen Daniels, and Charles Watkins, "Estate and Empire: Sir George Cornewall's Management of Moccas, Herefordshire and La Taste, Grenada, 1771-1819," *Journal of Historical Geography* 24, no. 3 (1998): 341.

29. Evidence of Robert Thomas and Thomas Norbury, cited in Lambert, *House of Commons*, 71:257, 72:300.

30. Lewis, *Journal*, 96.

31. Quoted in Craton, *Invisible Man*, 396.

32. For arguments in favor of slave women's attachment to their children, see Kenneth Morgan, "Slave Women and Reproduction in Jamaica, c. 1776–1834," *History* 91, no. 3 (2006): 247.

33. Bush, *Slave Women*, 147-49.

34. Jonathan Dalby, *Crime and Punishment in Jamaica: A Quantitative Analysis of the Assize Court Records, 1756–1856* (Kingston: Social History Project, Department of History, University of the West Indies, 2000), 42-43.

35. Quoted in Orlando Patterson, *The Sociology of Slavery: An Analysis of the Origins, Development, and Structure of Negro Slave Society in Jamaica* (London: MacGibbon and Kee, 1967), 106-7.

36. See the studies cited in Richard H. Steckel, "A Dreadful Childhood: The Excess Mortality of American Slaves" in *The African Exchange: Toward a Biological History*, ed. Kenneth F. Kiple (Durham, NC: Duke University Press, 1987), 291-329.

37. Craton, *Invisible Man*, 413n14.

38. Higman, *Slave Populations*, 626.

39. Calculated from the National Archives, Kew, T 71/274: Slave Registration records for Grenada and the Grenadines.

40. G. H. Beaton and J. M. Bengoa, "Practical Population Indicators of Health and Nutrition" in *Nutrition in Preventative Medicine*, ed. G. H. Beaton and J. M. Bengoa (Geneva: WHO, 1976), 507.

41. Derrick B. Jelliffe, "Interactions between Nutrition and Infection," in *Child Health in the Tropics*, ed. Derrick Jelliffe (London: Edward Arnold, 1968), 14.

42. Cicely D. Williams, Naomi Baumslag, and Derrick B. Jelliffe, *Mother and Child Health: Delivering the Services* (London: Oxford University Press, 1985), 70, 77.

43. Kiple, *Caribbean Slave*, 80-85; Hubert Carey Trowell, *Non-Infective Disease in Africa* (London: Edward Arnold, 1960), 127.

44. Robert Dirks, "Resource Fluctuations and Competitive Transformation in West Indian Slave Societies," in *Extinction and Survival in Human Populations*, ed. Charles D. Laughlin and Ivan A. Brady (New York: Columbia University Press, 1978), 146.

45. Lucius Nicholls, *Tropical Nutrition and Dietetics* (London: Baillière, Tindell and Cox, 1961), 310.

46. Barbara Bush, "Towards Emancipation: Women and Coercive Labour Regimes in the British West Indian Colonies, 1790-1838," *Slavery and Abolition* 5, no. 2 (1984): 225-26; Richard S. Dunn, "Sugar Production and Slave Women in Jamaica," in *Cultivation and Culture: Labor and the Shaping of Slave Life in the Americas*, ed. Ira Berlin and Philip D. Morgan (Charlottesville: University Press of Virginia, 1993), 62.

47. Isaac W. Orderson, *Directions to Young Planters for Their Care and Management of a Sugar Plantation in Barbadoes* (London: T. Bensley, 1800), 4.

48. [Philip Gibbes], "Instructions for the Treatment of Negroes," *Journal of the Barbados Museum and Historical Society* 2 (1934): 25.

49. Tara A. Inniss, "From Slavery to Freedom: Children's Health in Barbados, 1823-1838," *Slavery and Abolition* 27, no. 2 (2006): 253.

50. Anja Jabour, "Slave Health and Health Care in the British Caribbean: Profits, Racism and the Failure of Amelioration in Trinidad and British Guiana, 1824-1834," *Journal of Caribbean History* 28, no. 1 (1994): 7, 10. See also Gerald C. Friedman, "The Heights of Slaves in Trinidad," *Social Science History* 6, no. 4 (1982): 507.

51. Alvin O. Thompson, "Enslaved Children in Berbice, with Special Reference to the Government Slaves, 1803-1831," in *In the Shadow of the Plantation: Caribbean History and Legacy*, ed. Thompson (Kingston: Ian Randle, 2002), 178-79. For the dramatic impact of food shortages on child mortality in Barbados in the summer of 1841, see Laurence Brown and Tara A. Inniss, "The Slave Family in the Transition to Freedom: Barbados, 1834-1841," *Slavery and Abolition* 26, no. 2 (2005): 264-65.

52. Evidence of Gilbert Francklyn, cited in Lambert, *House of Commons*, 71:89.

53. D. B. Jelliffe, *Child Nutrition in Developing Countries: A Handbook for Fieldworkers* (Washington, DC: U.S. Government Printing Office, 1969), 77.

54. Quoted in Sheridan, *Doctors and Slaves,* 225-26.

55. Ibid., 8.

56. Higman, *Slave Populations,* 344; Sheridan, *Doctors and Slaves,* 236; Kenneth F. Kiple and Virginia H. Kiple, "Deficiency Diseases in the Caribbean," *Journal of Interdisciplinary History* 11, no. 1 (1980): 197-215.

57. Humphrey Grant to Roger Hope Elletson, 27 August 1770, Roger Hope Elletson: *Letters from Jamaica,* vol. 1, Henry E. Huntington Library, San Marino, California; Kiple, *Caribbean Slave,* 132; Sheridan, *Doctors and Slaves,* 236.

58. Humphrey Grant to Roger Hope Elletson, 18 May 1771, Roger Hope Elletson: *Letters from Jamaica,* vol. 1, Huntington Library. For other contemporary testimony on lockjaw as a cause of neonatal mortality, see evidence of Sir Ashton Warner Byam, Alexander Campbell, John Castles, Samuel Athill, and Robert Hibbert, in Lambert, *House of Commons,* 71:110, 156, 208; 72:323, 363; Bodleian Library, Oxford, [?] to Joseph Foster Barham, 10 April 1809, MS Clarendon Deposit, c. 358, bundle 1; Thomas Samson to Henry Goulburn, 18 January 1806, Goulburn Collection, 304/5/1/13(1), Surrey History Centre, Woking; Madeys estate plantation accounts, Grenada, 1799, C110/103, National Archives, Kew.

59. Pitt Papers, 30/8/155, 40, National Archives, Kew, *cited in Slavery, Abolition and Emancipation: Black Slaves and the British Empire: A Thematic Documentary,* ed. Michael Craton, James Walvin, and David Wright (London: Longman, 1976), 102.

60. John Hancock, "Observations on *Tetanum Infantum,* or Lock Jaw of Infants," *Edinburgh Medical and Surgical Journal* 35 (1831), 343.

61. Sheridan, *Doctors and Slaves,* 209.

62. Ibid., 238.

63. Thomas Dancer, *The Medical Assistant or Jamaica Practice of Physic designed chiefly for the use of families and plantations* (Kingston: Alexander Aikman, 1809), 269.

64. James Maxwell, *Observations on Yaws and its Influence in Originating Leprosy: Also Observations on Acute Traumatic Tetanus and Tetanus Infantum* (Edinburgh: Maclachlan, Stewart, 1839), 124.

65. Dancer, *Medical Assistant,* 269-70.

66. Evidence of John Greg, cited in Lambert, *House of Commons,* 71:227. A similar explanation is given in Gilbert Mathison, *Notices Respecting Jamaica in 1808-1809-1810* (London: Printed for John Stockdale, 1811), 27-28.

67. For example, Grainger, *West-India Diseases,* 15.

68. Edward Long, *A History of Jamaica,* 3 vols. (London: T. Lowndes, 1774), 3:436.

69. James Thomson, *A Treatise on the Diseases of Negroes as they occur in the island of Jamaica with Observations on the Country Remedies* (Jamaica: Alexander Aikman, 1820), 118; Maxwell, *Observations on Yaws,* 122; Jelliffe, *Child Nutrition,* 8.

70. D. Burman and D. S. McLaren, "Element Deficiency and Toxicity," in *Textbook of Paediatric Nutrition,* ed. D. S. McLaren and D. Burman, 2nd ed. (Edinburgh: Churchill Livingstone, 1982), 172.

71. Thomson, *Diseases of Negroes,* 119.

72. Stephen A. Roberts, Mervyn D. Cohen, and John O. Forfar, "Antenatal Factors Associated with Neonatal Hypocalcaemic Convulsions," *Lancet* 2 (7833) (October 13, 1973): 809-11.

73. Kiple, *Caribbean Slave*, 126.

74. Lewis, *Journal*, 97.

75. P. M. Dunn, "Sir Hans Sloane (1660-1753) and the Value of Breast Milk," *Archives of Disease in Childhood: Foetal and Neonatal Edition* 85 (2001): 73-74.

76. D. S. McLaren, "Protein Energy Malnutrition (PEM)," in McLaren and Burman, *Paedriatric Nutrition*, 103-4.

77. Higman, *Slave Populations*, 341.

78. Jerome S. Handler and Robert S. Corruccini, "Plantation Slave Life in Barbados: A Physical Anthropological Analysis," *Journal of Interdisciplinary History* 14, no. 1 (1983): 65-90.

79. Hans Sloane, *A Voyage to the Islands Madera, Barbados, Nieves, S. Christophers and Jamaica* . . . (London: printed by B.M. for the author, 1707), 1:cxxx. Sloane's views on slave infant health are summarized in Tara Alana Inniss, "La santé des enfants au sein de la société esclavagiste des Caraïbes britanniques: Descriptions médicales de Sir Hans Sloane à la fin du XVIIème siècle à la Jamaïque," *Cahiers des Anneaux de la Mémoire* 5 (2003): 183-94.

80. E. M. DeMayer, "Protein Energy Malnutrition" in Beaton and Bengoa, *Nutrition in Preventative Medicine*, 29.

81. Craton, *Invisible Man*, 124.

82. Long, *History of Jamaica*, 3:436.

83. Kiple, *Caribbean Slave*, 130.

84. Nicholls, *Tropical Nutrition*, 166. In Jamaica in the mid-twentieth century 50 to 85 percent of all children's deaths were related to kwashiorkor. See Kiple, *Caribbean Slave*, 130.

85. Thomas Roughley, *The Jamaica Planter's Guide; or, A System for Planting and Managing a Sugar Estate, or other Plantations in that Island, and throughout the British West Indies in General* (London: Longman, Hurst, Rees, Orme and Brown, 1823), 194.

86. B. W. Higman, *Slave Population and Economy in Jamaica, 1807-1834* (Cambridge: Cambridge University Press, 1976), 154.

87. Jelliffe, *Child Nutrition*, 8.

88. DeMayer, "Protein Energy Malnutrition," 23.

89. Maxwell, *Observations on Yaws*, 51-52.

90. Ibid.

91. Sheridan, *Doctors and Slaves*, 235-36. The Grenada records state the name and age of the slave, the doctor who certified the death, and, in nearly every case, the cause of death.

92. Calculated from National Archives, Kew, T 71/278-326.

93. Listed in ibid.

94. J. A. Stewart, *A View of the Past and Present State of the Island of Jamaica with Remarks on the Moral and Physical Condition of the Slaves and on the Abolition of Slavery in the Colonies* (Edinburgh: Oliver and Boyd, 1823), 303.

95. Higman, *Slave Populations*, 278-80.

96. Ward, *British West Indian Slavery*, 158.

97. Thomson, *Diseases of Negroes*, 10.

# 12

## LEFT BEHIND BUT GETTING AHEAD

*Antebellum Slavery's Orphans in the Chesapeake, 1820–60*

CALVIN SCHERMERHORN

Enslaved children left behind in the antebellum Chesapeake faced an unforgiving landscape of challenges as their parents were sold off to the cotton plantations of the Deep South. Forced separations orphaned countless youngsters, as slaveholders broke up, through sales, one in three marriages among the people they owned each decade between 1820 and the onset of the American Civil War in 1861. Slaveholders hired other spouses away at considerable distances and converted one in five enslaved people of any age into cash. Children witnessed thefts of fathers, dislocations of mothers, and the scattering of siblings, uncles, aunts, and cousins. In one of the largest forced migrations in modern history the market prized the fit and the fertile, which left children behind, bereft, but—as children—also innocent to the systemic implications of their losses.

Though these children experienced extreme domestic instability, were raised by grandparents or other kin or caregivers, and could themselves expect to be hired out alone at early ages, often at a distance, they made what they could of their abandonment. Children responded spontaneously by forming substitute networks of caregivers among the enslaved. Their initial bewilderment and senses of loss of one or both parents gave way to strategies to recruit others who could care for them. In the many additional cases where the young orphaned slaves were the products of white paternity and its corollary—the absence of a father in a position to act as a caregiver—the challenges were not diminished. But, rather than viewing the resulting social landscape as a dystopia of damaged psyches and scarred souls, we can see how pain and loss stimulated strategies for survival and even the building blocks of successful social reproduction, even if the means these children adopted did not match the norms of the intact nuclear families that other social groups around them were able to maintain. Each generation retained elders—like grandparents—who could take part in caring for babies of absented parents. Fathers and mothers remarried after their loss of a spouse, children gained stepsiblings and became stepchildren, and extended families provided child care. Enslaved children developed acute awareness of interpersonal situations and honed abilities to judge character and reliability among potential caregivers, all while realizing the pain of separation. There was not therefore a yawning gap between enslaved children, who could lose caregivers at any moment, and enslaved orphans. Even under severe constraints, children matured, formed lasting relationships, or at least continued to search for new connections with the potential to endure.[1]

By the mid-nineteenth century, childhood was just beginning to enter the cultural lexicon of middle-class Americans as an organic stage of development, and it would take another century for scientific theories of the concept to be fully articulated and for a culture of childhood to take shape. For the working classes, childhood meant a stage of preparation for a working life characterized by assisting in household, field, or even in wage-earning industrial production. Against that broad background, this chapter offers a historical assessment of the particular challenges that enslaved children faced and their responses. Since the early twentieth century, psychoanalytic or psychosexual theories stressing stages of child development have competed with cognitive theories stressing distinctively childlike patterns of thought. Behavioral approaches to child development have explained children's behavior with reference to environmental influences or inputs, and social development theories have located the vital importance of stable and trusting relationships with parental of other caregivers in shaping one's social relationships throughout later life.

It would be tempting to use the analytical tools of the last and current centuries to peer speculatively into the psyches of enslaved children in the nineteenth century and to ascribe pathologically effaced childhoods, brutally taken away by slaveholders, to the children they owned. However, it is difficult, if not impossible, to use twenty-first-century psychological tools and categories to read trauma and disorders back onto children of the nineteenth. It would be anachronistic (and perhaps teleological) thus to assume that enslaved children somehow anticipated a socially constructed childhood that slaveholders stole. Some scholars studying the effects of slavery on the sociology of African American families have attributed chronic social pathologies to slavery's legacy. Families destroyed by these forced separations, according to this interpretation, had ramifications far beyond the orphans created by the domestic antebellum slave trade. However, this chapter sets these enslaved children's experiences in their historical contexts, rather than hypothesizing damage to African American family structures over time.[2]

## HISTORICAL DEMOGRAPHICS

Slaves in the antebellum Chesapeake were very young. By 1830, the first year for which comprehensive age data are available, one in three of the people enslaved in Maryland and Virginia was under the age of ten. The same remained true in 1840. In 1850 and 1860, nearly half (45 percent) of enslaved residents of those two states were under fifteen.[3] When Charles Dickens visited the slave quarter of a plantation in Virginia's Tidewater region in the early 1840s, he reported, "All I saw of them, was, that they were very crazy, wretched cabins, near to which groups of half-naked children basked in the sun, or wallowed on the dusty ground."[4] If that description leaves a sense of an empty landscape, it is because we are accustomed—as Dickens evidently also was—to thinking about enslaved people as adults.[5]

The demographic processes that had made the Chesapeake effectively a vast orphanage of enslaved children by the antebellum decades were the incremental results of successful reproduction among enslaved African American families since the middle of the eighteenth century, followed by agricultural diversification and protoindustrial development after the turn of the nineteenth century. Since the late seventeenth century, Chesapeake slaveholders had bought men and women from Atlantic slavers in roughly equal proportions, and the enslaved population was increasing through natural reproduction by the 1750s. When the Tidewater planters shifted from tobacco cultivation requiring gangs of laborers to mixed grain and fruit agriculture in the upland Piedmont in the last quarter of the eighteenth century, they needed fewer hands from among their rapidly reproducing enslaved populations. Slaveholders initially hired out this surplus human property for a variety of local jobs, but by the 1820s they had found new employments in more remote incipient manufacturing economies and in expanding markets in distant woodlands in what was becoming the cotton kingdom in the Deep South.[6]

By the end of the War of 1812 slaveholders in the Chesapeake were selling off their disposable surplus of human property to the expanding southwestern cotton frontier while retaining local populations that reproduced. The United States' prohibition of the international slave trade in 1808 conferred a legal monopoly on slave sales to these slaveholders in the Chesapeake and rest of the upper South within a rapidly expanding political nation. Enslaved people realized their extreme vulnerability to sale, and members of one generation prepared the next for seemingly inevitable separation. Virginia native Henry "Box" Brown recalled his mother, "pointing to the forest trees which were then being stripped of their foliage by the winds of autumn," and counseling her young son, "as yonder leaves are stripped from off the trees of the forest, so are the children of the slaves swept away from them by the hands of cruel tyrants." Preparing children for journeys away from their parents was at least one family's response to the high likelihood of family separation. In the 1820s, when Brown had heard that advice, the rate of natural reproduction among enslaved people was peaking at just over 30 percent per decade, a rate that would have greatly increased the total numbers of people enslaved in the Chesapeake had they not been removed in high numbers. People among the enslaved in the deepest reproducing slave society in anglophone America, like Brown, who could name generations of ancestors, saw relatives sold off in numbers that approached their high rates of natural increase.[7]

As the generations rolled, and slaveholders continued to sell off their people in nearly direct proportions to their rates of reproduction, children who had lost parents became mothers and fathers whose children in turn saw them bound away. Enslaved children recalled those forced separations through a veil of tears in what Willie Lee Rose has termed a "traumatic moment" of separation.[8] "As near as I can remember," recalled Maryland native Leonard Black, "my mother and sister were sold and taken to New Orleans, leaving four brothers and myself behind."[9] Black was born in the 1810s to a generation who grew up amid a forced migration already well underway. His mother was among the one out of every five enslaved people in that decade bound away from the Maryland and Virginia Chesapeake. Black's contemporary, Jacob D. Green of Maryland, recalled, "my mother was sold to a trader named Woodfork, and where she was conveyed I have not heared [sic] up to the present time. This circumstance caused serious reflections in my mind, as to the situation of slaves."[10] Green's mother was most likely shipped in the coastwise trade to Georgia.

### INITIAL RESPONSES

Some children too young to take care of themselves idealized their lost parents to compensate in some partial, fantasized way for their absence. John Walker recalled that his father was sold away from Virginia in the 1850s, when he was seven. "He wouldn't let [the overseer] whip him," Walker recalled, "so several men overpowered him and put him on a horse and took him away. I sat on the fence a-cryin'." A child like Walker could initially do little else. The following year, at age eight, he was himself sold and put to work in fields, the first of five sales he endured before reaching adulthood during the Civil War. In memory of his father's courage and innocent to his father's reasons, he too refused to be whipped. "That's the reason I was sold so many times," he explained to an interviewer decades later.[11] Walker dried his eyes and kept alive the bonds with his absent father by emulating his defiant dignity.

With determination and responsibility like Walker's in view, it is tempting to see enslaved children as pint-size warriors on politicized battlefields of American slavery, as historians focused on slave resistance have portrayed them. However, enslaved children were not capable of a full awareness of the political ramifications of chattel slavery. They were taught elements of it in intensely personal ways, experiencing the loss of loved ones and learning to see themselves as saleable property. Orphans and those who retained parents alike learned to view themselves as disposable property, even if they did not grasp the broad historical processes and narrow contingencies that conspired to make it likely that they would join departing droves of loved ones. Tidewater Virginia native Robert Ellett, for instance, recalled a man laying $800 on his head and daring his owner to take it. That is how he learned how much he was worth to strangers, and implicitly also how little he could depend on his family to keep him. But enslaved children were still children whose brains had not yet developed the ability to form complex judgments or understand abstractions such as slavery, resistance, or the market.[12]

Enslaved children separated from caregivers confronted their abandonment in a variety of ways: some got ahead by ingratiating themselves to slaveholders, seizing opportunities to gain education, and to evade debilitating punishments and work regimes. Other children were utterly devastated and simply gave up. Eastern North Carolina native Moses Grandy had a young brother who was sold away from his parents to a master in a neighboring county. The man beat him for failing to perform tasks to his satisfaction. After repeated abuses the boy made himself a bed of leaves and lay down to die; his body was eventually found being picked at by a flock of turkey vultures. Symbolically, "these birds had pulled his eyes out," Grandy recalled.[13]

## CHILDREN AT WORK

Most orphaned children bore up under such adversities, endured punishments, and were put to work as soon as they could perform useful tasks.

Grandy was separated from his mother and, after his father and siblings were sold away, hired out to a series of employers. He first worked for a farmer who "flogged me naked with a severe whip made of a very tough sapling," Grandy recalled, because "I could not learn his way of hilling corn." The sapling splintered during the beating, and the resulting wound became infected and would not heal completely for years. The next employer "half-starved" him, prompting him to grind husks of corn to eat in famished desperation. In hard winter frosts, Grandy recalled, "I was compelled to go into the fields and woods to work, with my naked feet cracked and bleeding from extreme cold: to warm them, I used to rouse an ox or hog, and stand on the place where it had lain." Such ingenuity saved him from permanent disabilities resulting from exposure but not from punishments at the whims of employers. He was later hired by a gambler who beat him with a shovel, dislocating his shoulder, when he fell asleep after the man had kept him up "five nights together, without sleep night or day, to wait on the gambling table."[14]

The types of work that enslaved children were made to perform expanded in the nineteenth century, and sometimes children like Grandy were hired out to tradesmen who taught them skills and introduced them to potential allies or patrons. When Grandy was fourteen, after working for six employers since the age of eight, he learned riverine transportation trades, first as assistant on a ferry boat and later as a canal boat operator on the Dismal Swamp Canal connecting Albemarle Sound, in North Carolina, to Virginia ports. Reaching adulthood during the War of 1812, Grandy transported much-needed supplies to Norfolk, Virginia, then shut down by the British blockade of the Chesapeake, from ports on Albemarle Sound. Known fondly after that as Captain Grandy, he started a family and eventually saw his children and grandchildren sold away into the interstate slave trade.[15] Virginia native Lewis Charlton was born during that blockade, in 1814. Like Grandy he lost a father to sale before being sent to learn a trade. "My father was sold in Georgia when I was but a babe," he recalled. When he was seven, "my master died and I was sold far from my mother, to a man who intended to learn me to be a cooper."[16]

As the Chesapeake economy diversified following the War of 1812, enslaved children were put to work in factories, as well as in shops and fields. Cities like Baltimore and Norfolk grew as major coastal transportation centers, and enslaved people were sent there to work in the maritime trades. As a young man, Frederick Douglass became a journeyman ship's caulker. He worked in the construction of at least three coastal slaving vessels, which were built for the clandestine international slave trade in the

Caribbean and South America.[17] If the enslaved caulker noticed that the ballast tanks were constructed to carry freshwater rather than saltwater, he never commented on it.[18]

Inland, Richmond and Petersburg became centers of tobacco manufacturing and grain milling, and both relied on slave labor. Tobacco manufacturers hired children to work alongside men and women in dark, dusty, and dangerous conditions. But these factory environments also gave children opportunities to form associations with adults who could instruct them in the realities of enslavement and assist in their care, if only during the long hours of work. An enslaved boy named Laurence, his owner wrote in 1844, was "very anxious to be hired in Richmond for he has been in Richmond two years in one of the Tobac[co] Factorys & he would be pleased to go in one of them now." Whether the enslaved child was in fact "very anxious" to be hired—slaves worked fourteen to sixteen hours per day at relentlessly repetitive tasks—enslaved children were routinely hired out in urban manufacturing centers.[19] When Box Brown was separated from his parents at age thirteen, he was put to work in his master's Richmond tobacco factory, where he worked alongside children even younger than he.

Sometimes enslaved children could earn more than adults for their masters, and owners planned their financial futures around the employment of the children they owned. Two brothers, Anthony and Robert, were hired out to a Richmond tobacconist in the 1840s, while their mother Becky and three younger siblings were hired out to domestic service nearby. The two boys, combined, each year earned for their owner nine times what their mother did. John Washington, born in 1838, was apprenticed in his teens to learn the shoe trade in Fredericksburg, Virginia, while his mother and four siblings were removed some hundred miles away and hired to a schoolteacher. His owner saw the enslaved young man's future as a tobacco worker when he reached his early twenties, but the onset of the Civil War foreclosed that option after a year's employment.[20]

There was little gender division of labor in the fields, but more boys than girls were taught trades or employed in factories. Henrietta Right was among the girls hired out in the urban upper Chesapeake. Right was born free but bound out to service by the Baltimore Orphan's Court because her parents had either died, disappeared, or been judged destitute. In 1847, at age six, she was apprenticed "to be taught plain serving and housework" as well to be "taught to read during her apprenticeship, or in lieu thereof, to give her the sum of twenty dollars when free in addition to the freedom dues required by law." She was due to be freed at age eighteen (boys were typically freed at twenty-one). Right's indenture was sold and resold, however, as if she were a slave on the market. When the second master died, she fell into the hands of a man who trafficked in young African American "apprentices," seeking to sell them out of state into chattel slavery. With the assistance of a friend, fourteen-year-old Right testified in 1855 that she was "most cruelly treated," by her master; "that she has been dreadfully beaten and has been in fear of her life," and that her master "does not take that care of her or treat her as he should an apprentice. And that he is not a fit or proper person to have care of" a vulnerable young woman.[21] The master petitioned for dismissal of the case, but that Right's case made it to court at all was the result of her enlisting her "next friend," Maria Johnson, as an ally.

### SEXUAL EXPLOITATION, SEXUALITY AS STRATEGY

Like childhood, privacy was not a concept that enslaved children, and especially enslaved orphans, would have understood. Their sexual innocence was a result of elders' keeping information from them rather than from a lack of exposure to human bodies. Virginia native John Brown recalled that "the children of both sexes usually run about quite naked, until they are from ten to twelve years of age. I have seen them as old as twelve, going about in this state, or with only an old shirt, which they would put on when they had to go anywhere very particular for their mistress, or up to the great house." While Victorian-era children later were discovering their childhoods and wondering what lay beneath the copious layers of clothes that enveloped the respectably modest, the details of developing human bodies were no mystery to antebellum enslaved children. Leonard Black recalled that as a child he had "no hat, no pantaloons, but one pair of shoes, and wore a lindsey [linsey-woolsey] slip only." Frederick Douglass received his first pair of trousers at age eight and reported that children too young for field work received "neither shoes, stockings, jackets, nor trousers," and that "their clothing consisted of two coarse linen shirts per year. When these failed them, they went naked until the next allowance-day. Children from seven to ten years old, of both sexes, almost naked, might be seen at all seasons of the year."[22] The arrival of Douglass's clothing coincided with his removal to an urban setting, away from friends and family.

North American slave narratives do not go into detail about how enslaved people experienced their and others' sexuality, as distinct from widely reported rapes, probably because the middle-class readers of their abolition-oriented writings had developed an aversion to such personal issues, especially if their subjects were African American. Living conditions, however, imply that enslaved children were routinely exposed to adult sexuality, since there was no division between public and private spaces in enslaved families' quarters. Cabins were cramped, and four family groups typically lived in a slave cabin, clustered around two hearths partitioned off from each other by a thin wall. Most cabins had packed-dirt floors, drafty walls, and beds that were little more than rope and straw. Sparse and crude wooden furniture was clustered around tables where the sleeping area abutted the kitchen. Such cramped and open places left little room for personal modesty. In the cold of winter, all would sleep together huddled under blankets, as close to fireplaces as they dared. In steamy Chesapeake summers, the only use for bedclothes would be to keep mosquitoes and other pests at bay. Enslaved children would have grown up witnessing other children, older kin, non-family members in their most intimate moments. Children heard lovers in the throes of passion and mothers in the pains of childbirth. In cabins, they saw elders nursing infants and also injuries suffered in factories or at the hands of overseers and others burning with fever or suffering from the cholera and dysentery that was endemic in slave quarters. No bodily sound or smell would have been alien to them.[23]

Girls and boys alike were subject to physical ill-treatment under the arbitrary power of slaveholders, but girls were much more susceptible to being abused sexually as well. Eastern North Carolina native Harriet Jacobs was fifteen when her owner "peopled my young mind with unclean images" and then acted them out by attempting to rape her, which began nearly ten years of sexual abuse. Her memoirs merely suggest the existential torture to which she was subjected, abetted in some instances by her owner's jealous wife, who evidently could not stop her husband's abuses and so took her jealous rage out on his victim.

The sexual abuse that Jacobs suffered was common. Robert Ellett recalled many years later that "if you was a slave and has a good looking daughter," she would be taken and put in the "big house where the young masters could have the run of her." Girls without parents had no recourse in such situations, and neither law nor custom offered them protection. Enslaved children seem not to have been instructed extensively in sexual matters, however, and when they asked where babies came from they were sent looking in clover patches, in hollow logs, or awaiting the arrival of physician or midwife as a stork bearing a bundle. Even young women experiencing menarche seem to have been told only reluctantly what it signaled.[24]

Sexual experience came close on the heels of sexual innocence as girls suddenly became aware of their potential exploitation and collateral strategies to which sexuality gave rise. Without fully realizing the ramifications, then, some girls attempted to use men's sexual interests as defensive strategies aimed at recruiting a patron. At fifteen years old, Jacobs became the mistress of a white man whom she hoped could protect her, and she eventually bore two children by him. An enslaved girl named Maria was described as a "rather genteel looking colored girl, with a faultless form," who planned to ally herself to a slaveholder. In 1841 she was among several members of a coffle aboard a slave ship traveling from Norfolk to New Orleans, where she reportedly believed that "immediately on our arrival in New-Orleans, she had no doubt, some wealthy single gentleman of good taste would purchase her at once." Whether Maria realized that she planned to advertise herself as a sexual commodity, or not, slavery made her such.

Another woman on that ship had seen a similar sexual strategy fail in Maryland. Emily had allied herself with a slaveholder there, living as his concubine and bearing him a daughter, Emma, before his jealous relatives sold them in the Washington, D.C., slave market. The child Emma was described as "seven or eight years old, of light complexion, and with a face of admirable beauty." Upon reaching New Orleans, the slave trader who sold her mother and brother away from Emma decided to keep her since, he let it be known, "there were heaps and piles of money to be made of her" for sexual exploitation, "when she was a few years older." Like John Walker, Emily merely wailed "Come back" and "Don't leave me," through her tears.[25] Emily's father made no recorded effort to retrieve his offspring. The guilt (and family pressure) reflected in this man's inaction forced widespread sales of unrecognized offspring, in a pattern that Walter Johnson contends contributed significantly to peopling the lower South. The expediency of selling unrecognized progeny of sexual abuse and enslaved women's fertility out of sight and out of mind—and the hope of domestic tranquility in the legitimate family that came along with it—was a peculiar characteristic of the Second Middle Passage.[26]

For enslaved girls growing up in the Chesapeake, widespread rapes of African American women and girls were in the foreground of the social landscape, visible in a slave population with palpable European ancestry, even if particular fathers refused to acknowledge their paternity. Frederick Douglass recalled an enslaved man who "bore a very striking resemblance" to his master's son. The son prevailed upon the master to sell his half-sibling to avoid embarrassment, and the enslaved child was sold to Austin Woolfolk, a Baltimore slave trader. There were enough enslaved people whose light skin tones revealed European ancestry that those without evident European antecedents were noteworthy. John Brown recalled, as a child, meeting his Igbo grandfather "when he came to visit my mother. He was very black."[27]

## PHYSICAL CONDITIONS

Sexual abuse was one among many forms of psychic and physical exploitation that enslaved orphans endured. The void that lost loved ones left in their memories was complemented by empty stomachs, and abandoned child slaves routinely lacked adequate nourishment. Slaveholders rationed food by stinting children in order to feed productive adolescent and adult workers. As a result enslaved children were shorter in stature than typical American children, and other conditions contributing to malnutrition read like an index of social pathologies: overwork among pregnant women, insufficient neonatal care, and parasites and diseases abundant in unsanitary living conditions.[28]

Leonard Black, who was separated from his family and hired out, recalled his rations as a child, including "a pint of pot liquor" for breakfast, which was the water in which vegetables and meat had been cooked, along with "half a herring, and a little piece of bread." "For my dinner," he recalled, he had another "pint of pot liquor, and the skin off of the pork" and perhaps another small piece of bread. Jacobs recalled that if any enslaved child "could catch a bit of food while it was going [by], well and good," but that portions were spare, even in the household of a presumably well-off physician where he lived.[29]

Poor nutrition was accompanied by similarly insufficient allotments of clothing and inadequate shelter for enslaved children, especially orphans, with the result that many of them suffered from exposure. Black recalled that he slept on a piece of carpet, "spread down on the hearth, winter and summer. In the winter, when the fire got low, I used to burn my feet by getting them into the embers." When one cold winter day he strayed into the house to warm up, his master caught him and "warmed" him by branding his legs with a hot iron. Black remained with that employer for seven years.[30]

## AWAKENINGS:
### RECRUITING ALLIES AND LEARNING THE SOCIAL LANDSCAPE

The caregivers to whom enslaved orphans turned might include the very individuals responsible for orphaning them. Lack of awareness of the full circumstances of enslavement encouraged childish resiliency. Like so many others, young Frederick Douglass groped about for allies. His mother was hired out at twelve miles' distance and died when he was eight. His white father did not recognize him as a son, and his maternal grandmother took care of him until he was old enough to be put to work on the plantation, at age six, when he was separated from her. Douglass befriended the youngest son of the wealthy Maryland slaveholding family for whom his owner worked. The boy protected Douglass from bullies and shared food with him while his father was selling off enslaved people in staggering numbers.[31] Douglass recalled regular appearances by slave traders like Woolfolk. His owner, too, was selling off slaves. "The most valuable part of his property was his slaves," Douglass recalled, "of whom he could afford to sell one every year. This crop, therefore, brought him seven or eight hundred dollars a year, besides his yearly salary, and other revenue from his farms."[32] Innocent of the ramifications of what he was doing, Douglass also befriended the adult daughter of his first owner. She gave him extra food when he sang for it and selected him from among all the children to go and live in Baltimore, marking the occasion by presenting him with a pair of trousers.

Douglass and children like him formulated constructive responses to their isolation from family, such as learning to read as a way to augment their knowledge of the social geography. They also reached out to potential allies and teachers beyond kin or their owners, perhaps knowing only that they wanted friends or companions. Slavery's isolation became elemental loneliness through orphaning, and children sometimes embraced potential opportunities that arose from slaveholders' plans to profit from their labor. The Chesapeake's trading and manufacturing cities gave slaveholders new opportunities to hire out surplus slaves, and the urban environment also gave slaves opportunities to accumulate resources and connect with networks of potential sponsors or caregivers. Beyond the supervision of their owners, enslaved children sought out people whom they believed could help them learn and meet needs for friendship or even substitute parents. Douglass, after his master prohibited him from learning to read, sparked a desire to do the opposite, used his contacts in Baltimore, and turned to free neighborhood schoolchildren to acquire literate skills. "For a single biscuit," he recalled, "any of my hungry little comrades would give me a lesson more valuable to me than bread."[33]

Other enslaved children bought tuition with similar schemes. Richard H. Parker, youngest of fourteen children, was sold away from his mother near Yorktown, Virginia, in the 1810s and carried south to Norfolk. Conversion to Christianity prompted his awakening to literacy. Parker gathered iron nails and sold them until he could buy a school primer, which he carried in his hat until it "wore the hair from the top of his head." In search of teachers, he exchanged more nails for marbles and sought out white schoolchildren, with whom he traded the marbles for lessons until he could read words of two syllables. The daughter of his master was his next teacher, and though the two were caught and punished—the daughter reprimanded, the enslaved boy beaten—he eventually learned to read the Bible.[34]

Douglass found a substitute caregiver and a relationship of some depth with a free African American drayman who, according to a biographer, offered him spiritual guidance as "a surrogate physical father." Despite being illiterate himself, the drayman "strongly encouraged" Douglass's "efforts to improve his reading and writing skills," and "their mutual love and admiration grew, and in spite of [his master's] opposition to their relationship, they spent much time together exploring the mysteries and joys of Christianity." Other enslaved children replaced the wisdom of their lost parents by absorbing the wisdom of elders through observation. They were thus exposed to the weaponry of the weak, but children saw the tools their elders deployed to ameliorate slaveholders' demands for labor as tricks or mysteries. Discovery comes in stages, and before enslaved children awoke to the realization that these tricks could be used in power struggles, they merely delighted in them, much as contemporary middle-class children would have absorbed the aesthetics of a Punch-and-Judy show before awakening later to its meanings as a trickster satire. W. P. Jacobs recalled a slave who "had a red flannel jacket which he could make talk." The man would "hang the jacket on a nail, say something, squeeze it and the jacket would groan, moan, and carry on." Nobody else could effect the same result, and a frightened overseer spared him punishments. Jacobs also knew an enslaved man who kept rattlesnakes as pets. "They were huge snakes," he recalled, "and everyone feared them, especially the poor white overseer." The snake keeper "fed the snakes liquor every day," to "make them vicious." As a child, Jacobs would have absorbed such tales as lessons in how to dupe an adversary. The man with the jacket had sewn a bullfrog inside it and poked it with a pin to produce the commotion. The snake conjurer's fearsome gathering was actually harmless, since "when he caught them he pulled their fangs out."[35]

Children also learned a sense of humor from their elders and with it an idiom of potential protest. Francis Frederick witnessed an enslaved man pick up a Bible and, though unable to read, preach to his mistress: "Give your slaves plenty of bread and meat, and plenty of hot biscuit in a morning, also be sure and give him three horns of whiskey a-day." When asked to cite chapter and verse, he closed the book, remarking that there was more in the Bible than just those things written down on its pages. The child learned a subtle lesson, which at first was simply comic: the slave dissembling as he pretended to read. The seemingly trifling demands for meat and bread—and whiskey, too—would gradually give way to the realization that the recitation of scripture by an illiterate slave summoning up a biblical injunction to direct his mistress to be generous was in fact a veiled threat, or at least a criticism on and reversal of the common injunction, cited by slaveholders, for slaves to obey God by obeying their earthly masters.[36]

Other children responded by exploiting divisions among those around them. Jacob Green struck out when wronged. He was orphaned at the age of eight when his mother was sold, a moment that marked an awakening to his utter lack of control of his own fate and dissatisfaction with those surroundings. When Green's mother was about to be sold, she told him to be a "good boy," but his grief and desperation at their separation turned to anger after witnessing a white child stealing corn from his owner's stores. The owner blamed the black children on the property for the transgression, threatening to whip them until one confessed. Green later got into a fight with a white boy who was "continually stealing my tops and marbles," a contest over children's toys that was ended by a powerful kick from a white man, one of the lovers of Green's owner's wife. Green thought he had been kicked hard enough to arrest his growth. The incident "created such a feeling of revenge in my bosom," he recalled, "that I was determined when I became a man I would pay him back in his own coin."[37]

Green did not wait that long and instead embarked at once on a path that easily could have gotten him killed. Too young to groom horses, drive a cart, or work in the fields, he was tasked with housework and there came upon an opportunity for revenge. The man who had kicked him was one of two lovers carrying on affairs with his mistress and a "great smoker." One morning while working in the house of his mistress, Green happened upon a tobacco pipe on the mantelpiece, packed with tobacco and left out for the man who had kicked him. Knowing that his mistress was then entertaining the man's rival before receiving him, Green took a quantity of gunpowder from the pistols kept nearby and substituted the powder for the tobacco, adding a visible layer of tobacco on top. Before noon that day, there was a great alarm, and Green witnessed his assailant "lying back in the arm chair in a state of insensibility, his mouth bleeding profusely and from particulars given it appeared he took the pipe as usual and lighted it, and had just got it to his mouth when the powder exploded." The mistress's other lover was suspected, and the "master's wife came in for a deal of scandal." The heated suspicions led to a fight between the injured man's son and the rival, and the resulting legal disputes ended up costing all parties involved substantial amounts of money. Green had punished his assailant and embarrassed and financially injured the man who had sold his mother. Green was no closer to freedom, but his trickery had been rewarded.[38]

Viewed from Green's point of view, however, he had learned survival behavior in an environment that rewarded deception and developed a sense of self-worth by tricking others and acting vengefully on impulse. Green substituted trickery for trust in what under other circumstances would be a poor trade were it not for the practical necessity of honing everyday strategies of resistance as a way to keep a sense of self-worth. Having lost his mother and having been abused by others, he did what he could from his enforced isolation. His innocence of the full ramifications of his actions perhaps abetted his audacious behavior. Vacillating about whether to sabotage a to-bacco pipe might have exposed him to discovery. Most deceptions had less directly hostile intent. Fourteen-year-old John Washington skipped church one Sunday in the spring of 1852 to swim in the Rappahannock River with other slave children. He had taken to the habit of avoiding services when he became disillusioned with the Baptist Church in Fredericksburg, choos-ing instead to wait at the church door "until the minister would announce the text" on which he would preach, "then commit it to memory" so he could later give his mistress evidence of his attendance. When an overseer neared, the children hustled out of the water and spent the rest of the day playing among "wild flowers and black berries till near sundown [when] we went to our houses, most of us with a lie in our mouths."

Washington turned out to have been playing in poison oak, and when he broke out in sores the next week, he invented a story about having come into contact with the shrub while carrying firewood. The infection was widespread and the doctor was puzzled at its severity, advising Washington's owner to send him to the country for a month to recover. "I was delighted with the proposition and for fear She should change he[r] Mind," he recalled, "I very conveniently began to get Sicker than ever." However, Washington did not pitch his deception perfectly. "But hearing her remark one day that she thought I was too Sick to travel," he added, "I made haste to be almost well the next day." His temporary reunion with his mother and siblings, he remembered, "was a most happy one and long remembered."[39]

## THE INNOCENCE OF CHILDREN, THE RESILIENCE OF ADULTS

Orphans learned from the very slaveholders who had orphaned them the practical lessons in how to cope on their own with physical and psychologi-cal violence, including sexual exploitation, even if they did not understand the adult implications of what they were doing. The youthful landscape of antebellum slavery in the Chesapeake and the frequency of forced separa-tions infused the culture of slavery, and every enslaved child, whether an orphan or not, was affected by and responded to slaveholders' sales of so many would-be caregivers. Exposed to arbitrary authority, usually at the hands of employers or overseers, young children could do little but seize any opportunity to avoid hardships and endure the ones they could not. Vulnerability did not cripple enslaved children, but rather their wide-eyed curiosity gave rise to alternate strategies—strategies that would have seemed off limits to people who had reached the full age of reason. Their food and clothing were usually inadequate, but orphans found ways to take food and seek shelter when they needed it. To conclude that the children who grew up under such deprivation were left with permanently scarred psyches or damaged souls would draw on psychological theories of modern developmental normality for which we have no evidence from the early nineteenth century. Instead of seeing a wasteland of damage, a survey of the enslaved children in the Chesapeake made orphans by slavery reveals an elusive historical component of American slavery, namely the extent to which it forced children to form substitute ties to cope with the theft of parents and other caregivers.

Children whose natal families were disrupted by slaveholders patched together networks of caregivers through whom they obtained nutrition, shelter, and instruction, however minimally. From these substitute parents they learned such survival strategies as how to appraise potential allies or patrons, how to endure physical pain and punishments, how to dissemble when necessary, and—for girls—how to play on the sexual appetites and presumptions of their owners. In between the lines of their bitterest memories of slavery, we read how enslaved children could remember and even idealize the love of a lost parent who, for them, was absent in body but not in spirit. Children were resilient, and they formed attachments, even if only temporarily, and approached adulthood with an understanding of the particular adversities they faced, even if they did not understand such abstractions as markets, forced migration, national expansion, or slavery. The innocence often attributed to childhood, in that era more directly than in ours, was their greatest strength as well as their vulnerability. The adults such children grew into—such as Moses Grandy, Harriet Jacobs, and John Washington—committed themselves to collecting kin and keeping their families together. Moreover, the ubiquity of these experiences as children in the Chesapeake in the early decades of the nineteenth century produced the kinds of adults who survived sale and resettlement to the cotton South in the late antebellum decades. The resilience learned in the older areas of the South were crucial to remaking families in the newer, which may be responsible for the creative character of late antebellum slave culture. Left behind on an uncertain landscape of slavery, they got ahead by spontaneously developing alternative strategies that allowed them to reach the age of reason, awakening to the implications of their enslavement though using everyday strategies to avoid its most dehumanizing aspects.[40]

## NOTES

1. Susan Eva O'Donovan, "Traded Babies: Enslaved Children and America's Domestic Migrations, 1820-60," chap. 5, this volume; Edward E. Baptist, "'Stol' and Fetched Here': Enslaved Migration, Ex-Slave Narratives, and Vernacular History," in Edward E. Baptist and Stephanie M. H. Camp, eds., *New Studies in the History of American Slavery* (Athens: University of Georgia Press, 2006), 243-74; Herbert G. Gutman, *The Black Family in Slavery and Freedom, 1750-1925* (New York: Vintage Books, 1977); Brenda E. Stevenson, *Life in Black and White: Family and Community in the Slave South* (New York: Oxford University Press, 1996); Wilma A. Dunaway, *The African American Family in Slavery and Emancipation* (Cambridge: Cambridge University Press, 2003); Dunaway, *Slavery in the American Mountain South* (Cambridge: Cambridge University Press, 2003); Dylan C. Penningroth, *The Claims of Kinfolk: African American Property and Community in the Nineteenth-Century South* (Chapel Hill: University of North Carolina Press, 2003); Michael Tadman, *Speculators and Slaves: Masters, Traders, and Slave in the Old South* (Madison: University of Wisconsin Press, 1996), 134-35, 146-54, 169-78; Walter Johnson, *Soul by Soul: Life inside the Antebellum Slave Market* (Cambridge, MA: Harvard University Press, 1999); Steven Deyle, *Carry Me Back: The Domestic Slave Trade in American Life* (New York: Oxford University Press, 2005).

2. Steven Mintz, *Huck's Raft: A History of American Childhood* (Cambridge, MA: Harvard University Press, 2004), chap. 4; Joseph F. Kett, "Adolescence and Youth in Nineteenth Century America," *Journal of Interdisciplinary History* 2, no. 2 (1971): 283-98. On twentieth-century developments in child psychology, see, for instance, Sigmund Freud, *Three Essays on the Theory of Sexuality*, trans. James Strachey (New York: Basic Books, 1975); Jean Piaget, *Origins of Intelligence in the Child* (London: Heinemann, 1936); Erik H. Erikson, *Childhood and Society* (New York: Norton, 1963); B. F. Skinner, *Contingencies of Reinforcement: A Theoretical Analysis* (New York: Appleton-Century-Crofts, 1969); John Bowlby, *The Making and Breaking of Affectional Bonds* (New York: Routledge, 1989). On the sociology of African American families, see William E. Burghardt Du Bois, *The Negro American Family; Report of a Social Study Made Principally by the College Classes of 1909 and 1910 of Atlanta University* (Westport, CT: Greenwood, 1970); Du Bois, *The Negro American Family* (New York: Negro Universities, 1969); E. Franklin Frazier, *The Negro Family in the United States* (Chicago: University of Chicago Press, 1966); Daniel P. Moynihan, *The Negro Family: A Case for National Action* (Washington, DC: United States Department of Labor, Office of Policy Planning and Research, 1965); Herbert G. Gutman, "Persistent Myths about the Afro-American Family," *Journal of Interdisciplinary History* 6, no. 2, special issue "The History of the Family, III" (1975): 181-210; Frank F. Furstenberg Jr., Theodore Hershberg, and John Modell, "The Origins of the Female-Headed Black Family: The Impact of the Urban Experience," in ibid., 211-33. For a recent response to literature on African American family sociology, see Daryl Michael Scott, *Contempt and Pity: Social Policy and the Image of the Damaged Black Psyche, 1880-1996* (Chapel Hill: University of North Carolina Press, 1997).

3. Fifth, Sixth, Seventh, and Eighth United States Census, Historical Census Browser, University of Virginia, http://fisher.lib.virginia.edu/collections/stats/histcensus/index .html (accessed 18 September 2007).

4. Charles Dickens, *American Notes* (New York: Modern Library, 1996), 179.

5. Dickson J. Preston, *Young Frederick Douglass: The Maryland Years* (Baltimore: Johns Hopkins University Press, 1980); Gutman, *Black Family*; Wilma King, *African American Childhoods: Historical Perspectives from Slavery to Civil Rights* (New York: Palgrave Macmillan, 2005); King, *Stolen Childhood: Slave Youth in Nineteenth-Century America* (Bloomington: Indiana University Press, 1995); Penningroth, *Claims of Kinfolk*; Marie Jenkins Schwartz, *Born in Bondage: Growing Up Enslaved in the Antebellum South* (Cambridge, MA: Harvard University Press, 2000).

6. Luther Porter Jackson, *Free Negro Labor and Property Holding in Virginia, 1830–1860* (New York: D. Appleton-Century, 1942), 34-101; Lorena S. Walsh, "Slave Life, Slave Society, and Tobacco Production in the Tidewater Chesapeake, 1620-1820," in *Cultivation and Culture: Labor and the Shaping of Black Life in the Americas*, ed. Ira Berlin and Philip D. Morgan (Charlottesville: University Press of Virginia, 1993), 170-99; Allan Kulikoff, *Tobacco and Slaves: The Development of Southern Cultures in the Chesapeake, 1680-1800* (Chapel Hill: Institute of Early American History and Culture, 1986); Jennifer L. Morgan, *Laboring Women: Reproduction and Gender in New World Slavery* (Philadelphia: University of Pennsylvania Press, 2004).

7. Henry "Box" Brown, *Narrative of the Life of Henry Box Brown, Written by Himself* (Manchester: Printed by Lee and Glynn, 1851), 2, http://docsouth.unc.edu/neh/brownbox/brownbox.html (accessed 18 September 2007); Tadman, *Speculators and Slaves*, 77-108; Phillip David Troutman, "Slave Trade and Sentiment" (PhD diss., University of Virginia, 2000), 423; Adam Rothman, *Slave Country: American Expansion and the Origins of the Deep South* (Cambridge, MA: Harvard University Press, 2005); Loren Schweninger, "The Underside of Slavery: The Internal Economy, Self-Hire, and Quasi-Freedom in Virginia, 1780-1865," *Slavery and Abolition* 12, no. 2 (1991): 1-22; Jonathan D. Martin, *Divided Mastery: Slave Hiring in the American South* (Cambridge, MA: Harvard University Press), 2004.

8. Willie Lee Rose, *Slavery and Freedom*, ed. William W. Freehling (New York: Oxford University Press, 1982), 37-38.

9. Leonard Black, *The Life and Sufferings of Leonard Black, a Fugitive from Slavery* (New Bedford: Benjamin Lindsey, 1847), 6, http://docsouth.unc.edu/neh/black/black.html (accessed 23 August 2007).

A methodological note: the authors of slave narratives emphasized sufferings of enslaved people and the indifference or depravity of slaveholders and other slavers for dramatic effect. Commentators, in other words, cannot be separated from witnesses. I attempt here to use incidental details in those narratives to illustrate the arguments and use voices of enslaved autobiographers—and their amanuenses—with as little as possible of the rhetoric that often surrounds descriptions of events.

10. Jacob D. Green, *Narrative of the Life of J. D. Green, a Runaway Slave, from Kentucky, Containing an Account of His Three Escapes, in 1839, 1846, and 1848* (Huddersfield, UK: Printed by Henry Fielding, Pack Horse Yard, 1864), 5, http://docsouth.unc.edu/neh/greenjd/greenjd.html (accessed 23 August 2007).

11. Adeline Henderson and John Walker, interview by Beth Walters, 1930, in *Slave Testimony: Two Centuries of Letters, Speeches, Interviews, and Autobiographies*, ed. John W. Blassingame (Baton Rouge: Louisiana State Press, 1977), 565.

12. Robert Ellett, interview by Claude W. Anderson, in *Weevils in the Wheat: Interviews with Virginia Ex-Slaves*, ed. Charles L. Perdue, Thomas E. Barden, and Robert K. Phillips (Charlottesville: University Press of Virginia, 1976), 85; King, *Stolen Childhood*; Baptist, "'Stol' and Fetched,'" offers a useful way to conceptualize how children thought about their enslavement and experiences of forced separation.

13. Moses Grandy, *Narrative of the Life of Moses Grandy, Late a Slave in the United States of America* (London: Gilpin, 1843), 9, http://docsouth.unc.edu/fpn/grandy/grandy.html (accessed 18 September 2007).

14. Ibid., 10–12.

15. Ibid., 21; William L. Andrews, ed., *North Carolina Slave Narratives: The Lives of Moses Roper, Lunsford Lane, Moses Grandy, and Thomas H. Jones* (Chapel Hill: University of North Carolina Press), 133–55.

16. Lewis Charlton, *Sketch of the Life of Mr. Lewis Charlton, and Reminiscences of Slavery* (daily press print, Portland, ME, n.d.), 1–2, http://docsouth.unc.edu/neh/charlton/charlton.html (accessed 23 August 2007).

17. Preston, *Young Frederick Douglass*, 146.

18. William S. McFeely, *Frederick Douglass* (New York: Norton, 1991), 63, 391n.

19. W. Storke to Lewis Hill, 5 January 1844, Lewis Hill Papers, Robert Alonzo Brock Collection, Mss BR box 92, Huntington Library, San Marino, CA.

20. Box Brown, *Narrative*, 36–37; Jeffrey Ruggles, *The Unboxing of Henry Brown* (Richmond: Library of Virginia, 2003), 5–13; Taliaferro Papers, 1820–1920, sec. 1, item 7, MSS 1 T1438 a, 1–5, Virginia Historical Society, Richmond; John Washington, "Memorys of the Past," unpublished manuscript, Manuscripts Division, Library of Congress.

21. Baltimore, City Register of Wills (Petitions), *Right v. Moan*, petition, 24 January 1855, answer 8 February 1855; copy of indenture, 24 January 1855; petition for dismissal 13 February 1855, MSA SC 4239-14-259 M11026, Maryland State Archives, Annapolis.

22. Frederick Douglass, *Narrative of the Life of Frederick Douglass, An American Slave, Written by Himself* (Boston: Anti-Slavery Office, 1845), 10, http://docsouth.unc.edu/neh/douglass/douglass.html (accessed 18 September 2007); Black, *Life and Sufferings*, 8.

23. On privacy as a value, see Rhys Isaac, *The Transformation of Virginia, 1740–1790* (Chapel Hill: University of North Carolina Press, 1982), chaps. 2, 4, 13; Anne Elizabeth Yentsch, *A Chesapeake Family and Their Slaves: A Study in Historical Archaeology* (New York: Cambridge University Press, 1994), chs. 15, 16.

24. Anthony S. Parent Jr. and Susan Brown Wallace, "Childhood and Sexual Identity under Slavery," *Journal of the History of Sexuality* 3, no. 3, special issue "African American Culture and Sexuality" (1993): 363–401; John Brown, *Slave Life in Georgia: A Narrative of the Life, Sufferings, and Escape of John Brown, a Fugitive Slave, Now in England* (London: [W. M. Watts], 1855), 2, http://docsouth.unc.edu/neh/jbrown/jbrown.html (accessed 18 September 2007); Harriet Jacobs, *Incidents in the Life of a Slave Girl: Written by Herself* (Boston: published for the author, 1861), 44–47, http://docsouth.unc.edu/fpn/jacobs/jacobs.html (accessed 18 September 2007); Christina Accomando, "'The Laws Were Laid Down to Me Anew': Harriet Jacobs and the Reframing of Legal Fictions," *African American Review* 32, no. 2 (1998): 229–45; Joshua D. Rothman, *Notorious in the Neighborhood: Sex and Families across the Color Line in Virginia* (Chapel Hill: University of North Carolina Press, 2003), chap. 4; Ellett interview, 84.

25. Jean Fagan Yellin, *Harriet Jacobs: A Life* (New York: Basic Civitas Books, 2004), 23-27; Solomon Northup, *Twelve Years a Slave: Narrative of Solomon Northup, a Citizen of New-York, Kidnapped in Washington City in 1841, and Rescued in 1853* (Auburn, NY: Derby and Miller, 1853), 50, 65, 86-87, 88, http://docsouth.unc.edu/fpn/northup/northup.html (accessed 18 September 2007); for slave traders' activities in the sex trade, see Edward E. Baptist, "'Cuffy,' 'Fancy Maids,' and 'One-Eyed Men,': Rape, Commodification, and the Domestic Slave Trade," *American Historical Review* 106, no. 5 (2001): 1619-50; Robert H. Gudmestad, *A Troublesome Commerce: The Transformation of the Interstate Slave Trade* (Baton Rouge: Louisiana State University Press, 2003), chap. 1.

26. Walter Johnson, at "The Suppression of the Atlantic Slave Trade: A Bicentennial Reexamination, 1807–2007, Part 1: New Directions in the Study of Abolition: A Multi-National Approach," roundtable discussion at the 121st annual meeting of the American Historical Association, 4-7 January 2007, Atlanta.

27. Thelma Jennings, "'Us Colored Women Had to Go Through a Plenty': Sexual Exploitation of African-American Slave Women," *Journal of Women's History* 1, no. 3 (1990): 45-74; John Brown, *Slave Life*, 2 (http://docsouth.unc.edu/neh/jbrown/jbrown.html, accessed: 18 September 2007); Frederick Douglass, *My Bondage and My Freedom* (New York: Miller, Orton, and Mulligan, 1855), 115, http://docsouth.unc.edu/neh/douglass55/douglass55.html (accessed 18 September 2007).

28. Mintz, *Huck's Raft*, 96-100.

29. Richard H. Steckel, "Stature and the Standard of Living," *Journal of Economic Literature* 33, no. 4 (1995): 1903-40; Philip R. P. Coelho and Robert A. McGuire, "Diets versus Disease: The Anthropometrics of Slave Children," *Journal of Economic History* 60, no. 1 (2000): 232-46; Black, *Life and Sufferings*, 8-9.

30. John Brown, *Slave Life*, 4; Black, *Life and Sufferings*, 9.

31. By 1830, when Douglass was twelve, the boy's father owned 558 human beings, including 175 children (31 percent of the total). Ten years later he owned 224 individuals, including 72 children (32 percent). Online database: Ancestry.com, *1830 United States Federal Census* (Provo, UT: Generations Network, 2004), original data: United States, Bureau of the Census, *Fifth Census of the United States, 1830* (Washington, DC: National Archives and Records Administration, 1830), M19, 201 rolls, Talbot County, Maryland, 1830, roll 58, p. 14; online: Ancestry.com, *1840 United States Federal Census* (Provo UT: Generations Network, 2004), original: Bureau of the Census, *Sixth Census of the United States, 1840* (Washington, DC: National Archives and Records Administration, 1840), M704, 580 rolls, Talbot County, Maryland, 1840, roll 171, p. 4 (accessed 17 August 2007).

32. Douglass, *Bondage and Freedom*, 78.

33. Ibid., 155; Daneen Waldrop, "'While I Am Writing': Webster's 1825 *Spelling Book*, the Ell, and Frederick Douglass's Positioning of Language," *African American Review* 32, no. 4 (1998): 469-660; Janet Cornelius, "'We Slipped and Learned to Read': Slave Accounts of the Literary Process, 1830-1865," *Phylon* 44, no. 3 (1983): 171-86; David W. Blight, ed., *The Columbian Orator* (New York: New York University Press, 1998), xiii-xxix.

34. Richard H. Parker, in Blassingame, *Slave Testimony*, 465-66.

35. Waldo E. Martin Jr., *The Mind of Frederick Douglass* (Chapel Hill: University of North Carolina Press, 1984), 9; W. P. Jacobs, in Perdue, *Weevils in the Wheat*, 155-56.

36. Francis Fedric [Frederick], *Slave Life in Virginia and Kentucky; or, Fifty Years of Slavery in the Southern States of America* (London: Wertheim, Macintosh, and Hunt, 1863), 13, http://docsouth.unc.edu/neh/fedric/fedric.html (accessed 30 August 2007).

37. Green, *Narrative*, 5–7.

38. Ibid., 7–8.

39. Washington, *Memorys*, 30, 42–45.

40. Andrews, *North Carolina Slave Narratives*, 133–45; Yellin, *Harriet Jacobs*; David W. Blight, *A Slave No More: Two Men Who Escaped to Freedom, Including Their Own Narratives of Emancipation* (New York: Harcourt, 2007), 128–62.

# CONTRIBUTORS

RICHARD B. ALLEN is the author of *Slaves, Freedmen, and Indentured Laborers in Colonial Mauritius* (1999) and numerous articles on European slave trading in the Indian Ocean and the social and economic history of Mauritius during the eighteenth and nineteenth centuries. He is currently working on a book-length manuscript on African and Asian free men and women of color and the development of a Creole society in Mauritius between 1721 and 1830, and continuing a project on British and French slave trading in the Indian Ocean during the seventeenth, eighteenth, and early nineteenth centuries.

PIERRE H. BOULLE retired from McGill University in 2001. He has written numerous articles on French commerce, the first French empire, the slave trade and, more recently, on race, as well as edited books on Canada and the French Revolution. In 2007 he published *Race et esclavage dans la France de l'Ancien Régime*. He is preparing a study of the 1777 census of nonwhite residents in France.

GWYN CAMPBELL holds a Canada Research Chair and is director of the Indian Ocean World Centre in the Department of History, McGill University. Born in Madagascar and raised in Wales (where he worked as a BBC radio producer in English and Welsh), he holds degrees in economic history from the universities of Birmingham and Wales. He has taught in India, Madagascar, Britain, South Africa, Belgium, France, and Canada and served as an academic consultant to the South African Government in the lead-up to the 1997 formation of an Indian Ocean regional association. He has organized a series of international conferences on slavery following the "Avignon format" (after the place where they were inaugurated); the latest, "Sex, Power, and Slavery," at McGill University in 2007, marked the Bicentenary of the British Anti-Slave Trade Act. As author, editor, or coeditor, he has over 100 publications, a significant proportion of which are on the theme of unfree labor and slavery.

BOK-RAE KIM received her doctorate in History from the University of Paris I. She is currently an assistant professor at the Andong National University, South Korea. She is the author of several articles and ten books in Korean.

GEORGE MICHAEL LA RUE is a professor of history at Clarion University of Pennsylvania (larue@clarion.edu). He conducted field research in Dar Fur province of Sudan on the *hakura* system (a precolonial land tenure system), and the sultanate's social and economic history. He has written on trans-Saharan trade from Bagirmi and Dar Fur. Most recently, he has been using French medical sources to investigate African slavery in nineteenth-century Egypt, and gathering slave narratives and biographical material.

ANTÓNIO DE ALMEIDA MENDES is currently an assistant professor at the University of Nantes and researcher at the CIRESC (Centre International de Recherches sur les Esclavages, Paris) and the CHAM (Centro de História de Além-Mar, Lisbon). He obtained his doctorate in history from the Ecoles des Hautes en Sciences Sociales, Paris, in 2007. His research interests are the early modern Atlantic world, the Iberian peninsula, and slavery. Further details are available at http://www.esclavages.cnrs.fr/spip.php?article322.

SUZANNE MIERS, professor emerita of history at Ohio University, is a specialist in the history of slavery, and has served as a trustee on the board of Anti-Slavery International. Her publications include *Slavery in the Twentieth Century: The Evolution of a Global Problem* (2003) and *Britain and the Ending of the Slave Trade* (1975). She has also coedited (with Gwyn Campbell and Joseph C. Miller) *Women and Slavery*, 2 vols. (2007); (with Martin Klein) *Slavery and Colonial Rule in Africa* (1999); (with Maria Jaschok) *Women and Chinese Patriarchy: Submission, Servitude and Escape* (1994); (with Richard Roberts) *The End of Slavery in Africa* (1988); and (with Igor Kopytoff) *Slavery in Africa: Historical and Anthropological Perspectives* (1977).

JOSEPH C. MILLER is the T. Cary Johnson Professor of History at the University of Virginia, where he has taught since 1972. He is a historian of early Africa with training at the University of Wisconsin–Madison under Jan Vansina and Philip D. Curtin. His early research on oral traditions in Angola led to Atlantic-scaled interests in the Angola-Brazil trade in slaves and a 1988 monograph, *Way of Death: Merchant Capitalism and the Angolan Slave Trade, 1730–1830*; to a comprehensive bibliography of slavery and slaving throughout the world about to appear (sponsored by the Virginia Center for Digital History) in searchable online format; and to a long-term effort to historicize the study of slavery on a global scale, developed significantly through his participation in the series of Avignon conferences that have led to the current, and other, volumes of papers. Further details are available at http://www.virginia.edu/history/user/44.

KENNETH MORGAN is a professor of history at Brunel University, London. His research focuses on the social and economic history of Britain's colonies and on music history. His two most recent books are *Slavery and the British Empire: From Africa to America* (2007) and *The Bright-Meyler Papers: A Bristol–West India Connection, 1732–1837* (2007).

FRED MORTON is a professor of history (retired), Loras College, Dubuque, Iowa, and lives in Botswana. He is a scholar of East African nineteenth-century Kenya coastal history and nineteenth-century South African and Botswana history. His 1990 book, *Children of Ham: Freed Slaves and Fugitive Slaves on the Kenya Coast, 1873–1907*, has been reprinted by iUniverse in 2008. He is the coeditor of *Slavery in South Africa: Captive Labor on the Dutch Frontier* (1994), also scheduled for reprint with iUniverse in 2009. His latest book—*When Rustling was an Art: Pilane's Kgatla, 1840–1902*—is in press.

SUSAN EVA O'DONOVAN is an assistant professor of history at the University of Memphis. She is the author of *Becoming Free in the Cotton South* (2007) and coeditor of *Freedom: A Documentary History of Emancipation, 1861–1867*, ser. 3, vol. 1, *Land & Labor, 1865* (2008). Besides being one of the lead investigators in a collaborative examination of labor, politics, and race in the postemancipation Carolinas, she is currently working on a book-length study of enslaved women and men in antebellum America and how, in advancing their own interests, they helped to destabilize a world their owners would soon go to war to save.

PAULINE PUI-TING POON obtained her MPhil degree at the University of Hong Kong in 2000. She was a research assistant for a Chinese emigration project at the university in 1999–2000. Her dissertation was extracted and published as an article entitled "The Political Maneuverings of the Early Twentieth-Century Hong Kong revealed by the Mui Tsai System" in the *E-Journal on Hong Kong Cultural and Social Studies* of the Centre of Asian Studies, the University of Hong Kong, in 2004. She has been working with the Antiquities and Monuments Office in Hong Kong since 2001. Her recent research interest lies in the traditional house forms of South China.

KRISTINA RICHARDSON is an assistant professor of history at Queens College, City University of New York. She received her AB in history and Near Eastern studies from Princeton University and her PhD in Near Eastern studies from the University of Michigan-Ann Arbor. Her dissertation,

"Blighted Bodies and Physical Difference in Cairo, Damascus and Mecca, 1400-1550," investigated the ways in which scholarly male friendship influenced the transmission of ideas about disability in the late medieval and early modern Arab Islamicate lands. Her forthcoming projects include investigations of intimacy and marital relations; medical and scientific discourses; and the relationships between body and authority in early modern Damascus and Cairo.

CALVIN SCHERMERHORN is an assistant professor of history at Arizona State University, specializing on slavery in the Chesapeake and African American forced migration in the early United States.

GULAY YILMAZ is a PhD student at the Institute of Islamic Studies, McGill University. Her dissertation title is "The Social and Economic Roles of Janissaries in a Seventeenth-Century Ottoman City: The Case of Istanbul." She worked as a researcher on a project funded by the Social Sciences and Humanities Research Council, "Citizenship after Orientalism: Ottoman Citizenship." She is now working on "The Dragoman Renaissance: Venetian-Ottoman Diplomatic Interpreters in the Early Modern Mediterranean."

# INDEX